U0904357

英释 国学经典选读

English Interpretation of Chinese Classics: Selected Readings

主　编：侯先绒　刘胜兵
副主编：陈　晖　欧阳婷　袁　圆
编　者：(按单元顺序)
侯先绒　陈　晖　欧阳婷　旷剑敏
王　昱　吴　莎　刘胜兵　袁　圆
审　校：范武邱　彭金定

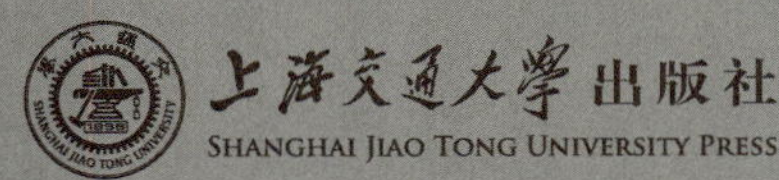
上海交通大学出版社
SHANGHAI JIAO TONG UNIVERSITY PRESS

图书在版编目(CIP)数据

英释国学经典选读/侯先绒,刘胜兵主编. —上海:上海交通大学出版社,2018(2019 重印)
ISBN 978-7-313-19575-3

Ⅰ.①英…　Ⅱ.①侯…②刘…　Ⅲ.①英语–高等学校–教材　Ⅳ.①H319.39

中国版本图书馆 CIP 数据核字(2018)第 129159 号

英释国学经典选读

主　　编:侯先绒　刘胜兵
出版发行:上海交通大学出版社　　地　　址:上海市番禺路 951 号
邮政编码:200030　　电　　话:021-64071208
印　　制:上海万卷印刷股份有限公司　　经　　销:全国新华书店
开　　本:889mm×1194mm　1/16　　印　　张:10.75
字　　数:271 千字
版　　次:2019 年 7 月第 2 版　　印　　次:2019 年 7 月第 2 次印刷
书　　号:ISBN 978-7-313-19575-3/H
定　　价:39.00 元

前　言

在中国政治经济正在深刻影响世界历史的今天，建设文化强国，让中国文化走出去，已经成为提升我国竞争力和软实力的一项战略国策。作为国家文化教育、科学研究重镇的大学应当在文化传播中担任重要角色。高校学生作为国际交流不可忽视的一支生力军，对传播中国文化具有不可估量的作用。大学英语课程的主要目标之一是培养学生具有国际视野的跨文化能力。《英释国学经典选读》正是在这一形势下，本着学国学、讲经典、练英语、传文化的初心编撰而成的。

《英释国学经典选读》课题组从璨如星海的传统国学经典中精心选出《周易》《庄子》《论语》《中庸》《史记》《孙子兵法》《黄帝内经》和《聊斋志异》八部经典，既有百经之首、医之始祖，又有儒道瑰宝、兵学圣典，还有史家绝唱、短篇巨著，横贯历史长河，纵览上下数千年。不仅如此，这些国学经典均在不同历史时期由国内外译者屡次翻译推介，可见其在中国文化史和人类文明史上具有举足轻重的地位。课题组选择这些经典及其译文可以帮助学生体会经典的魅力、文化的影响力和翻译的创作力，为讲好中国故事、传播中国文化做好准备。

全书各单元从作品及选读简介入手，旨在让学生通过简介(Introduction)了解该著作在中国文化史上的地位和影响，然后设立学习目标(Learning Objectives)，帮助学生以目标为导向进行学习，也有助于教师设计翻转课堂教学活动。课题组针对每部经典的多个今译本和英译本进行仔细对比甄选后，选择有代表性的今译本，和在国际国内接受度高的中国译者和西方译者各一篇英译本，与节选的原著(Selected Readings)组成每单元的阅读主体材料。为了提供更好的阅读体验，编者们对文中艰涩的古汉字和较难的英语单词都做了注释。

除此之外，每单元还设有中国哲学板块，就所选国学经典中涉及的哲学思想(Chinese Philosophy)做出英语阐释，帮助学生更好地用英语表达中国传统文化价值观中的精华部分。在练习部分(Practice)，既安排了帮助学生学英语的经典词汇和翻译练习，又设计了促进学生文化思考的批判性思维问题。

教师在使用此书时可以先布置课前预习任务，包括简介、节选原文、今译本和两篇英译本，并安排教学小组做好课件进行课堂展示。在课堂上根据教学目标，一方面可以引导学生关注各译本对原著的不同解读，在学习英语的同时帮助学生认识翻译创作对文化传播的影响和再造功能；另一方面可以针对经典中蕴含的文化思想激发学生进行思考，结合国家的发展、社会的进步，探讨这些思想在当今时代的新的价值和意义。

本书是2016年中南大学精品教材立项建设教材，是大学英语高级阶段《英释国学经典选读》选修课教材。编者都是有着丰富教学经验的一线教师，有着深厚的应用语言学和翻译学学术涵养。第一单元《周易》由侯先绒教授编写，第二单元《庄子》由陈晖老师编写，第三单元《论语》由欧阳婷博士编写，第四单元《中庸》由旷剑敏（博士在读）编写，第五单元《史记》由王昱老师（博士在读）编写，第六单元《孙子兵法》由吴莎博士编写，第七单元《黄帝内经》由刘胜兵副教授编写，第八单元《聊斋志异》由袁圆博士编写。在编撰过程中大家数次组织研讨，从指导思想、编写理念到选材、体例都进行了深入的交流，在这个思维碰撞的过程中每个人都获益良多。所选材料确定后在选修课上试用了初稿，从各个方面收集了教与学的反馈意见，进行了有针对性的修改。每位成员在成书过程中严谨细致、努力奉献的学术精神令人振奋。

在编写过程中我们还得到了多位专家和同行的支持和帮助。彭金定、李清平、鄢宏福和傅晓燕等专家和老师在教材设计、选材、推荐出版等方面给予了大力支持和帮助。本教材在交稿前有幸得到北京外国语大学孙有中教授的指导和中南大学范武邱教授的亲自审订。孙教授对教材提出了非常中肯的修改意见和建议，范教授、彭教授亲自进行修改。三位专家为教材质量把住最后的关口。在此，我们致以诚挚的感谢！在交付出版的过程中，我们一直得到出版社编辑的帮助和鼓励。对于他们的贡献和付出，在此一并表示感谢。此外，本教材的编撰和出版还得到了中南大学本科生院“2016年中南大学教材立项”资助和中南大学外国语学院省级重点学科“外国语言文学”基金资助，在此我们对中南大学本科生院和外国语学院的大力支持致以诚挚的感谢！

在编写过程中，我们无时无刻不感恩生长在这个有着浓厚文化底蕴的文明国度，无时无刻不感念先祖们闪耀的智慧和前辈译者们的卓越贡献。如果本书能给读者提供传播中国文化、用英语讲好中国故事的学习和参考材料，为中国文化走出去贡献一份绵薄之力，我们将倍感欣慰。

鉴于编者水平、时间和经验等方面的因素，虽已竭尽全力，但错漏之处恐难避免。祈请读者朋友不吝赐教，我们将不胜感激。

《英释国学经典选读》课题组
2018年4月
于中南大学外国语学院

Contents

Unit 1

The Zhou Book of Change[①]

Introduction

The Zhou Book of Change, also translated as *The Classic of Changes* (*Yijing*), *Changes of the Zhou* (*Zhouyi*), *I Ching*, etc., is hailed as a book of wisdom as well as the source of *Dao* (or Way) and the origin of Chinese Classics. It consists of 64 hexagrams (*gua*) and the related texts as the Ten Wings (*Shiyi*). The hexagrams, formed by combinations of 2 trigrams (also *gua*), are composed of 6 lines (*yao*), each arranged one atop the other in vertical sequence and read from bottom to top. Each line is either solid (*yang*—) or broken (*yin*--). Each hexagram is accompanied basically by a hexagram name (*guaming*), a hexagram statement (*guaci*), and a line statement (*yaoci*) for each of the 6 lines.

One of the Ten Wings, On the Trigrams, also translated as Explaining the Trigrams (*Shuogua*), is a treatise on the origin and use of the *The Zhou Book of Change* and on the nature and meaning of the 8 classic trigrams (*bagua*), the permutations of which form the 64 hexagrams. Understanding On the Trigrams is quite helpful for the understanding of *The Zhou Book of Change*. Hence the selected readings in this unit.

Learning Objectives

After learning this unit, you will be able to

1. learn generally about the content and the genre of *The Zhou Book of Change*;
2. understand deeply the schema and the symbolic meaning related to each of the eight trigrams;

---

① The original text of *Shuogua* and its modern Chinese version in this unit are excerpted from *Zhouyi* interpreted by Huang Shouqi and Zhang Shanwen published by Shanghai Classics Publishing House in 2007. English version 1 (On the Trigrams) in this unit is excerpted from *The Zhou Book of Change* translated by Fu Huisheng which was published by Hunan People's Publishing House in 2008, while English version 2 (Explaining the Trigrams [Shuogua]) is excerpted from *The Classic of Changes—A New Translation of the I Ching as Interpreted by Wang Bi* translated by Richard John Lynn which was published by Columbia University Press in 1994.

3. interpret critically the texts of On the Trigrams in English;
4. explore the traditional Chinese philosophy out of the selected treatise On the Trigrams.

Selected Readings

说 卦 传

第一章

◈【原文】

昔者圣人之作《易》也，幽赞于神明而生**蓍**，**参**天两地而倚数，观变于阴阳而立卦，发挥于刚柔而生爻，和顺于道德而理于义，穷理尽性以至于命。

蓍[shī] 名词，(植)蓍草
参[sān] 数词，同"叁"[sān]，即"三"

◈【今译】

从前圣人创作《周易》的时候，凭着精深的智虑赞祝神奇光明的造化而创造出用蓍草来揲筮的方法，于是采取天的"三"数与地的"两"数而建立阴阳奇偶数的象征(来配合蓍占)，并且观察天地阴阳的变化规律而演算成立卦形，发动挥散卦中刚柔两画而产生各爻的变迁，然后和谐顺成其道德而运用合宜的方法治理天下，又能穷极奥理，尽究万物的性质，以至通晓自然命运。

◈ [Version 1]

On the Trigrams

Chapter One①

Of old when the **sages** wrote *The Zhou Book of Change*, they silently prayed to the bright and miraculous nature and produced **yarrow stalks** for **divination**. At the same time they used heavenly and earthly numbers such as three and two to **signify** odd and even numbers. They operated to produce the trigrams through observation of changes of yin and yang and elaborated **alternation** of the firm line and the yielding line to **manifest** changes of lines. Then the sages associated them harmoniously with the ways and virtue of heaven and earth and applied the principles of change

① As for the number of chapters in the treatise On the Trigrams, there are different divisions in history with various versions. Of the selected readings, it is divided into 11 chapters while in other versions it is not the case, for example, Feng Guochao (2016) divides it into 6 chapters. As for the translation of the chapter numbers, in some of the versions, they are translated as "Chapter 1" to "Chapter 11" (as in Fu Huisheng, 2008), while in other versions, they may be just numbered as "1" through "11" (as in Richard John Lynn, 1994).

appropriately to the rule of the land, thus they attained a thorough mastery of the **esoteric** principles, a full knowledge of nature of all things of creation and even fate.

sage /seɪdʒ/ *n*. *literary* someone, especially an old man, who is very wise 圣人;贤人;哲人

yarrow /ˈjærəʊ/ *n*. a widely naturalized strong-scented Eurasian composite herb (Achillea millefolium) with finely dissected leaves and small (usually white) corymbose flowers 蓍草

stalk /stɔːk/ *n*. a long narrow part of a plant that supports leaves, fruits, or flowers (植物的)茎,秆;(支持叶子、果实和花的)梗,柄

divination /ˌdɪvəˈneɪʃən/ *n*. the ability to say what will happen in the future, or the act of doing this 预测;占卜

signify /ˈsɪgnɪfaɪ/ *vt*. to represent, mean, or be a sign of something 表示;意味;预示

alternation /ˌɔːltəˈneɪʃən/ *n*. successive change from one condition or action to another and back again repeatedly 交替;轮流;间隔

manifest /ˈmænəfest/ *vt*. *formal* to show a feeling, an attitude, etc. 证明,表明;显示

esoteric /ˌesəˈterɪk/ *adj*. known and understood by only a few people who have special knowledge about something 秘传的;限于圈内人的;难懂的

◈ [Version 2]

Explaining the Trigrams

(Shuo gua)

1. In the distant past, the way the sage made the *Changes* is as follows: He was mysteriously assisted by the gods (*shenming*, literally, "the numinous and the bright") and so initiated the use of yarrow stalks. He made Heaven three and Earth two and so provided the numbers with a basis. He observed the changes between yin and yang and then established the trigrams. As the trigrams are begun and are **dispersed** through the movement of the hard and soft lines, he initiated the use of such lines. He was in complete **accord** with the Dao and with Virtue, and the principles involved **conform** to rightness. He exhausted principles to the utmost and dealt thoroughly with human nature, and in doing so arrived at the workings of fate.

disperse /dɪˈspɜːs/ *v*. 1. if a group of people disperse or are dispersed, they go away in different directions 驱散;散开 2. if something disperses or is dispersed, it spreads in different directions over a wide area 使分散;扩散

accord /əˈkɔːd/ *n*. *formal* a situation in which two people, ideas, or statements agree with each other 符合;一致;协议;自愿

conform /kənˈfɔːm / *vi*. 1. to behave in the way that most other people in your group or society behave 守规矩 2. to obey a law, rule, etc. (与法律、愿望等)相符合

第二章

◈【原文】

昔者圣人之作《易》也，将以顺性命之理。是以立天之道曰阴与阳，立地之道曰柔与刚，立人之道曰仁与义。兼三才而两之，故《易》六画而成卦；分阴分阳，迭用柔刚，故《易》六位而成章。

◈【今译】

从前圣人创作《周易》的时候，是用它来顺合万物的性质和自然命运的变化规律。所以确立天的道理有“阴”和“阳”两方面，确立地的道理有“柔”和“刚”两方面，确立人的道理有“仁”和“义”两方面。(作《易》者)兼合(三画的八卦符号中)天地人的象征而每两卦相重，所以《周易》卦体必须具备六画才形成一卦；六画又分阴位阳位，更迭运用柔爻和刚爻来布局，所以《周易》的卦体必须具备六位才蔚成章理。

◈［Version 1］

Chapter Two

Of old when the sages wrote *The Zhou Book of Change*, they intended to **simulate** obediently the principles of nature and fate of all things of creation. Therefore, they set alternation of yin and yang as the way of heaven, alternation of yieldingness and firmness as the way of earth and benevolence and righteousness as the way of man. They doubled the eight trigrams of the three **cardinal** ways into different combinations of the sixty four hexagrams. Therefore, in *The Zhou Book of Change*, one hexagram consists of six lines. The six lines are subdivided into three pairs of yin and yang positions and distributed with alternation of yielding and firm lines, therefore, a hexagram of six lines in *The Zhou Book of Change* forms a pattern.

simulate /ˈsɪmjəleɪt/ *vt*. to make or produce something that is not real but has the appearance or feeling of being real 模拟

cardinal /ˈkɑːdənəl/ *adj*. (only before noun) very important or basic 首要的

◈［Version 2］

2. In the distant past, the way the sages made the *Changes* was as follows: It was to be used as a means to stay in accord with the principles of nature and of fate. It was for this reason that they determined what the Dao of Heaven was, which they defined in terms of yin and yang, what the Dao of Earth was, which they defined in terms of hard and soft, and what the Dao of Man was, which they defined in terms of benevolence and righteousness. They brought these three powers together and doubled them; this is why the *Changes* forms its hexagrams out of six lines.

They provided yin **allotments** and yang allotments, so their functions alternate between soft and hard; this is why the *Changes* forms its patterns out of six positions.

allotment /əˈlɒtmənt/ *n*. the act of distributing by allotting or apportioning 分配

第三章

◆【原文】

天地定位,山泽通气,雷风相薄,水火不相**射**,八卦相错。数往者顺,知来者逆,是故《易》逆数也。

射[yì] 动词,厌弃

◆【今译】

天地设定上下配合的位置,山泽一高一低气息流通,雷风各自与动以交相潜入应和,水火异性不相厌弃而相资助:八卦就是这样(既对立又统一地)互相错杂。(掌握这种对立统一的运动规律),欲明过去的事理可以顺着推算,欲晓将来的事理可以逆着推知,(将来的事理隐奥难测),所以《周易》的主要功用是逆推来事。

◆[Version 1]

Chapter Three

Heaven and earth determine their own positions; mountain and lake **interchange** with each other through air and vapor; thunder rumbles and wind blows, they echo and mix with each other; fire and water are not opponents but assistants to each other; and the eight trigrams **mingle** in a unity of opposites. A mastery of the principles of change in *The Zhou Book of Change* enables one to trace back and understand the history and to predict and know what will happen in the future. Therefore, the main function for *The Zhou Book of Change* is to predict the future.

interchange /ˌɪntəˈtʃeɪndʒ/ *v*. to put each of two things in the place of the other, or to be exchanged in this way 互换

mingle /ˈmɪŋgəl/ *v*. if two feelings, sounds, smells etc. mingle, they mix together with each other 混合

◆[Version 2]

3. As Heaven (*Qian*, Pure Yang) and Earth (*Kun*, Pure Yin) establish positions, as Mountain (*Gen*, **Restraint**) and Lake (*Dui*, Joy) **reciprocally circulate** material force, as Thunder

(*Zhen*, Quake) and Wind (*Sun*, **Compliance**) give rise each to the other, and as Water (*Kan*, Sink Hole) and Fire (*Li*, Cohesion) do not fail to complement each other, the eight trigrams combine with one another in such a way that, to reckon the past, one follows the order of their progress, and, to know the future, one works backward through them. Therefore, the Changes allow us to work backward (from the future) and reckon forward (from the past).

restraint /rɪˈstreɪnt/ *n*. rules or conditions that limit or restrict someone or something 限制
reciprocally /riˈsiprəkli/ *adv*. in a mutual or shared manner 相互地;相反地;互惠地
circulate /ˈsɜːkjəleɪt/ *v*. to move around within a system, or to make something do this 循环
compliance /kəmˈplaɪəns/ *n*. *formal* when someone obeys a rule, agreement, or demand 顺从;服从

第四章

◈【原文】

雷以动**之**,风以散之;雨以润之,日以**烜**之;艮以止之,兑以**说**之;乾以君之,坤以藏之。

之[zhī] 代词,指代万物
烜[xuān] 动词,晒干
说[yuè] 动词,同"悦"

◈【今译】

(震为)雷用来振奋鼓动万物,(巽为)风用来散布流通万物;(坎为)雨水用来滋润万物,(离为)太阳用来干燥万物;艮(为山)用来抑止万物,兑(为泽)用来欣悦万物;乾(为天)用来君临万物,坤(为地)用来处藏万物。

◈ [Version 1]

Chapter Four

Thunder **invigorates** all things of creation, wind scatters them, rain **moistens** them, the sun dries them, mountain stops them, lake pleases them, heaven **reigns** over them and earth **hoards** them up.

invigorate /ɪnˈvɪgəreɪt/ *vt*. if something invigorates you, it makes you feel healthier, stronger, and have more energy 鼓舞;增加活力
moisten /ˈmɔɪsən/ *vt*. to make something slightly wet 弄湿;使……湿润
reign /reɪn/ *v*. to rule a nation or group of nations as their king, queen, or emperor 在位统治

hoard /hɔːd/ (also hoard up) *v*. to collect and save large amounts of food, money, etc. especially when it is not necessary to do so 贮藏

◈ [Version 2]

4. It is by Thunder (*Zhen*, Quake) that things are caused to move, by Wind (*Sun*, Compliance) that they are dispersed, by the Rain (*Kan*, Sink Hole, i.e., Water) that they are moistened, by the Sun (*Li*, Cohesion, i.e., Fire) that they are dried, by Restraint (*Gen*) that they are made to stop, by Joy (*Dui*) that they are made happy, by Pure Yang (*Qian*, i.e., Heaven) that they are provided with a sovereign, and by Pure Yin (*Kun*, i.e., Earth) they are harbored.

第五章

◈【原文】

帝出乎震,齐乎巽,相见乎离,致役乎坤,说言乎兑,战乎乾,劳乎坎,成言乎艮。万物出乎震,震东方也。齐乎巽,巽东南也;齐也者,言万物之絜齐也。离也者,明也,万物皆相见,南方之卦也;圣人南面而听天下,向明而治,盖取诸此也。坤也者,地也,万物皆致养焉,故曰致役乎坤。兑,正秋也,万物之所说也,故曰说言乎兑。战乎乾,乾西北之卦也,言阴阳相薄也。坎者,水也,正北方之卦也,劳卦也,万物之所归也,故曰劳乎坎。艮,东北之卦也,万物之所成终而所成始也,故曰成言乎艮。

帝[dì] 名词,(主宰大自然生机的)元气

◈【今译】

主宰大自然生机的元气使万物出生于(象征东方和春分的)震,生长整齐于(象征东南和立夏的)巽,纷相显现于(象征南方和夏至的)离,致力用事于(象征西南和立秋的)坤,成熟欣悦于(象征西方和秋分的)兑,交配结合于(象征西北和立冬的)乾,勤勉劳倦于(象征北方和冬至的)坎,最后成功而又重新萌生于(象征东北和立春的)艮。万物出生于震,因为震卦是象征(万物由以萌生的)东方。生长整齐于巽,因为巽卦是象征(万物和顺生长的)东南方;生长整齐,是说万物的成长状态整洁一致。离卦是光明的象征,万物都旺盛而纷相呈现,这是代表南方的卦;圣人坐北朝南而听政于天下,面向光明而治理事务,大概是吸取了这一卦的象征吧。坤卦,是地的象征,万物都致力养育于大地,所以说致力用事于坤。兑卦,象征正秋时节,万物成熟欣悦于此时,所以说成熟欣悦于兑。交配结合于乾,乾卦是象征西北(阴方)的卦,说明阴阳于此交相潜入应和。坎卦,是水的象征,是代表正北方的卦,又是代表勤勉劳倦的卦,万物劳倦必当归藏休息,所以说勤勉劳倦于坎。艮卦是象征东北(终而复始之位)的卦,万物于此成就其终而更发其始,所以说最后成功而又重新萌生于艮。

◈ [Version 1]

Chapter Five

The **primordial** qi of all things of creation **permeating** in nature begins to take shape in the direction and season of the Zhen trigram (a symbol of east and spring **equinox**), they grow evenly in the direction and season of the Xun trigram (a symbol of southeast and the beginning of summer), manifest themselves in the direction and season of the Li trigram (a symbol of south and summer **solstice**), dedicate themselves to full development in the direction and season of the Kun trigram (a symbol of southwest and the beginning of autumn), enjoy maturity in the direction and season of Dui trigram (a symbol of west and autumn equinox), **copulate** in the direction and season of the Qian trigram (a symbol of northwest and the beginning of winter), work diligently in the direction and season of the Kan trigram (a symbol of north and winter solstice), finally they complete their cycles and start a new life in the direction and season of the Gen trigram (a symbol of northeast and spring equinox①). All things of creation are born in the direction of the Zhen trigram, which is a symbol of east. They grow evenly in the direction of Xun trigram, which is a symbol of southeast. Even growth here means all things of creation grow **exuberantly** in the same height. The Li trigram symbolizes light. All things of creation thrive in full and it is a trigram in the direction of south. The sages faced the south and received audience under heaven. They faced light and ruled the land, and perhaps drew inspiration from this trigram. The Kun trigram is a symbol of earth, all things of creation grow and thrive fully on earth, therefore, they dedicated themselves to growth in the direction of the Kun trigram. The Dui trigram symbolizes the season of autumn, all things of creation become ripe and joyful, and thus they are ripe and joyful in the direction of the Dui trigram. Copulation between yin and yang takes place in the direction of the Qian trigram. The Qian trigram symbolizes the direction of northwest, a time that yin and yang penetrate and mix with each other. It symbolizes hard work and exhaustion. All things of creation come to a rest after hard work, thus they work hard and become exhausted in the direction of the Kan trigram. The Gen trigram symbolizes the direction of northeast, when all things of creation complete their cycles and start for a new one. Therefore, they succeed in the end and start a new life in the direction of the Gen trigram.

---

primordial /praɪˈmɔːdiəl/ *adj*. *formal* existing at the beginning of time or the beginning of the Earth 原始的;远古的

permeate /ˈpɜːmieɪt/ *vi*./*vt*. (liquid, gas, etc.) to enter something and spread through every part of it (液体、气体等)渗透,渗入;弥漫(于)

equinox /ˈiːkwənɒks/ *n*. one of the two times in a year when night and day are of equal length 昼夜平分日(指春分或秋分)

solstice /ˈsɒlstɪs/ *n*. the time when the sun is furthest north or south of the equator 至,至日;至点 the summer/winter solstice (= the longest or shortest day of the year) 夏至/冬至

copulate /ˈkɒpjəleɪt/ *v*. *technical* to have sex 交配;交媾

① Here "spring equinox" should be "beginning of spring".

exuberant /ɪɡˈzjuːbərənt/ *adj*. happy and full of energy and excitement 繁茂的；生气勃勃的，充溢的

◈ [Version 2]

5. The Divine Ruler (*shangdi*) comes forth in *Zhen* (Quake) and sets all things in order in *Sun* (Compliance), makes them visible to one another in *Li* (Cohesion, i. e., the Sun, Fire), gives them maximum support in *Kun* (Pure Yin, i. e., Earth), makes them happy then in *Dui* (Joy), has them do battle in *Qian* (Pure Yang), finds them thoroughly worn out in *Kan* (Water Hole), and has them reach final maturity in *Gen* (Restraint).

The **myriad** things come forth in *Zhen* (Quake); *Zhen* corresponds to the east. They are set in order in *Sun* (Compliance); Sun corresponds to the southeast. "Set in order" means that they are fresh and neat. *Li* (Cohesion, Fire, i. e., the Sun) here means brightness. That the myriad things are made visible to one another here signifies that this is the trigram of the south. The fact that the sage (king) faces the south to listen to the whole world and that he turns toward the brightness there to rule is probably derived from this. *Kun* (Pure Yin, Earth) here means the Earth. The myriad things all are nourished to the utmost by it. This is why it says: "gives them maximum support in *Kun*." *Dui* (Joy) here means autumn at its height, something in which the myriad things all find cause to rejoice. This is why it says: "makes them happy then in Dui." (As for) "has them do battle in *Qian*," Qian here is the trigram of the northwest, so this signifies where yin and yang exert pressure on each other. *Kan* (Sink Hole) here means water. It is the trigram of due north. It is the trigram of **wearisome** toil. It is here that the myriad things all find refuge. This is why it says: "finds them thoroughly worn out in *Kan*." *Gen* (Restraint) is the trigram of the northeast. It is here that the myriad things reach the end of their development, but it is also the beginning of that development. This is why it says: "has them reach final maturity in *Gen*."

myriad /ˈmɪriəd/ *adj*. *written* (usually before noun) very many 无数的；种种的

wearisome /ˈwɪərisəm/ *adj*. *formal* making you feel bored, tired, or annoyed 使疲倦的；使厌倦的；乏味的

第六章

◈【原文】

神也者，妙万物而为言者也。动万物者莫疾乎雷，**桡**万物者莫疾乎风，燥万物者莫**熯**乎火，说万物者莫说乎泽，润万物者莫润乎水，终万物始万物者莫盛乎艮。故水火相**逮**，雷风不相**悖**。山泽通气，然后能变化，既成万物也。

神[shén] 名词，神奇，此处指大自然运化规律的神奇功能

桡[ráo] 动词，曲木；木头弯曲；泛指弯曲，此处指风吹拂万物或使抒发、或使摧折

熯[hàn] 形容词，燥热，炎热

逮[dài] 动词，到；及

悖[bèi] 动词，相反；违反

◈【今译】

所谓大自然的神奇造化，是说它能够奇妙地化育万物。鼓动万物者没有比雷更迅猛的，吹拂万物者没有比风更疾速的，干燥万物者没有比火更炎热的，欣悦万物者没有比泽更和悦的，滋润万物者没有比水更湿润的，最终成就万物又重新萌生万物者没有比艮更美盛的。所以水火异性而相互济及，雷风异动而不相违逆，山泽异处而流通气息，然后自然界才能变动运化而形成万物。

◈ [Version 1]

Chapter Six

Miracle means miraculous creation and development of all things of creation. Nothing is swifter and more violent than thunder in invigorating all things of creation, nothing is speedier than wind in bending them, nothing is hotter than fire in drying them, nothing is more joyful than lake in pleasing them, nothing is more humid than water in moistening them, and nothing is more exuberant than mountain, a symbol of the Gen trigram, where all things of creation complete their cycles and start **anew**. Therefore, water and fire can benefit each other, thunder and wind do not go against each other, and mountain and lake interchange with each other through air and vapor. Then in these complicated changes, nature creates and develops all things of creation.

anew /əˈnjuː/ *adv*. *written* if you do something anew, you start doing it again 重新；再

◈ [Version 2]

6. As for ***the numinous***, it is the term used for that which invests the myriad things with the marvel of what they are and do. Of things that make the myriad things move, none is swifter than Thunder. Of things that make the myriad things bend, none is swifter than the Wind. Of things that make the myriad things dry, none is a better drying agent than Fire. Of things that make the myriad things **rejoice**, none is more joy giving than the Lake. Of things that moisten the myriad things, none is more effective than Water. Of things that provide the myriad things with ends and beginnings, none is more resourceful than Restraint. This is why Water and Fire drive each other on, why Thunder and Wind do not work against each other, and why "Mountain and Lake reciprocally circulate". Only in consequence of all this can change and transformation take place, thus allow the myriad things to all that they can be.

numinous /ˈnjuːmɪnəs/ *adj*. *literary* having a mysterious and holy quality, which makes you feel that God is present 神圣的；神秘的

rejoice /rɪˈdʒɔɪs/ *v*. *literary* to feel or show that you are very happy 欣喜；使高兴

第七章

◈【原文】

乾，健也；坤，顺也；震，动也；巽，入也；坎，陷也；离，**丽**也；艮，止也；兑，说也。

丽[lì] 名词，附着；依附

◈【今译】

乾，表示强健；坤，表示温顺；震，表示奋动；巽，表示潜入；坎，表示险陷；离，表示附丽；艮，表示静止；兑，表示欣悦。

◈ [Version 1]

Chapter Seven

The Qian trigram symbolizes vigor, the Kun trigram obedience, the Zhen trigram vigorous movement, the Xun trigram stealthy penetration, the Kan trigram dangerous trap, the Li trigram attachment, the Gen trigram **tranquility** and the Dui trigram joy.

tranquility /træŋˈkwiləti/ *n*. a state of being pleasantly calm, quiet, and peaceful 宁静；平静

◈ [Version 2]

7. *Qian* (Pure Yang) means strength and dynamism (*jian*); *Kun* (Pure Yin) means **submissiveness** and **pliancy**; *Zhen* (Quake) means energizing; *Sun* (Compliance) means **accommodation**; *Kan* (Water) means **pitfall**; *Li* (Cohesion) means attachment; *Gen* (Restraint) means **cessation**; *Dui* (Joy) means to delight.

submissiveness /səbˈmɪsɪvnɪs/ *n*. the trait of being willing to yield to the will of another person or a superior force, etc. 柔顺；服从

pliancy /ˈplaiənsi/ *n*. 1. the property of being pliant and flexible 柔软；柔顺 2. adaptability of mind or character 适应性

accommodation /əˌkɔməˈdeiʃən/ *n*. making or becoming suitable; adjusting to circumstances 适应；

适应性调节

pitfall /ˈpɪtfɔːl/ *n*. a problem or difficulty that is likely to happen in a particular job, course of action, or activity 陷阱,圈套;缺陷;诱惑

cessation /seˈseɪʃən/ *n*. *formal* a pause or stop 停止;中止;中断

第八章

◈【原文】

乾为马,坤为牛,震为龙,巽为鸡,坎为豕,离为雉,艮为狗,兑为羊。

豕[shǐ] 名词,猪

◈【今译】

乾为马象,坤为牛象,震为龙象,巽为鸡象,坎为猪象,离为雉鸟象,艮为狗象,兑为羊象。

◈[Version 1]

Chapter Eight

The Qian trigram symbolizes horse, the Kun trigram cow, the Zhen trigram dragon, the Xun trigram rooster, the Kan trigram pig, the Li trigram **pheasant**, the Gen trigram dog and the Dui trigram **ram**.

pheasant /ˈfezənt/ *n*. a large bird with a long tail, often shot for food, or the meat of this bird 野鸡;雉科鸟

ram /ræm/ *n*. an adult male sheep 公羊

◈[Version 2]

8. *Qian* (Pure Yang) has the nature of the horse, *Kun* (Pure Yin) that of the ox, *Zhen* (Quake) that of the dragon, *Sun* (Compliance) that of the cock, *Kan* (Water Hole) that of the pig, *Li* (Cohesion) that of the pheasant, *Gen* (Restraint) that of the dog, and *Dui* (Joy) that of the sheep.

第九章

◈【原文】

乾为首,坤为腹,震为足,巽为股,坎为耳,离为目,艮为手,兑为口。

◈【今译】

乾为头象，坤为腹象，震为足象，巽为大腿象，坎为耳象，离为目象，艮为手象，兑为口象。

◈ [Version 1]

Chapter Nine

The Qian trigram symbolizes head, the Kun trigram belly, the Zhen trigram foot, the Xun trigram thigh, the Kan trigram ear, the Li trigram eye, the Gen trigram hand and the Dui trigram mouth.

◈ [Version 2]

9. *Qian* (Pure Yang) works like the head, *Kun* (Pure Yin) like the stomach, *Zhen* (Quake) like the foot, *Sun* (Compliance) like the thigh, *Kan* (Water Hole) like the ear, *Li* (Cohesion) like the eye, *Gen* (Restraint) like the hand, and *Dui* (Joy) like the mouth.

第十章

◈【原文】

乾，天也，故称乎父；坤，地也，故称乎母。震一**索**而得男，故谓之长男；巽一索而得女，故谓之长女；坎再索而男，故谓之中男；离再索而得女，故谓之中女；艮三索而得男，故谓之少男；兑三索而得女，故谓之少女。

索[suǒ] 动词，求，文中犹言"求合"，指阴阳相求

◈【今译】

乾，是天的象征，所以称作父；坤，是地的象征，所以称作母；(父母阴阳互求，阳求合于阴得男，阴求合于阳得女。)震是初次求合所得的男性，所以叫做长男；巽是初次求合所得的女性，所以叫做长女；坎是再次求合所得的男性，所以叫做中男；离是再次求合所得的女性，所以叫做中女；艮是三次求合所得的男性，所以叫做少男；兑是三次求合所得的女性，所以叫做少女。

◈ [Version 1]

Chapter Ten

The Qian trigram symbolizes heaven, that is why it is called father; and the Kun trigram symbolizes earth, that is why it is called mother. The Zhen trigram is an image of son **begotten** for the first time the father seeks copulation, so it is the eldest son; and the Xun trigram an image of daughter begotten for the first time the mother seeks copulation, so it is called the eldest daughter. The Kan is an image of son begotten for the second time the father seeks copulation, so it is the second son; and the Li trigram an image of daughter begotten for the second time the mother seeks copulation, thus it is called the second daughter. The Gen trigram is an image of son for the third time the father seeks copulation, so it is called the youngest son; and the Dui trigram an image of daughter begotten for the third time the mother seeks copulation, so it is called the youngest daughter.

beget /bɪˈget/ *vt*. (begot; begotten; begetting) 1. *old use* to become the father of a child 成为……的父亲 2. to cause something or make it happen 导致

◈ [Version 2]

10. *Qian* (Pure Yang) is Heaven, thus it corresponds to the Father, and *Kun* (Pure Yin) is Earth, thus it corresponds to the Mother. As for *Zhen* (Quake), (*Kun*) here seeks (*Qian*) for the first time and gets a son, thus we call it the Eldest Son, and as for *Sun* (Compliance), (*Qian*) here seeks (*Kun*) for the first time and gets a daughter, thus we call it the Eldest Daughter. As for *Kan* (Water Hole), (*Kun*) here seeks (*Qian*) for the second time and gets a son, thus we call it the Middle Son, and as for *Li* (Cohesion), (*Qian*) here seeks (*Kun*) for the second time and gets a daughter, thus we call it the Middle Daughter. As for *Gen* (Restraint), (*Kun*) here seeks (*Qian*) for the third time and gets a son, thus we call it the Youngest Son, and as for *Dui* (Joy), (*Qian*) here seeks (*Kun*) for the third time and gets a daughter, thus we call it the Youngest Daughter.

第十一章

◈【原文】

乾为天,为**圜**,为君,为父,为玉,为**金**,为寒,为冰,为**大赤**,为良马,为老马,为瘠马,为驳马,为木果。

坤为地,为母,为**布**,为釜,为吝啬,为均,为子母牛,为大**舆**,为**文**,为众,为柄,其于地也为黑。

震为雷,为龙,为**玄黄**,为**旉**,为大涂,为长子,为决躁,为**苍筤**竹,为**萑苇**,其于马也,为善鸣,为**馵足**,为**作足**,为**的颡**,其于稼也,为反生,其究为健,为蕃鲜。

巽为木,为风,为长女,为绳直,为工,为白,为长,为高,为进退,为不果,为臭,其于人也,为寡发,为广颡,为多白眼,为近利市三倍,其究为躁卦。

坎为水,为沟渎,为隐伏,为矫輮,为弓轮,其于人也为加忧,为心病,为耳痛,为血卦,为赤,其于马也为美脊,为亟心,为下首,为薄蹄,为曳,其于舆也为多**眚**,为通,为月,为盗,其于木也,为坚多心。

离为火,为日,为电,为中女,为甲胄,为戈兵,其于人也为大腹,为乾卦,为鳖,为蟹,为**蠃**,为蚌,为龟,其于木也为科上槁。

艮为山,为径路,为小石,为门阙,为果**蓏**,为**阍寺**,为指,为狗,为鼠,为**黔喙**之属,其于木也,为坚多节。

兑为泽，为少女，为巫，为口舌，为毁折，为附决，其于地也，为刚卤，为妾，为羊。

圜[yuán] 名词，圆
金[jīn] 名词，青铜或纯铜(铸成的钟鼎等)
大赤[dà chì] 名词，大红色
布[bù] 名词，古代的一种钱币
舆[yú] 名词，大车
文[wén] 名词，纹理，花纹，文中指大地万物之色杂
玄黄[xuán huáng] 名词，青黄相杂之色
旉[fū] 名词，花朵
苍筤[cāng láng] 形容词，竹色青嫩
萑苇[huán wěi] 名词，两种芦类植物，蒹长成后为萑，葭长成后为苇
馵足[zhù zú] 名词，(马)白色的左后足
作足[zuò zú] 名词，(马)双前足举起
的颡[dì sǎng] 名词，(马)白额
眚[shěng] 名词，灾异
蠃[luǒ] 名词，蚌属水生物
蓏[luǒ] 名词，瓜类植物的果实
阍寺[hūn sì] 名词，阍人和寺人，指古代宫中掌管门禁的官
黔[qián] 形容词，黑
喙[huì] 名词，鸟嘴，“黔喙”指猛禽

◈【今译】

乾为天象，为圆环象，为君主象，为父象，为玉象，为金象，为寒象，为冰象，为大红颜色象，为良马象，为老马象，为瘠马象，为驳马象，为树木果实象。

坤为地象，为母象，为钱币流布之象，为锅釜象，为吝啬象，为平均象，为子牛母牛象，为大车象，为文采章理象，为众多象，为柯柄象，对于地来说为黑色土壤之象。

震为雷象，为龙象，为青黄颜色交杂之象，为花朵象，为宽阔大路象，为长子象，为刚决躁动象，为青嫩幼竹象，为萑苇象，对于马来说为擅长鸣啸的马象，为左后足长白毛的马象，为前两足腾举的马象，为额首斑白的马象，对于禾稼来说为顶着种子的甲壳萌生之象，此卦发展至极则化为刚健之象，为草木繁育鲜明之象。

巽为树木象，为风象，为长女象，为笔直的准绳象，为工巧象，为白色象，为长象，为高象，为抉择进退之象，为迟疑不决之象，为气味象，对于人来说为头发稀少象，为额首宽广象，为多以白眼视人之象，为亲近于利而购物必获三倍利益者之象，此卦发展至极则化为急躁卦。

坎为水象，为沟洼渎泊象，为隐伏象，为矫揉屈曲象，为弯弓转轮象，为深加忧虑象，为内心患病象，为耳中疾痛象，为鲜血卦，为赤色象，对于马来说为脊背美丽的马象，为内心焦急的马象，为头部下

垂的马象，为脚蹄频频踢地的马象，为艰难拖曳的马象，对于车辆来说为多灾多难的车象，为通行象，为月亮象，为盗贼象，对于树木来说为坚硬而多生小刺之象。

离为火象，为太阳象，为闪电象，为中女象，为护身甲胄象，为戈矛兵器象，对于人来说为妇女大腹怀孕象，为干燥卦，为鳖象，为蟹象，为螺象，为蚌象，为龟象，对于树木来说为柯干中空上部枯槁之象。

艮为山象，为斜径小路象，为小石象，为崇门高阙象，为果蓏象，为阍人寺人象，为手指象，为狗象，为鼠象，为黑嘴刚猛的禽类象，对于树木来说为坚硬而多生节纽之象。

兑为泽象，为少女象，为巫师象，为口舌象，为毁灭摧折象，为附从决断象，对于地来说为土壤刚硬不生植物之象，为妾象，为羊象。

◈ [Version 1]

Chapter Eleven

The Qian trigram symbolizes heaven, a ring, a king, father, jade, bronze, cold, ice, bright red, a strong horse, an old horse, a **lean** horse, a **dappled** horse, and fruit on a tree.

The Kun trigram symbolizes earth, mother, a circulating coin, a **cauldron**, misery, equality, a cow milking a **calf**, a cart, a rich and bright-colored pattern, multitude, a handle. As for earth, it is a symbol of black soil.

The Zhen trigram symbolizes thunder, a dragon, mixed color of black and yellow, a flower, a wide road, the eldest son, self-willed hot-temper, a green bamboo shoot, rush and **reed**. As for a horse, the trigram symbolizes a good **neigher**, a horse with a white-haired left hind leg, a horse holding up its two front legs, a horse with a white forehead. As for a crop, it symbolizes a seed sprouting with its shell. In the extreme, the trigram symbolizes vigor, and exuberance of grass and trees.

The Xun trigram symbolizes a tree, wind, the eldest daughter, to be straight like a rope, deft craftsmanship, white, to be long, to be high, decision of advance or retreat, hesitation, smell. For a man, it symbolizes a head with few hairs, a man with broad forehead, an eye with more white, a deal with nearly triple profits. In the extreme, the trigram symbolizes a quick temper trigram.

The Kan trigram symbolizes water, a **ditch** or a pool, concealment, bend, bow and wheel. As for a man, it symbolizes frequent worries, chronic heart disease, pains in the ear, a bloody trigram, and red. As for a horse, it symbolizes a horse with a good-looking back, an anxious horse, a horse lowering its head, a horse that frequently kicks ground, a horse that drags itself along. As for a carriage, it symbolizes many troubles on the road. It symbolizes smoothness, the moon and a thief. As for a tree, it symbolizes being hard with small **thorns**.

The Li trigram symbolizes fire, the sun, lightning, the second daughter, **armor**, **dagger-axe** and weapons. As for a woman, it symbolizes pregnancy with a big belly. It symbolizes a dry trigram, a turtle, a crab, a **conch**, a **clam** and a tortoise. As for a tree, it symbolizes an empty

trunk with a **withered** top.

The Gen trigram symbolizes a mountain, a short cut, a **pebble**, a palace gate with watch towers, fruit and melon, a door keeper or a **eunuch**, a finger, a dog, a mouse, a bird of prey with a black beak. As for a tree, it symbolizes a hard tree with knots.

The Dui trigram symbolizes lake, the youngest daughter, a witch or a **sorcerer**, mouth and tongue, ruin or break, obedience to other's decision. As for earth, it symbolizes hard and salty **barren** soil. It symbolizes a **concubine** and a ram.

---

lean /liːn/ *adj*. thin in a healthy and attractive way 瘦的

dappled /ˈdæpəld/ *adj*. marked with spots of colour, light, or shade 斑纹的;有斑点的;花的

cauldron /ˈkɔːldrən/ *n*. a large round metal pot for boiling liquids over a fire (金属)大锅

calf /kɑːf/ *n*. (plural calves /kɑːvz/) the baby of a cow, or of some other large animals, such as an elephant 牛犊;(大象等大型动物的)幼兽

reed /riːd/ *n*. a type of tall plant like grass that grows in wet places 芦苇

neigh /neɪ/ *v*. if a horse neighs, it makes a long loud noise 马嘶

ditch /dɪtʃ/ *n*. a long narrow hole dug at the side of a field, road, etc. to hold or remove unwanted water 沟渠;壕沟

thorn /θɔːn/ *n*. a sharp point that grows on the stem of a plant such as a rose 刺;[植] 荆棘

armor /ˈɑːmə/ *n*. metal or leather clothing that protects your body, worn by soldiers in battles in past times [军] 装甲;盔甲

dagger-axe /ˈdægə æks/ *n*. a type of pole weapon that was in use from the Shang dynasty until the Han dynasty in China 戈

conch /kɒntʃ/ *n*. the large twisted shell of a tropical sea animal that looks like a snail 贝壳;海螺壳

clam /klæm/ *n*. a shellfish you can eat that has a shell in two parts that open up 蛤蜊

withered /ˈwɪðəd/ *adj*. being drier and smaller and even dead or dying 枯萎的;凋谢的

pebble /ˈpebəl/ *n*. a small smooth stone found especially on a beach or on the bottom of a river 卵石

eunuch /ˈjuːnək/ *n*. a man whose testicles have been removed, especially someone who guarded a king's wives in some Eastern countries in the past 太监;阉人

sorcerer /ˈsɔːsərə/ *n*. a man in stories who uses magic and receives help from evil forces 魔术师;男巫士

barren /ˈbærən/ *adj*. land or soil that is barren has no plants growing on it 荒芜的

concubine /ˈkɒŋkjəbaɪn/ *n*. a woman in the past who lived with and had sex with a man who already had a wife or wives, but who was socially less important than the wives 妾;情妇;姘妇

◈ [Version 2]

11. *Qian* (Pure Yang) is Heaven, is round, is the sovereign, is father, is jade, is metal, is coldness, is ice, is pure red, is a fine horse, an old horse, an **emaciated** horse, a **piebald** horse, is

fruit of the tree.

Kun (Pure Yin) is Earth, is mother, is cloth, is a cooking pot, is **frugality**, is **impartiality**, is a cow with calf, is a great cart, is the markings on things, is the multitude of things themselves, and is the handle of things. In respect to soils, it is the kind that is black.

Zhen (Quake) is thunder, is the dragon, is black and yellow, is overspreading, is the great highway, is the Eldest Son, is decisiveness and **impetuosity**, a green, lush bamboo, and the reed plants. In respect to horses, it is those that excel at neighing, those that have white rear legs, those that work the legs (i. e., run fast), and those that have white foreheads. In respect to cultivated plants, it is the kind that grows back (i. e., **pod-sprouting** plants, **legumes**, etc.). At the end point of its development, it is soundness and **sturdiness** (i. e., it turns into Qian (Pure Yang)) and is luxuriant and fresh growth.

Sun (Compliance) is wood, is the wind, is the Eldest Daughter, is the straightness of a marking **cord**, is the carpenter (or "carpenter's square"), is the spotless and pure, is the lengthy, is the high, is the now-advancing and now-receding, is the unresolved, and is odor. In respect to men, it is the balding, the broad in forehead, the ones with much white in their eyes, the ones who keep close to what is profitable and who market things for **threefold** gain. At the end point of its development it is the trigram of impetuosity, i. e., it turns into Zhen (Quake).

Kan (Sink Hole) is water, is the **drains** and ditches, is that which lies low, is the now-straightening and now-bending, and is the bow and the wheel. In respect to men, it is the increasingly anxious, the sick at heart, the ones with earaches. It is the trigram of blood, of the color red. In respect to horses, it is those with beautiful backs, those that put their whole hearts into it, those that keep their heads low, those with thin **hooves**, and those that **shamble** along. In respect to carriages, it is those that often have calamities, i. e., breakdowns/accidents. It is penetration, is the moon, and is the stealthy thief. In respect to trees, it is those that are strong with dense centers.

Li (Cohesion) is fire, is the sun, is lightning, is the Middle Daughter, is the **mail** and **helmet**, is the **halberd** and the sword. In respect to men, it is those with big bellies. It is the trigram of dryness. It is the turtle, is the crab, is the snail, is the clam, and is the tortoise. In respect to trees, it is the hollow ones with tops withered.

Gen (Restraint) is the mountain, is the footpath, is the small stone, is the gate tower, is the tree fruit and vine fruit, is the gatekeeper and the palace guard, is the fingers, is the dog, is the rat, is the black **maws** of species of birds and beasts of prey. In respect to trees, it is the kind that is sturdy and much gnarled.

Dui (Joy) is the lake, is the Youngest Daughter, is the **shamaness**, is the mouth and tongue, is the deterioration of plant life, and the breaking off of what had been attached. In respect to soils, it is the kind that is hard and **alkaline**. It is the concubine, the sheep.

---

emaciated /ɪˈmeɪʃieɪtəd/ *adj*. extremely thin from lack of food or illness 瘦弱的;憔悴的

piebald /ˈpaɪbɔːld/ *adj*. a piebald animal has black and white areas on its body 花斑的;杂色的

frugality /fruːˈɡæləti/ *n*. prudence in avoiding waste 节俭,节约,俭朴

impartiality /ɪmˌpɑːʃɪˈæləti/ *n*. a state of being not involved in a particular situation, and therefore able to give a fair opinion or piece of advice 公正,公平;不偏不倚

impetuosity /ɪmˌpetʃuˈɒsəti/ *n*. 性急,冲动;冲力,猛烈

pod /pɒd/ *n*. a long narrow seed container that grows on various plants, especially peas and beans 豆荚

sprout /spraʊt/ *v*. if vegetables, seeds, or plants sprout, they start to grow, producing shoots, buds, or leaves 发芽;长芽

legume /ˈlegjuːm/ *n*. *technical* a plant such as a bean plant that has seeds in a pod (= a long thin case) 豆类;豆科植物;豆荚

sturdiness /ˈstəːdɪnɪs/ *n*. the state of being vigorous and robust 坚固;强健,雄壮

cord /kɔːd/ *n*. a line made of twisted fibers or threads 绳索

threefold /ˈθriːfəʊld/ *adj*. three times as much or as many 三倍的;三重的,有三部分的

drain /dreɪn/ *n*. *especially British English* a pipe that carries water or waste liquids away 排水管;下水道;排水沟

hoof /huːf/ *n*. (*plural* hoofs or hooves /huːvz/) the hard foot of an animal such as a horse, cow, etc. (马等动物的)蹄

shamble /ˈʃæmbəl/ *v*. to walk slowly and awkwardly, not lifting your feet much, for example because you are tired, weak, or lazy 蹒跚地走;摇晃不稳;摇摇晃晃地走

mail /meɪl/ *n*. armor made of small pieces of metal, worn by soldiers in the ancient times 铠甲

helmet /ˈhelmɪt/ *n*. a strong hard hat that soldiers, motorcycle riders, the police, etc., wear to protect their heads 钢盔,头盔

halberd /ˈhælbəd/ *n*. a type of sword that was used as a weapon in the past 戟

maw /mɔː/ *n*. *literary* an animal's mouth or throat (像吞噬一切的)大嘴

shamaness /ˈʃɑːmənɪs/ *n*. a woman in some tribes who is a religious leader and is believed to be able to talk to spirits and cure illnesses 女巫

alkaline /ˈælkəlaɪn/ *adj*. containing an alkali 碱的;碱性的

Chinese Philosophy

1.【阴阳】

Yin-Yang, or *yin* and *yang*, is one of the dominant concepts shared by different schools of Chinese philosophy throughout the history. In traditional view, *yin* and *yang* represent the most basic antagonistic relationship of all things. It is the objective law of nature, the origin of the movement of all things, and the basic law of human understanding of things. The concept of *yin* and *yang* originates from the ancient Chinese people's view of nature. The ancients observed the natural phenomena of the unity of opposites in nature, such as heaven and earth, the sun and the moon, the day and the night, the summer and the winter, the men and the women, and the upper and the lower, and then summed up the concept of "*yin* and *yang*" in a philosophical way.

2.【变化】

Every hexagram of the sixty-four hexagrams of *The Zhou Book of Change* is composed of six lines. The six lines are subdivided into three pairs of *yin* and *yang* positions and distributed with alternation of yielding and firm lines. It is because of the alternation and alteration of the *yin* and *yang* lines at different positions that the *Zhou Book of Change* turns out to be a complicated system full of variety and change. From ancient to modern times, the book has been providing people with much wisdom as to how to live a harmonious life in a world of uncertainty.

3.【天道阴阳,地道柔刚,人道仁义】

It is said that "when the sages wrote *The Zhou Book of Change*, they intended to simulate obediently the principles of nature and fate of all things of creation". Thus, *The Zhou Book of Change* encompasses "the way of heaven" (yin and yang), "the way of earth" (yieldingness and firmness) and "the way of man" (benevolence and righteousness). Hence, the origin of the philosophical notion and practical pursuit of "harmony between heaven and man".

4.【八卦相错】

It goes without saying that *The Zhou Book of Change* entails the philosophical thought of "a unity of opposites". After listing the relationships of four pairs of trigrams in Chapter Three ("Heaven and earth determine their own positions; mountain and lake interchange with each other through air and vapor; thunder rumbles and wind blows, they echo and mix with each other; fire and water are not opponents but assistants to each other"), it comes to the conclusion that "the eight trigrams mingle in a unity of opposites".

Practice

I. Vocabulary

Choose a proper word or phrase to complete each of the following sentences, changing the form when necessary.

divination	signify	manifest	simulate	mingle
invigorate	penetrate	moisten	symbolize	beget

1. Interviews can be ________ in the classroom.
2. The magic will be used in organized or private rituals for healing, and ________ for guidance when important decisions loom.
3. A dog's protective instincts are ________ in increased alertness.
4. Hunger ________ crime.
5. Explorers ________ deep into unknown regions.

6. The image of the lion ________ power and strength.
7. Wedding rings ________ a couple's commitment to each other.
8. Add just enough water to ________ the cake mixture without making it too watery.
9. Her excitement was ________ with a slight feeling of fear.
10. He felt ________ after a day in the country.

II. Translation

Translate the following sentences and the passage into English.

1. 是以立天之道曰阴与阳，立地之道曰柔与刚，立人之道曰仁与义。

____

2. 天地定位，山泽通气，雷风相薄，水火不相射，八卦相错。

____

3. 圣人南面而听天下，向明而治，盖取诸此也。

____

4. 神也者，妙万物而为言者也。

____

5. 有天地然后有万物，有万物然后有男女，有男女然后有夫妇，有夫妇然后有父子，有父子然后有君臣，有君臣然后有上下，有上下然后礼义有所错。

____

____

6.《易》之为书也，广大悉备：有天道焉，有人道焉，有地道焉。兼三才而两之，故六；六者非它也，三才之道也。道有变动，故曰爻；爻有等，故曰物；物相杂，故曰文；文不当，故吉凶生焉。

____

____

____

III. Critical Thinking

Discuss the following questions in groups and give your group presentation in class on the basis of your discussion.

1. What do you think of the symbolism of the trigrams? Please support your opinion in your own words.
2. How do you understand the traditional Chinese theory that man is an integral part of nature?

References

[1] Lynn, Richard John. The Classic of Changes—A New Translation of the I Ching as

Interpreted by Wang Bi [M]. New York: Columbia University Press, 1994.
[2] 冯国超译注.(国学经典规范读本)周易(普及版)[M].北京：商务印书馆，2016.
[3] 黄寿祺，张善文译注.周易[M].上海：上海古籍出版社，2007.
[4] (魏)王弼著，楼宇烈校释.王弼集校释(下)[M].北京：中华书局，2012.
[5] 张善文今译，傅惠生英译.(大中华文库)周易(全2卷)[M].长沙：湖南人民出版社，2008.

Unit 2

Zhuangzi the Book[①]

Introduction

Zhuangzi the Book (also known as *Chuang-tzu*), named after "Master Zhuang" was, along with the *Laozi*, one of the earliest texts to contribute to the philosophy that has come to be known as Daoism, though it originally had nothing to do with religion at all. It began to be circulated before the Qin dynasty. Among all the circulated versions, Guo Xiang's edition which is composed of 33 chapters was the most popular one, which has been handed down up to the present day. It can be divided into three parts: "Inner Chapters" (7), "Outer Chapters" (15) and "Miscellaneous Chapters" (11).

The text of *Zhuangzi the Book* is ranked among the greatest literary and philosophical masterpieces. Its style is mythical, poetic, narrative, humorous, indirect, and polysemic. Much of the text espouses a holistic philosophy of life, encouraging disengagement from the artificialities of socialization, and cultivation of our natural "ancestral" potencies and skills, to live a simple and natural, but full and flourishing life.

Learning Objectives

After learning this unit, you will be able to

1. know the content and genre of *Zhuangzi the Book* in general;
2. understand the selected quotations from *Zhuangzi the Book* in detail;
3. interpret critically the materials related to *Zhuangzi the Book*'s philosophy in English;
4. understand and develop the traditional Chinese values based on *Zhuangzi the Book*.

① The excerpts from *Zhuangzi the Book* in this unit is from the first chapter. The ancient Chinese version is by Guo Xiang, the modern Chinese translation is by Chen Guying, and the first English version by Burton Watson and the second by Fung Yulan.

Selected Readings

逍 遥 游[1]

Free and Easy Wandering[2]

◈【原文】

北冥有鱼,其名为鲲。鲲之大,不知其几千里也;化而为鸟,其名为鹏。鹏之背,不知其几千里也;怒而飞,其翼若垂天之云。是鸟也,海运则将徙于南冥。南冥者,天池也。《齐谐》者,志怪者也。《谐》之言曰:"鹏之徙于南冥也,水击三千里,**抟**扶摇而上者九万里,去以六月息者也。"野马也,尘埃也,生物之以息相吹也。天之苍苍,其正色邪?其远而无所至极邪?其视下也,亦若是则已矣。且夫水之积也不厚,则其负大舟也无力。覆杯水于坳堂之上,则芥为之舟;置杯焉则胶,水浅而舟大也。风之积也不厚,则其负大翼也无力,故九万里,则风斯在下矣。而后乃今培风,背负青天,而莫之夭阏者,而后乃今将图南。**蜩**与学鸠笑之曰:"我**决**起而飞,**抢**榆枋,时则不至,而控于地而已矣;奚以之九万里而南为?"适莽苍者,三飡而反,腹犹果然;适百里者,宿舂粮;适千里者,三月聚粮。之二虫又何知!小知不及大知,小年不及大年。奚以知其然也?朝菌不知晦朔,蟪蛄不知春秋,此小年也。楚之南有冥灵者,以五百岁为春,五百岁为秋;上古有大椿者,以八千岁为春,八千岁为秋。而彭祖乃今以久特闻,众人匹之,不亦悲乎?

汤之问棘也是已:"穷发之北有冥海者,天池也。有鱼焉,其广数千里,未有知其修者,其名为鲲。有鸟焉,其名为鹏,背若太山,翼若垂天之云;抟扶摇、羊角而上者九万里,绝云气,负青天,然后图南,且适南冥也。斥鴳笑之曰:'彼且奚适也?我腾跃而上,不过数仞而下,翱翔蓬蒿之间,此亦飞之至也。而彼且奚适也?'"此小大之辩也。

故夫知效一官、行比一乡、德合一君、而徵一国者,其自视也,亦若此矣。而宋荣子犹然笑之。且举世而誉之而不加劝,举世而非之而不加沮,定乎内外之分,辩乎荣辱之境,斯已矣。彼其于世,未数数然也。虽然,犹有未树也。夫列子御风而行,泠然善也,旬有五日而后反。彼于致福者,未**数数然**也。此虽免乎行,犹有所待者也。若夫乘天地之正,而御六气之辩,以游无穷者,彼且**恶**乎待哉?故曰:至人无己,神人无功,圣人无名。

抟[tuán] 动词,击

蜩[tiáo] 名词,蝉

决[xuè] 名词,通作"翅",迅疾的样子

抢[qiāng] 动词,突过

---

① This chapter is divided into three parts, explaining a state of happiness of the perfect man who is absolutely free, because he has transcended all distinctions and is happy in any form of existence. Zhuangzi used imaginative fables to explain profound philosophy.

② This title is Burton Waston's translation; Feng's version of the title is "The Happy Excursion". Wang Rongpei, though, translated this title as "Wandering in Absolute Freedom".

数数[shuò]**然** 形容词，急急忙忙的样子

恶[wū] 文言叹词，何，什么

◈【今译】

北方的大海里有一条鱼，它的名字叫做鲲。鲲的体积，真不知道大到几千里；变化成为鸟，它的名字就叫鹏。鹏的脊背，真不知道长到几千里；当它奋起而飞的时候，那展开的双翅就像天边的云。这只鹏鸟呀，随着海上汹涌的波涛迁徙到南方的大海。南方的大海是个天然的大池。《齐谐》是一部专门记载怪异事情的书，这本书上记载说："鹏鸟迁徙到南方的大海，翅膀拍击水面激起三千里的波涛，海面上急骤的狂风盘旋而上直冲九万里高空，离开北方的大海用了六个月的时间方才停歇下来。"春日林泽原野上蒸腾浮动犹如奔马的雾气，低空里沸沸扬扬的尘埃，都是大自然里各种生物的气息吹拂所致。天空是那么湛蓝湛蓝的，难道这就是它真正的颜色吗？抑或是高旷辽远没法看到它的尽头呢？鹏鸟在高空往下看，不过也就像这个样子罢了。

再说水汇积不深，它浮载大船就没有力量。倒杯水在庭堂的低洼处，那么小小的芥草也可以给它当做船；而搁置杯子就粘住不动了，因为水太浅而船太大了。风聚积的力量不雄厚，它托负巨大的翅膀便力量不够。所以，鹏鸟高飞九万里，狂风就在它的身下，然后方才凭借风力飞行，背负青天而没有什么力量能够阻遏它了，然后才像现在这样飞到南方去。寒蝉与小灰雀讥笑它说："我从地面急速起飞，碰着榆树和檀树的树枝，常常飞不到而落在地上，为什么要到九万里的高空而向南飞呢？"到迷茫的郊野去，带上三餐就可以往返，肚子还是饱饱的；到百里之外去，要用一整夜时间准备干粮；到千里之外去，三个月以前就要准备粮食。寒蝉和灰雀这两个小东西懂得什么！小聪明赶不上大智慧，寿命短比不上寿命长。怎么知道是这样的呢？清晨的菌类不会懂得什么是晦朔，寒蝉也不会懂得什么是春秋，这就是短寿。楚国南边有叫冥灵的大龟，它把五百年当做春，把五百年当做秋；上古有叫大椿的古树，它把八千年当做春，把八千年当做秋，这就是长寿。可是彭祖到如今还是以年寿长久而闻名于世，人们与他攀比，岂不可悲可叹吗？

商汤询问棘的话是这样的："在那草木不生的北方，有一个很深的大海，那就是'天池'。那里有一种鱼，它的脊背有好几千里，没有人能够知道它有多长，它的名字叫做鲲，有一种鸟。它的名字叫鹏，它的脊背像座大山，展开双翅就像天边的云。鹏鸟奋起而飞，翅膀拍击急速旋转向上的气流直冲九万里高空，穿过云气，背负青天，这才向南飞去，打算飞到南方的大海。斥鴳讥笑它说：'它打算飞到哪儿去？我奋力跳起来往上飞，不过几丈高就落了下来，盘旋于蓬蒿丛中，这也是我飞翔的极限了。而它打算飞到什么地方去呢？'"这就是小与大的不同了。

所以，那些才智足以胜任一个官职，品行合乎一乡人心愿，道德能使国君感到满意，能力足以取信一国之人的人，他们看待自己也像是这样的。而宋荣子却讥笑他们。世上的人们都赞誉他，他不会因此越发努力，世上的人们都非难他，他也不会因此而更加沮丧。他清楚地划定自身与外物的区别，辨别荣誉与耻辱的界限，不过如此而已呀！宋荣子他对于整个社会，从来不急急忙忙地去追求什么。虽然如此，他还是未能达到最高的境界。列子能驾风行走，那样子实在轻盈美好，而且十五天后方才返回。列子对于寻求幸福，从来没有急急忙忙的样子。他这样做虽然免除了行走的劳苦，可还是有所依凭。至于遵循宇宙万物的规律，把握"六气"的变化，遨游于无穷无尽的境域，他还仰赖什么呢！因此说，道德修养高尚的"至人"能够达到忘我的境界，精神世界完全超脱物外的"神人"心目中没有功名和事业，思想修养臻于完美的“圣人”从不去追求名誉和地位。

◈ [Version 1]

In the northern darkness there is a fish and his name is Kun. The Kun is so huge I don't know how many thousand *li* he measures. He changes and becomes a bird whose name is Peng. The back of the Peng measures I don't know how many thousand li across, and when he rises up and flies off, his wings are like clouds all over the sky. When the sea begins to move, this bird sets off for the southern darkness, which is the Lake of Heaven.

The Universal Harmony records various wonders, and it says: "When the Peng journeys to the southern darkness, the waters are **roiled** for three thousand li. He beats the whirlwind and rises ninety thousand li, setting off on the sixth month **gale**." Wavering heat, bits of dust, living things blowing each other about—the sky looks very blue. Is that its real color, or is it because it is so far away and has no end? When the bird looks down, all he sees is blue, too.

If water is not piled up deep enough, it won't have the strength to bear up a big boat. Pour a cup of water into a hollow in the floor, and bits of trash will sail on it like boats. But set the cup there, and it will stick fast, for the water is too shallow and the boat too large. If wind is not piled up deep enough, it won't have the strength to bear up great wings. Therefore, when the Peng rises ninety thousand li, he must have the wind under him like that. Only then can he mount on the back of the wind, shoulder the blue sky, and nothing can hinder or block him. Only then can he set his eyes to the south.

The **cicada** and the little dove laugh at this, saying, "When we make an effort and fly up, we can get as far as the **elm** or the **sapanwood** tree, but sometimes we don't make it and just fall down on the ground. Now how is anyone going to go ninety thousand li to the south!"

If you go off to the green woods nearby, you can take along food for three meals and come back with your stomach as full as ever. If you are going a hundred li, you must grind your grain the night before; and if you are going a thousand li, you must start getting the provisions together three months in advance. What do these two creatures understand? Little understanding cannot come up to great understanding; the short-lived cannot come up to the long-lived.

How do I know this is so? The morning mushroom knows nothing of twilight and dawn; the summer cicada knows nothing of spring and autumn. They are the short-lived. South of Chu there is a **caterpillar** which counts five hundred years as one spring and five hundred years as one autumn. Long, long ago there was a great **rose of Sharon** that counted eight thousand years as one spring and eight thousand years as one autumn. They are the long-lived. Yet P'eng-tsu alone is famous today for having lived a long time, and everybody tries to **ape** him. Isn't it pitiful!

Among the questions of Tang to Ch'i we find the same thing. In the bald and barren north, there is a dark sea, the Lake of Heaven. In it is a fish which is several thousand li across, and no one knows how long. His name is Kun. There is also a bird there, named Peng, with a back like

Mount Tai and wings like clouds filling the sky. He beats the whirlwind, leaps into the air, and rises up ninety thousand li, cutting through the clouds and mist, shouldering the blue sky, and then he turns his eyes south and prepares to journey to the southern darkness.

The little **quail** laughs at him, saying, "Where does he think he's going? I give a great leap and fly up, but I never get more than ten or twelve yards before I come down **fluttering** among the weeds and **brambles**. And that's the best kind of flying, anyway! Where does he think he's going?" Such is the difference between big and little.

Therefore a man who has wisdom enough to fill one office effectively, good conduct enough to impress one community, virtue enough to please one ruler, or talent enough to be called into service in one state, has the same kind of self-pride as these little creatures. Sung Jung-tzu would certainly burst out laughing at such a man. The whole world could praise Sung Jung-tzu and it wouldn't make him exert himself; the whole world could condemn him and it wouldn't make him **mope**.

He drew a clear line between the internal and the external, and recognized the boundaries of true glory and disgrace. But that was all. As far as the world went, he didn't **fret** and worry, but there was still ground he left unturned.

Lieh Tzu could ride the wind and go soaring around with cool and breezy skill, but after fifteen days he came back to earth. As far as the search for good fortune went, he didn't fret and worry. He escaped the trouble of walking, but he still had to depend on something to get around. If he had only mounted on the truth of Heaven and Earth, ridden the changes of the six breaths, and thus wandered through the boundless, then what would he have had to depend on?

Therefore I say, the Perfect Man has no self; the Holy Man has no merit; the Sage has no fame.

---

roil /rɔɪl/ *v*. make turbid by stirring up the sediments of （水）激荡，翻滚，翻腾

gale /geɪl/ *n*. an extremely strong wind 大风；飓风

cicada /sɪˈkɑːdə/ *n*. a large insect with transparent wings, common in hot countries 蝉，知了

elm /elm/ *n*. a tall tree with broad leaves, also the hard wood of the elm tree 榆树

sapanwood /ˈsæpənwʊd/ *n*. a variant spelling of sappan wood, a small leguminous tree, Caesalpinia sappan, of S Asia producing wood that yields a red dye 苏木

caterpillar /ˈkætəpɪlə/ *n*. a small creature like a worm with legs, that develops into a butterfly or moth 毛虫

the rose of Sharon /ˈʃærən/ *phr*. flowering plant 鲜花

ape /eɪp/ *v*. to do sth in the same way as sb else, especially when it is not done very well 模仿，仿效

quail /kweɪl/ *n*. a small brown bird, whose meat and eggs are used for food; the meat of this bird 鹌鹑；鹌鹑肉

flutter /ˈflʌtə/ *v*. fly somewhere moving the wings quickly and lightly 飞来飞去

bramble /ˈbræmbl/ *n*. (especially British English) a wild bush with thorns on which blackberries grow 荆棘

mope /məʊp/ *v*. to spend your time doing nothing and feeling sorry for yourself 闷闷不乐；自怨自艾

fret /fret/ *v*. to be worried or unhappy and not able to relax 苦恼；烦躁；焦虑不安

◈ [Version 2]

In the Northern Ocean, there is a fish, by the name of Kun, which is many thousand *li* in size. This fish **metamorphoses** into a bird by the name of Peng, whose back is many thousand li in breadth. When the bird rouses itself and flies, its wings obscure the sky like clouds. When this bird moves itself in the sea, it is preparing to start for the Southern Ocean, the **Celestial** Lake.

A man named Chi Hsieh, who recorded novel occurrences, said: "When the Peng is moving to the Southern Ocean, it flaps along the water for three thousand li. Then it ascends on a whirlwind up to a height of ninety thousand li, for a flight of six months' duration."

There is the wandering air; there are the **motes**; there are living things that blow one against another with their breath. We do not know whether the blueness of the sky is its original color or is simply caused by its infinite height. When the Peng sees the earth from above, just as we see the sky from below, it will stop rising and begin to fly to the south. Without sufficient depth, the water would not be able to float a large boat. Upset a cup of water into a small hole, and a mustard seed will be the boat. Try to float the cup, and it will stick, because the water is shallow and the vessel is large. Without sufficient density, the wind would not be able to support the large wings. Therefore, when the Peng ascends to the height of ninety thousand li, the wind is all beneath it. Then, with the blue sky above, and no obstacle on the way, it mounts upon the wind and starts for the south.

A cicada and a young dove laugh at the Peng, saying: "When we make an effort, we fly up to the trees. Sometimes, not able to reach, we fall to the ground midway. What is the use of going up ninety thousand li in order to start for the south?"

He who goes to the grassy suburbs, taking enough food for three meals with him, comes back with his stomach as full as when he started. But he who travels a hundred li must grind flour enough for a night's halt. And he who travels a thousand li must supply himself with provisions for 3 months.

What do these two creatures know?

Small knowledge is not to be compared with the great nor a short life to a long one. How do we know that this is so? The morning mushroom knows not the end and the beginning of a month. The **chrysalis** knows not the alternation of spring and autumn. These are instances of short life. In the south of the Chu state, there is Ming-ling, whose spring is 500 years and whose autumn is equally long. In high **antiquity**, there was Ta-chun, whose spring was 8000 years and whose autumn was equally long. Peng Tsu was the one specially renowned until the present day for his

length of life. If all men were to match him, would they not be miserable?

In the question put by Tang to Chi, there was a similar statement: "In the barren north, there is a sea, the Celestial Lake. In it there is a fish, several thousand li in breadth, and no one knows how many li in length. Its name is the Kun. There is also a bird, named the Peng, with a back like Mount Tai, and wings like clouds across the sky. Upon a whirlwind it soars up to a height of ninety thousand li. Beyond the clouds and atmosphere, with the blue sky above it, it then directs its flight to the south, and thus proceeds to the ocean there.

"A quail laughs at it, saying: 'Where is that bird going? I spring up with a bound, and when I have reached not more than a few yards I come down again. I just fly about among the brushwood and the bushes. This is also the perfection of flying. Where is that bird going?'" This is the difference between the great and the small. There are some men whose knowledge is sufficient for the duties of some office. There are some men whose conduct will secure unity in some district. There are some men whose virtue befits him for a ruler. There are some men whose ability wins credit in the country. In their opinion of themselves, they are just like what is mentioned above.

Yet Sung Yung Tzu laughed at it. If the whole world should admire him, he would not be encouraged thereby, nor if the whole world should blame him would he thereby be discouraged. He held fast the difference between the internal and the external. He marked distinctly the boundary of honor and disgrace. This was the best of him. In the world, such a man is rare, yet there is still something which he did not establish.

Lieh Tzu could ride upon the wind and pursue his way, in a refreshing and good manner, returning after fifteen days. Among those who attained happiness, such a man is rare. Yet, although he was able to dispense with walking, he still had to depend upon something.

But suppose there is one who **chariots** on the normality of the universe, rides on the transformation of the six elements and thus makes **excursion** into the infinite, what has he to depend upon?

Therefore, it is said that the perfect man has no self; the spiritual man has no achievement; the true sage has no name.

---

metamorphose /ˌmetəˈmɔːfəʊz/ *v*. to change or make sth/sb change into sth completely different, especially over a period of time (使)变形,变化,发生质变

celestial /səˈlestiəl/ *adj*. of the sky or of heaven 天空的;天上的

mote /məʊt/ *n*. a very small piece of dust 尘埃;微粒

chrysalis /ˈkrɪsəlɪs/ *n*. (also chrysalid) the form of an insect, especially a butterfly or moth , while it is changing into an adult inside a hard case, called a chrysalis 蛹,蛹壳

antiquity /ænˈtɪkwəti/ *n*. the state of being very old or ancient 古老,古

chariot /ˈtʃæriət/ *n*. an open vehicle with two wheels, pulled by horses, used in ancient times in battle and for racing （古代用于战斗或比赛的）双轮敞篷马车；*v*. ride a carriage 驾驭马车

excursion /ɪkˈskəːʃn/ *n*. a short journey made for pleasure, especially one that has been organized for a group of people （尤指集体）远足，短途旅行

◈【原文】

尧让天下于许由，曰："日月出矣，而爝火不息；其于光也，不亦难乎？时雨降矣，而犹浸灌；其于泽也，不亦劳乎？夫子立而天下治，而我犹尸之；吾自视缺然，请致天下。"许由曰："子治天下，天下既已治也；而我犹代子，吾将为名乎？名者，实之宾也；吾将为宾乎？**鹪鹩**巢于深林，不过一枝；偃鼠饮河，不过满腹。归休乎君，予无所用天下为！庖人虽不治庖，尸祝不越樽俎而代之矣！"

肩吾问于连叔曰："吾闻言于接舆，大而无当，往而不反。吾惊怖其言。犹河汉而无极也；大有径庭，不近人情焉。"连叔曰："其言谓何哉？"曰："'**藐姑射**之山，有神人居焉。肌肤若冰雪，**淖约**若处子，不食五谷，吸风饮露，乘云气，御飞龙，而游乎四海之外；其神凝，使物不**疵疠**而年谷熟。'吾以是狂而不信也。"连叔曰："然。瞽者无以与乎文章之观，聋者无以与乎钟鼓之声。岂唯形骸有聋盲哉？夫知亦有之！是其言也，犹时女也。之人也，之德也，将旁礴万物以为一，世**蕲**乎乱，孰**弊弊焉**以天下为事！之人也，物莫之伤，大浸稽天而不溺，大旱金石流，土山焦而不热。是其尘垢粃糠，将犹陶铸尧舜者也，孰肯以物为事？"

宋人资章甫而适诸越，越人断发文身，无所用之。尧治天下之民，平海内之政，往见四子藐姑射之山，汾水之阳，**窅然丧**其天下焉。

鹪鹩[jiāoliáo] 名词，一种善于筑巢的小鸟

藐[miǎo] 形容词，遥远的样子

姑射[yè] 名词，传说中的山名

淖[chuò]**约** 形容词，柔弱、美好的样子

疵疠[lì] 名词，疾病

蕲[qí] 动词，通祈；求的意思

乱[luàn] 这里作"治"讲，这是古代同词义反的语言现象

弊弊焉[bì bì yān] 形容词，忙忙碌碌、疲惫不堪的样子

窅[yǎo]**然** 形容词，怅然若失的样子

丧[shàng] 动词，丧失、忘掉

◈【今译】

尧打算把天下让给许由，说："太阳和月亮都已升起来了，可是小小的炬火还在燃烧不熄；它要跟太阳和月亮的光亮相比，不是很难吗？季雨及时降落了，可是还在不停地浇水灌地；如此费力的人工灌溉对于整个大地的润泽，不显得徒劳吗？先生如能居于国君之位，天下一定会获得大治，可是我还空居其位；我自己越看越觉得能力不够，请允许我把天下交给你。"许由回答说："你治理天下，天下已经获得了大治，而我却还要去替代你，我难道为了名声吗？'名'是'实'所派生出来的次要东西，我难道去追求这次要的东西吗？鹪鹩在森林中筑巢，不过占用一根树枝；鼹鼠到大河边饮水，不过喝满肚

子。你还是打消念头回去吧，天下对于我来说没有什么用处啊！厨师即使不下厨，祭祀主持人也不会越俎代庖的！”

肩吾向连叔求教：“我从接舆那里听到谈话，大话连篇没有边际，一说下去就回不到原来的话题上。我十分惊恐他的言谈，就好像天上的银河没有边际，跟一般人的言谈差异甚远，确实是太不近情理了。”连叔问：“他说的是些什么呢？”肩吾转述道：“‘在遥远的姑射山上，住着一位神人，皮肤润白像冰雪，体态柔美如处女，不食五谷，吸清风饮甘露，乘云气驾飞龙，遨游于四海之外。他的神情那么专注，使得世间万物不受病害，年年五谷丰登’。我认为这全是虚妄之言，一点也不可信。”连叔听后说：“是呀！对于瞎子没法同他们欣赏花纹和色彩，对于聋子没法同他们聆听钟鼓的乐声。难道只是形骸上有聋与瞎吗？思想上也有聋和瞎啊！这话似乎就是说你肩吾的呀。那位神人，他的德行，与万事万物混同一起，以此求得整个天下的治理，谁还会忙忙碌碌把管理天下当成回事！那样的人呀，外物没有什么能伤害他，滔天的大水不能淹没他，天下大旱使金石熔化、土山焦裂，他也不感到灼热。他所留下的尘埃以及瘪谷糠麸之类的废物，也可造就出尧舜那样的圣贤人君来，他怎么会把忙着管理万物当做己任呢！”

北方的宋国有人贩卖帽子到南方的越国，越国人不蓄头发，满身刺着花纹，没什么地方用得着帽子。尧治理好天下的百姓，安定了海内的政局，到姑射山上、汾水北面，去拜见四位得道的高士，不禁怅然若失，忘记了自己居于治理天下的地位。

◆ [Version 1]

Yao wanted to **cede** the empire to Xu You. “When the sun and moon have already come out,” he said, “it’s a waste of light to go on burning the torches, isn’t it? When the seasonal rains are falling, it’s a waste of water to go on irrigating the fields. If you took the throne, the world would be well ordered. I go on occupying it, but all I can see are my failings. I beg to turn over the world to you.” Xu You said, “You govern the world and the world is already well governed. Now if I take your place, will I be doing it for a name? But name is only the guest of reality—will I be doing it so I can play the part of a guest? When the **tailorbird** builds her nest in the deep wood, she uses no more than one branch. When the **mole** drinks at the river, he takes no more than a **bellyful**. Go home and forget the matter, my lord. I have no use for the rulership of the world! Though the cook may not run his kitchen properly, the priest and the **impersonator** of the dead at the sacrifice do not leap over the wine casks and sacrificial stands and go take his place.”

Jian Wu said to Lian Shu, “I was listening to Jie Yu’s talk—big and nothing to back it up, going on and on without turning around. I was completely **dumbfounded** at his words—no more end than the Milky Way, wild and wide of the mark, never coming near human affairs!”

“What were his words like?” asked Lian Shu.

“He said that there is a Holy Man living on faraway Gushe Mountain, with skin like ice or snow and gentle and shy like a young girl. He doesn’t eat the five grains but sucks the wind, drinks the dew, climbs up on the clouds and mist, rides a flying dragon, and wanders beyond the four seas. By concentrating his spirit, he can protect creatures from sickness and plague and make the harvest plentiful. I thought this all was insane and refused to believe it."

"You would!" said Lian Shu. "We can't expect a blind man to appreciate beautiful patterns or a deaf man to listen to bells and drums. And blindness and deafness are not confined to the body alone—the understanding has them, too, as your words just now have shown. This man, with this virtue of his, is about to embrace the ten thousand things and roll them into one. Though the age calls for reform, why should he wear himself out over the affairs of the world? There is nothing that can harm this man. Though floodwaters pile up to the sky, he will not drown. Though a great drought melts metal and stone and **scorches** the earth and hills, he will not be burned. From his dust and leavings alone, you could **mold** a Yao or a Shun! Why should he consent to bother about mere things?"

A man of Song who sold ceremonial hats made a trip to Yue, but the Yue people cut their hair short and tattooed their bodies and had no use for such things. Yao brought order to the people of the world and directed the government of all within the seas. But he went to see the Four Masters of the faraway Gushe Mountain, [and when he got home] north of the Fen River, he was dazed and had forgotten his kingdom there.

---

cede /siːd/ *v*. to give sb control of sth or give them power, a right, etc., especially unwillingly 让给;退让

tailorbird /ˈteɪləbɜːd/ *n*. tropical Asian warbler that stitches leaves together to form and conceal its nest 缝叶莺

mole /məʊl/ *n*. a small animal with dark grey fur, that is almost blind and digs tunnels under the ground to live in 鼹鼠

bellyful /ˈbelɪfʊl/ *n*. an undesirable overabundance 满肚子;过分,过量

impersonator /ɪmˈpɜːsəneɪtə(r)/ *n*. a person who copies the way another person talks or behaves in order to entertain people 演员,模仿明星的艺人

dumbfounded /dʌmfaʊndɪd/ *adj*. unable to speak because of surprise 惊呆的;*v*. 使发愣

scorch /skɔːtʃ/ *v*. to burn and slightly damage a surface by making it too hot; to be slightly burned by heat 烤焦;使枯萎

mold /məʊld/ *n*. the distinctive form in which a thing is made 模式;*v*. form in clay, wax, etc. 浇筑,塑造;shape or influence; give direction to 对……产生影响

◈ [Version 2]

Yao wished to resign as the ruler of the empire in Hsu Yu's favour, saying: "If, when the sun and moon have come forth, one insists on lighting the torches, would it not be difficult for them to give light? If, when the seasonal rains have come down, one still continues to water the ground, would this not be a waste of labour? Now, you, master, just stand before the throne, and the empire will be in peace; yet I still preside over it. I am conscious of my deficiency, and beg to

give to you the empire." "You, sir, govern the empire," said Hsu Yu, "and it is already in peace. Suppose I were to take your place, would I do it for the name? Name is the shadow of real gain. Would I do it for real gain? The **tit**, building its nest in the **mighty** forest, occupies but a single **twig**. The **tapir**, **slaking** its thirst from the river, drinks only enough to fill its belly. You return and be quiet. I have no need of the empire. Though the cook were not attending to his kitchen, the boy **impersonating** the dead, and the officer of prayer would not step over the cups and stands to take his place."

Chien Wu said to Lien Shu: "I heard from Chieh Yu some utterances that were great but could not be justified. Once stated, there is no end of his tale. I was greatly startled at what he said. It seemed to be as boundless as the Milky Way. It was very improbable and far removed from human experience."

"What did he say?" asked Lien Shu.

"He said," replied Chien Wu, "far away on the mountain of Ku Yi, there lived a spiritual man. His flesh and skin were like ice and snow. His manner was elegant and graceful as that of a maiden. He did not eat any of the five grains, but inhaled the wind and drank the dew."

"He rode on clouds, drove along the flying dragons, and thus rambled beyond the four seas."

"His spirit is compact."

"'Yet he could save things from corruption and secure every year a plentiful harvest.' I thought all these sayings were nonsense and refused to believe in them."

"Yes," said Lien Shu, "the blind have nothing to do with beauty, nor the deaf with music. There are not only physical blindness and deafness, there are also the intellectual. Of the latter you yourself supply an illustration. That man, with those virtues, would embrace all things. According to him, everything in the world is longing for peace; why should there be some who address themselves laboriously to govern the empire?"

"That man, nothing can hurt. In a flood reaching the sky, he would not be drowned. In a drought, though metals ran liquid and mountains were scorched, he would not feel hot."

"Even his dust and **siftings** could still fashion and mold Yao and Shun. How should he will to occupy himself with things?"

A man of the Sung state carried some ceremonial caps to the Yueh state. But the men of Yueh used to cut off their hair and paint their body, so that they had no use of such things. Yao ruled the people of the empire and maintained a perfect government within the four seas. He went to see the four sages in the distant mountain of Ku Yi. On returning to his capital south of the Fen River, he silently forgot his empire.

---

tit /tɪt/ *n*. a small bird （鸟）山雀

mighty /ˈmaɪti/ *a*. large and impressive; (especially literary) very strong and powerful 巨大的；强有力的；浩瀚的

twig /twɪg/ *n*. a small, very thin branch that grows out of a larger branch on a bush or tree 细枝，嫩枝

tapir /ˈteɪpə(r)/ *n*. an animal like a pig with a long nose, that lives in Central and S America and SE Asia 貘(生活在中南美洲和东南亚的长鼻猪状动物)

slake /sleɪk/ *v*. to drink so that you no longer feel thirsty 解(渴)；消除；to satisfy a desire 满足

impersonate /ɪmˈpɜːsəneɪt/ *v*. to pretend to be sb in order to trick people or to entertain them 扮演；模仿；拟人，人格化

sift /ˈsɪftɪŋ/ *v*. to put flour or some other fine substance through a sieve/sifter 筛，过滤

◈【原文】

惠子谓庄子曰："魏王贻我大瓠之种，我树之成，而实五石。以盛水浆，其坚不能自举也。剖之以为瓢，则瓠落无所容。非不**呺然**大也，吾为其无用而掊之。"庄子曰："夫子固拙于用大矣！宋人有善为不龟手之药者，世世以**洴澼**为事。客闻之，请买其方以百金。聚族而谋曰：'我世世为洴澼**絖**，不过数金；今一朝而**鬻**技百金，请与之。'客得之，以说吴王。越有难，吴王使之将，冬与越人水战，大败越人，裂地而封之。能不龟手，一也，或以封，或不免于洴澼絖，则所用之异也。今子有五石之瓠，何不虑以为大樽，而浮于江湖，而忧其瓠落无所容？则夫子犹有蓬之心也夫！"

惠子谓庄子曰："吾有大树，人谓之**樗**。其大本拥肿而不中绳墨，其小枝卷曲而不中规矩，立之涂，匠人不顾。今子之言，大而无用，众所同去也。"庄子曰："子独不见狸狌乎？卑身而伏，以候敖者；东西跳梁，不辟高下；中于机辟，死于罔**罟**。今夫**斄**牛，其大若垂天之云。此能为大矣，而不能执鼠。今子有大树，患其无用，何不树之于无何有之乡，广莫之野，彷徨乎无为其侧，逍遥乎寝卧其下。不夭斤斧，物无害者，无所可用，安所困苦哉！"

呺[xiāo]**然** 形容词，庞大而又中空的样子

洴[píng] 动词，浮

澼[pì] 动词，在水中漂洗。

絖[kuàng] 名词，丝絮

鬻[yù] 动词，卖，出售

樗[chū] 名词，一种高大的落叶乔木，但木质粗劣不可用

罟[gǔ] 名词，网的总称

斄[lí] 名词，牛，牦牛

◈【今译】

惠子对庄子说："魏王送我大葫芦种子，我将它培植起来后，结出的果实有五石之大。用大葫芦去盛水浆，可是它的坚固程度承受不了水的压力。把它剖开做瓢也太大了，没有什么地方可以放得下。这个葫芦不是不大呀，我因为它没有什么用处而砸烂了它。"庄子说："先生实在是不善于使用大东西啊！宋国有一善于调制不皲手药物的人家，世世代代以漂洗丝絮为职业。有个游客听说了这件事，愿意用百金的高价收买他的药方。全家人聚集在一起商量：'我们世世代代在河水里漂洗丝絮，所得不

过数金，如今一下子就可卖得百金。还是把药方卖给他吧。'游客得到药方，来游说吴王。正巧越国发难，吴王派他统率部队，冬天跟越军在水上交战，大败越军，吴王划割土地封赏他。能使手不皲裂，药方是同样的，有的人用它来获得封赏，有的人却只能靠它在水中漂洗丝絮，这是使用的方法不同。如今你有五石容积的大葫芦，怎么不考虑用它来制成腰舟，而浮游于江湖之上，却担忧葫芦太大无处可容？看来先生你还是心窍不通啊！"

惠子又对庄子说："我有棵大树，人们都叫它'樗'。它的树干却疙疙瘩瘩，不符合绳墨取直的要求，它的树枝弯弯扭扭，也不适应圆规和角尺取材的需要。虽然生长在道路旁，木匠连看也不看。现今你的言谈，大而无用，大家都会鄙弃它的。"庄子说："先生你没看见过野猫和黄鼠狼吗？低着身子匍匐于地，等待那些出洞觅食或游乐的小动物。一会儿东，一会儿西，跳来跳去，一会儿高，一会儿低，上下窜越，不曾想到落入猎人设下的机关，死于猎网之中。再有那斄牛，庞大的身体就像天边的云；它的本事可大了，不过不能捕捉老鼠。如今你有这么大一棵树，却担忧它没有什么用处，怎么不把它栽种在什么也没有生长的地方，栽种在无边无际的旷野里，悠然自得地徘徊于树旁，优游自在地躺卧于树下。大树不会遭到刀斧砍伐，也没有什么东西会去伤害它。虽然没有派上什么用场，可是哪里又会有什么困苦呢？"

◈ [Version 1]

Hui Tzu said to Chuang Tzu, "The king of Wei gave me some seeds of a huge gourd. I planted them, and when they grew up, the fruit was big enough to hold five **piculs**. I tried using it for a water container, but it was so heavy that I couldn't lift it. I split it in half to make **dippers**, but they were so large and **unwieldy** that I couldn't dip them into anything. It's not that the **gourds** weren't fantastically big—but I decided they were no use and so I **smashed** them to pieces."

Chuang Tzu said, "You certainly are **dense** when it comes to using big things! In Sung there was a man who was skilled at making a **salve** to prevent **chapped** hands, and generation after generation his family made a living by **bleaching** silk in water. A traveler heard about the salve and offered to buy the prescription for a hundred measures of gold. The man called everyone to a family council. 'For generations we've been bleaching silk and we've never made more than a few measures of gold,' he said. 'Now, if we sell our secret, we can make a hundred measures in one morning. Let's let him have it!' The traveler got the salve and introduced it to the king of Wu, who was having trouble with the state of Yueh. The king put the man in charge of his troops, and that winter they fought a naval battle with the men of Yueh and gave them a bad beating. A portion of the conquered territory was awarded to the man as a **fief**. The salve had the power to prevent chapped hands in either case; but one man used it to get a fief, while the other one never got beyond silk bleaching because they used it in different ways. Now you had a gourd big enough to hold five piculs. Why didn't you think of making it into a great tub so you could go floating around the rivers and lakes, instead of worrying because it was too big and unwieldy to dip into things! Obviously, you still have a lot of underbrush in your head!"

Hui Tzu said to Chuang Tzu, "I have a big tree, men called it shu. Its trunk is too **gnarled** and

bumpy to apply a measuring line to, its branches too bent and twisty to match up to a compass or square. You could stand it by the road and no carpenter would look at it twice. Your words, too, are big and useless, and so everyone alike **spurns** them!"

Chuang Tzu said, "Maybe you've never seen a wildcat or a **weasel**. It **crouches** down and hides, watching for something to come along. It leaps and races east and west, not hesitating to go high or low—until it falls into the trap and dies in the net. Then again there's the **yak**, big as a cloud covering the sky. It certainly knows how to be big, though it doesn't know how to catch rats. Now You have this big tree, and you're distressed because it's useless. Why don't you plant it in Not-Even-Anything Village, or the field of Broad-and-Boundless, relax and do nothing by its side, or lie down for a free and easy sleep under it? Axes will never shorten its life, nothing can ever harm it. If there's no use for it, how can it come to grief or pain?"

---

picul /ˈpɪkʌl/ *n*. a unit of weight used in some parts of Asia; approximately equal to 133 pounds (the load a grown man can carry) 石;担(计量单位)

dip /dɪp/ *v*. put something into a container and take something out 伸进(……里取东西)

unwieldy /ʌnˈwiːldi/ *adj*. difficult to move or control because of its size, shape or weight 笨重的;笨拙的;不灵巧的

gourd /gɔːd/ *n*. a type of large fruit, not normally eaten, with hard skin and soft flesh. Gourds are often dried and used as containers 葫芦

smash /smæʃ/ *v*. to break sth, or to be broken, violently and noisily into many pieces (哗啦一声)打碎,打破,破碎

dense /dens/ *adj*. stupid 愚笨的;迟钝的;笨拙的

salve /sælv/ *n*. a substance that you put on a wound or sore skin to help it heal or to protect it 药膏;软膏;油膏

chapped /tʃæpt/ *adj*. (of the skin or lips 皮肤或唇) rough, dry and sore, especially because of wind or cold weather (尤指因风吹或天冷而)皲裂的,开裂的

bleach /bliːtʃ/ *v*. to make sth white or pale by a chemical process or by the effect of light from the sun; to become white or pale in this way (使)变白,漂白,晒白,退色

fief /fiːf/ *n*. an area of land, especially a rented area for which the payment is work, not money 领地;(尤指)采邑,封地

gnarled /nɑːl/ *adj*. (of trees) twisted and rough; covered with hard lumps (树木)扭曲的;多节瘤的;疙疙瘩瘩的

bumpy /ˈbʌmpi/ *adj*. (of a surface) not even; with a lot of bumps 不平的;多凸块的

spurn /spɜːn/ *v*. to reject or refuse sb/sth, especially in a proud way (尤指傲慢地)拒绝

weasel /ˈwiːzl/ *n*. a small wild animal with reddish-brown fur, a long thin body and short legs 鼬;黄鼠狼

crouch /kraʊtʃ/ *v*. to put your body close to the ground by bending your legs under you 蹲;蹲下;

蹲伏

yak /jæk/ *n*. an animal of the cow family, with long horns and long hair, that lives in central Asia 牦牛

◈ [Version 2]

Hui Tzu said to Chuang Tzu: "The king of Wei sent me some **calabash** seeds. I planted them and they bore a fruit as big as a five-bushel measure. I used it as a vessel for holding water, but it was not solid enough to hold it. I cut the calabash in two for **ladles**, but each of them was too shallow to hold anything. Because of this uselessness, I knocked them to pieces."

"Sir," said Chuang Tzu, "it was rather you who did not know how to use large things. There was a man of Sung who had a recipe for salve for chapped hands. From generation to generation, his family made silk washing their occupation. A stranger heard of this and proposed to offer him 100 ounces of gold for the recipe. The **kindred** all came together to consider this proposal. 'We have,' said they, 'been washing silk for generations. What we gained is not more than a few ounces of gold. Now in one morning we can sell this art for 100 ounces. Let us give it to the stranger.' So, the stranger got it. He went and informed the king of Wu. When Wu and Yueh were at war, the king of Wu gave him the command of his fleet. In the winter he had a naval engagement with Yueh, in which the latter was totally defeated.

"The stranger was rewarded with a fief and a title. Thus while the efficiency of the salve to cure the chapped hands was the same in both cases, yet here it secured him a title, there, nothing more than a capacity for washing silk. This was because its application was different. Now you, sir, have this five-bushel calabash; why did you not make of it a large bottle gourd, by means of which you could float in rivers and lakes? Instead of this, you were sorry that it was useless for holding anything. I think your mind is rather **wooly**."

Hui Tzu said to Chuang Tzu: "I have a large tree, which men call the **ailanthus**. Its trunk is so irregular and knotty that a carpenter cannot apply his line to it. Its small branches are so twisted that the square and compasses cannot be used on them. It stands by the roadside, but is not looked at by any carpenter. Now your words, sir, are big but useless and also not wanted by anybody."

Chuang Tzu said: "Have you not seen a wild cat or a weasel? It lies, crouching down, in wait for its prey. East and west it leaps about, avoiding neither what is high nor what is low. At last it is caught in a trap or dies in a net. Again there is the yak, which is as large as the clouds across the sky. But it cannot catch mice. Now you have a large tree and are anxious about its uselessness. Why do you not plant it in the domain of nonexistence, in a wide and barren wild? By its side you may wander in nonaction; under it you may sleep in happiness. Neither bill nor ax would shorten its term of existence. Being of no use to others, it itself would be free from harm."

calabash /ˈkæləbæʃ/ *n*. a container made from the hard covering of a fruit or vegetable 葫芦

ladle /ˈleɪdl/ *n*. a large deep spoon with a long handle, used especially for serving soup 长柄勺；汤勺

kindred /ˈkɪndrəd/ *n*. family and relatives （统称）家人，亲属

wooly /ˈwʊli/ *adj*. confused and vague; used especially of thinking 糊涂的；不清楚的

ailanthus /eɪˈlænθəs/ *n*. any of several deciduous Asian trees of the genus Ailanthus 臭椿树

Chinese Philosophy

1.【小大之辩】

Everything has its proper nature. The nature of everything has its proper limitation. The difference among things is just like that between small and great knowledge, short and long life.... All believe in their own sphere, and none is intrinsically superior to others. After giving different illustrations, Chuang Tzu concluded with the independent man who forgets his own self and its other, and ignores all the differences. All things enjoy themselves in different spheres, but the independent man has neither achievement nor name. Therefore, he who unites the great and the small is one who ignores the distinction of the great and the small. If one insists on the distinction, the peng, the cicada, the small officer, and Lieh Tzu riding on the wind—all are troublesome things. He who equalizes life and death is one who ignores the distinction of life and death. If one insists on the distinction, Ta-chun, the chrysalis, Peng Tsu, and the morning mushroom, all suffer early death. Therefore, he who makes excursion in the nondistinction of the great and the small has no limitation. He who ignores the distinction of life and death, has no terminal. Those whose happiness is attached within the finite sphere will certainly have limitation. Though they are allowed to make excursion, they are not able to be independent.—Kuo Hsiang.

2.【有待无待】

If things enjoy themselves only in their finite spheres, their enjoyment must also be finite. For instance, if one enjoys only in life, he would suffer in death. If one enjoys only in power, he would suffer at the loss of it. The "independent man" transcends the finite. He "store the universe in the universe," as mentioned in Chapter VI. He thus becomes infinite, and so is his happiness. "The perfect man has no self," because he has transcended the finite and identified himself with the universe. "The spiritual man has no achievement," because he follows the nature of things and lets everything enjoy itself. "The true sage has no name," because his virtue is perfect; every name is a determination, a limitation.—Feng Yu-lan.

3.【至人无己，神人无功，圣人无名】

Yao had no need of the empire, just as the man of Yueh had no need for ceremonial caps. Yet he who has no need of the empire is just the man whom the empire needs for its ruler. Though the empire took Yao as its ruler, Yao himself did not consider the empire as his. He therefore silently forgot it, and let his mind wander in the realm of non-distinction. Though he sat on the throne and controlled all things, there was nothing which could disturb his happiness."—Kuo Hsiang.

4.【无用之用】

These stories in the third part are to show that everything has its particular fitness. Everything is useful in a certain way and useless in another. —Feng Yu-lan.

Practice

I. Vocabulary

Choose a proper word or phrase to complete each of the following sentences, changing the form when necessary.

ape (v.)	flutter	mope	fret	wooly
spurn	unwieldy	smash	crouch	gnarled

1. They were in the hotel room, only now there were trees all around, thin and ________ and leafless.
2. "I'll be here studying," Kristen ________. "I'm getting quizzed tonight on Socrates."
3. Superstition and ________ thinking are still bad even if they were practiced by well-meaning people.
4. Because he was ________ by Hollywood, he set up his own film studios at a compound in Southern California.
5. Mrs. Thatcher, of course, ________ about the reunification of Germany, as did many of her generation who recalled the megalomaniacal wickedness of Hitler, his conquests and his genocide.
6. He was old enough to be their father, and they liked him and looked up to him. Trent even tried sometimes to ________ the way he talked.
7. A few weeks ago, when his wife's body became so ________ that she could only waddle with a hand pressed against her aching back, he had brought another woman from the village to take on tasks he felt she should not do.
8. Gravity is so dense down there, they would be ________ as flat as paper if they fell.
9. Vestigial wings ________ on its back and the small hands attached to them reached out sideways as if pulling on the air.
10. McCuskey ________ beside the bed, gun in hand, wearing only the bottom half of a pair of long red underwear.

II. Translation

Translate the following sentences and the passage into English.

1. 吾闻言于接舆,大而无当,往而不反。

____

2. 吾惊怖其言，犹河汉而无极也，大有径庭，不近人情矣。

____

3. 吾以是狂而不信也。

____

4. 瞽者无以与乎文章之观，聋者无以与乎钟鼓之声。

____

5. 岂唯形骸有聋盲哉？夫知亦有之。

____

6. 尧让天下于许由，曰："日月出矣，而爝火不息；其于光也，不亦难乎？时雨降矣，而犹浸灌；其于泽也，不亦劳乎？夫子立，而天下治，而我犹尸之；吾自视缺然，请致天下。"许由曰："子治天下，天下既已治也；而我犹代子，吾将为名乎？名者实之宾也；吾将为宾乎？鹪鹩巢于深林，不过一枝；偃鼠饮河，不过满腹。归休乎君，予无所用天下为！庖人虽不治庖，尸祝不越樽俎而代之矣！"

____

____

____

____

____

III. Critical Thinking

Discuss the following questions in groups and do your group presentation in class on the basis of your discussion.

1. Do you know any famous stories in *Zhuangzi the Book*? Prepare to tell a story in *Zhuangzi the Book* and explain its implied meaning in English.
2. What do you think of the philosophy in *Zhuangzi the Book* and its application in current China?

References

[1] Burton Watson. The Complete Works of Zhuangzi [M]. New York: Columbia University Press, 2013: 1-6.

[2] Feng Yu-lan. Chuang-Tzu A New Selected Translation with an Exposition of the Philosophy of Guo Hsiang [M]. Foreign Language Teaching and Research Press, China & Springer International Publishing AG, 2016: 1-8.

[3] 陈鼓应. 庄子今注今译(上下册)[M]. 北京：商务印书馆，2007：5-40.

[4] 汪榕培英译，秦旭卿、孙雍长今译.（大中华文库）庄子(I)(II)[M]. 长沙：湖南人民出版社，1999：1-13.

Unit 3

The Analects of Confucius[①]

Introduction

The Analects of Confucius, also known as *The Analects*, or *Lunyu* (《论语》—literally, the "Classified Teachings"), is a collection of sayings and ideas attributed to the central Chinese philosopher Confucius and his contemporaries. It is an anthology of brief passages that presents the words of Confucius and his disciples, describes Confucius as a man, and recounts some of the events of his life.

The Analects of Confucius is written during the Spring and Autumn Period (770BC—476BC) through the Warring States Period (475 BC—221 BC). It is the representative work of Confucianism and continues to have a tremendous influence on Chinese and East Asian thought and values today. Since Confucius' time, *The Analects* has heavily influenced the philosophy and moral values of China and later other East Asian countries as well[②].

---

① The Chinese version comes from Yang Bojun, the edition of Zhonghua Book Company; English version one is translated by James Legge, who was the authority on Chinese studies during 1828 - 1893; English version two is translated by A. Charles Muller, a famous Chinese studies scholar who was devoted to introducing Chinese culture to Westerners.

② The philosophy conveyed through ***The Analects*** is basically an ethical perspective, and the text has always been understood as structured on a group of key ethical terms. There is a group of key terms whose meaning seems to be so flexible, subtle, and disputed that it seems best to leave them untranslated, simply using transcription for them. These include:

Loyalty (zhong 忠) denoting not only loyalty to one's superiors or peers, or to individuals, but also to office; an alignment of self with the interests of others, or of the social group as a whole.

Trustworthiness/Faithfulness (xin 信) derived from the concept of promise keeping, meaning reliability for others, but also unwavering devotion to principle.

Respectfulness/Attentiveness (jing 敬) derived from the notion of alertness, and fusing the attentiveness to task characteristic of a subordinate and the respect for superiors that such attentiveness reflects.

Filiality (xiao 孝) a traditional cultural imperative, obedience to parents, raised to a subtle level of fundamental self-discipline and character building.

Valor (yong 勇) in a feudal era marked by incessant warfare, bold warriors and adventurers were common: for Confucians, valor concerns risk taking on behalf of ethnical principle.

Learning Objectives

After learning this unit, you will be able to

1. learn generally about the content and genre of *The Analects*;
2. understand deeply the selected quotations from *The Analects* in detail;
3. interpret critically the materials in English related to the theory of Mean, and the knowledge about Chinese spirit;
4. explore the traditional Chinese values based on the Chinese classics.

Selected Readings

教育篇

◈【原文】

子曰:"学而时习之,不亦说乎? 有朋自远方来,不亦乐乎?"(《论语·学而》)

◈【今译】

孔子说:"学习了,而能按时去实践,不也高兴吗? 有朋友自远方来,(切磋学理),不也快乐吗?"

Education

◈ [Version 1]

The Master said, "Is it not pleasant to learn with a constant **perseverance** and application? Is it not delightful to have friends coming from distant quarters?"

perseverance /ˌpɜːsəˈvɪərəns/ *n.* determination **to keep trying to** achieve **something in** spite **of** difficulties 毅力;韧性;不屈不挠的精神

◈ [Version 2]

The Master said: "Isn't it a pleasure to study and practice what you have learned? Isn't it also great when friends visit from distant places?"

◈【原文】

子曰:"君子食无求饱,居无求安,敏于事而慎于言,就有道而正焉,可谓好学也已。"(《论语·学而》)

◈【今译】

孔子说:"有道德有学问的人不贪图饮食的满足、居室的舒适(不把精力放在吃住上),而求做事勤快、说话谨慎,向有道德有学问的人请教,这样做,就可以说是一个好学的人了。"

◈ [Version 1]

The Master said, "He who aims to be a man of complete virtue in his food does not seek to **gratify** his appetite, nor in his dwelling place does he seek the appliances of ease; he is earnest in what he is doing, and careful in his speech; he frequents the company of men of principle that he may be **rectified**—such a person may be said indeed to love to learn."

gratify /ˈgrætɪfaɪ/ *vt*. to make someone feel pleased and satisfied 使高兴;使满意
rectify /ˈrektɪfaɪ/ *vt*. to correct something or make something right 改正,校正

◈ [Version 2]

The Master said: "When the noble man eats he does not try to stuff himself; at rest he does not seek perfect comfort; he is diligent in his work and careful in speech. He **avails** himself to people of the Way and thereby corrects himself. This is the kind of person of whom you can say, 'he loves learning.'"

avail /əˈveɪl/ *vt*. & *vi*. use, purpose, advantage, or profit 有益于;使对某人有利

◈【原文】

子曰:"学而不思则罔,思而不学则**殆**。"(《论语·为政》)

殆[dài] 动词,此字有两解释。(1)危殆,亦疑。思而不学,则事无征验,疑不能定,危殆不安。(2)疲怠。徒使精神疲怠,而无所得。

◈【今译】

孔子说:"只读书却不思考,就会感到迷惑而无所得;只是空想却不认真学习,就会弄得精神疲倦而无所得。"

◈ [Version 1]

The Master said, "Learning without thought is labor lost; thought without learning is **perilous**."

perilous /ˈperələs/ *adj*. extremely dangerous 危险的,冒险的

◈ [Version 2]

The Master said: "To study and not think is a waste. To think and not study is dangerous."

◈【原文】

子曰:"温故而知新,可以为师矣。"(《论语·为政》)

◈【今译】

孔子说:"温习已知的旧知识,又能领悟到新的东西,可以凭借这一点做老师了。"

◈[Version 1]

The Master said, "If a man keeps cherishing his old knowledge, so as continually to be acquiring new, he may be a teacher of others."

◈[Version 2]

The Master said: "Reviewing what you have learned and learning anew, you are fit to be a teacher."

◈【原文】

子曰:"吾十有五而志于学,三十而立,四十而不惑,五十而知天命,六十而耳顺,七十而从心所欲,不逾矩。"(《论语·为政》)

◈【今译】

孔子说:"我十五岁时开始立志学习,三十岁时能立足于社会,四十岁时能通情达理,遇事不再疑惑,五十岁时懂得了天命的道理,六十岁能听得进不同的意见,到了七十岁时已经达到随心所欲,想怎么做就怎么做,也不会超出规矩。"

◈[Version 1]

The Master said, "At fifteen, I had my mind bent on learning. At thirty, I stood firm. At forty, I had no doubts. At fifty, I knew the decrees of Heaven. At sixty, my ear was an **obedient** organ for the reception of truth. At seventy, I could follow what my heart desired, without transgressing what was right."

---

obedient /əˈbiːdɪənt/ *adj*. doing, or willing to do, what you have been told to do by someone in authority 顺从的,服从的;忠顺的

◈[Version 2]

The Master said: "At fifteen my heart was set on learning; at thirty I stood firm; at forty I had no more doubts; at fifty I knew the mandate of heaven; at sixty my ear was obedient; at seventy I could follow my heart's desire without transgressing the norm."

◈【原文】

子曰:"朝闻道,夕死可矣。"(《论语·里仁》)

◈【今译】

孔子说:“早上懂得了真理,晚上就死去,也是可以的(爱真理胜于爱生命)。”

◈ [Version 1]

The Master said, “If a man in the morning hear the right way, he may die in the evening without regret.”

◈ [Version 2]

The Master said:“If I can hear the Way in the morning, in the evening I can die content.”

◈【原文】

子曰:“不愤不启,不悱不发,举一隅不以三隅反,则不复也。”(《论语·述而》)

悱[fěi] 动词,口欲言而未能

◈【今译】

孔子说:“(教学生)不到他苦思冥想怎么也弄不明白的时候,不去开导他;不到他想说而又说不出来的时候,不去启发他。告诉他(四方形)的一个角,他不能由此推出另外三个角,就不再往下教他(新知识)了。”

◈ [Version 1]

The Master said, “I do not open up the truth to one who is not eager to get knowledge, nor help out any one who is not anxious to explain himself. When I have presented one corner of a subject to any one, and he cannot from it learn the other three, I do not repeat my lesson.”

◈ [Version 2]

The Master said:“If a student is not eager, I won't teach him; if he is not struggling with the truth, I won't reveal it to him. If I lift up one corner and he can't come back with the other three, I won't do it again.”

◈【原文】

叶公问孔子于子路,子路不对。子曰:“女奚不曰,其为人也,发愤忘食,乐以忘忧,不知老之将至**云尔**。”(《论语·述而》)

云尔[yún ěr] 名词,尔,如此。云尔,犹如此说

◈【今译】

叶公向子路问孔子为人怎么样,子路不回答。孔子对子路道:“你为什么不这样说:他发奋时候

竟忘记吃饭,快乐时候就忘记了忧愁,把自己就要老了这件事也不放在心上,如此罢了。”

◈ [Version 1]

The Duke of She asked Zi Lu about Confucius, and Zi Lu did not answer him. The Master said, “Why did you not say to him, “He is simply a man, who in his eager pursuit of knowledge forgets his food, who in the joy of its attainment forgets his sorrows, and who does not perceive that old age is coming on?”

◈ [Version 2]

The Duke of Sheh asked Zi Lu about Confucius. Zi Lu didn't answer him. The Teacher said, “Why didn't you just tell him that I am a man who in eagerness for study forgets to eat, in his enjoyment of it, forgets his problems and who is unaware of old age setting in?”

◈【原文】

子曰:“古之学者为己,今之学者为人。”(《论语·宪问》)

◈【今译】

孔子说:“古代读书人学习的目的,在于修养自己的学问道德(然后去为国家、人民服务),现在读书人学习的目的,在于给别人看(希望得到别人的赞美和任用)。”

◈ [Version 1]

The Master said, “In ancient times, men learned with a view to their own improvement. Nowadays, men learn with a view to the **approbation** of others.”

---

approbation /ˌæprəˈbeɪʃən/ *n*. official praise or approval 认可,批准

◈ [Version 2]

The Master said: “The ancient scholars studied for their own improvement. Modern scholars study to impress others.”

◈【原文】

子贡问为仁。子曰:“工欲善其事,必先利其器。居是邦也,事其大夫之贤者,友其士之仁者。”(《论语·卫灵公》)

◈【今译】

子贡问为仁之方。孔子说:“工匠要想做好自己的工作,必须事先磨快工具。”比喻要胜任工作,必须先学好本领。

◈ [Version 1]

Zi Gong asked about the practice of virtue. The Master said, "The mechanic, who wishes to do his work well, must first sharpen his tools. When you are living in any state, take service with the most worthy among its great officers, and make friends of the most **virtuous** among its scholars."

virtuous /ˈvɜːtʃuəs/ *adj*. behaving in a very honest and moral way 有德行的，有道德的

◈ [Version 2]

Zi Gong asked about humaneness. Confucius said, "When a craftsman wants to do a nice piece of work, he will always sharpen his tools first. When you live in a certain district, get into the service of the most worthy officers, and seek friends among scholars who are steeped in humaneness."

仁 义 篇

◈【原文】

曾子曰："士不可以不弘毅，任重而道远。仁以为己任，不亦重乎？死而后已，不亦远乎？"(《论语·泰伯》)

◈【今译】

曾子说："读书的人不可以不抱负远大，意志坚强，因为他重任在身而路程遥远。以实现仁德于天下为己任，不也沉重吗？到死方休，不也遥远吗？"

Benevolence

◈ [Version 1]

The philosopher Zeng said, "The officer may not be without breadth of mind and vigorous endurance. His burden is heavy and his course is long. Perfect virtue① is the burden which he

① Perfect virtue, or other, Ren (仁) No terms is more important in Confucianism than ren. Prior to the time of Confucius, the term Humanity does not seem to have been much used. In those pre-philosophical days, the word seems to have meant "manly", an adjective of high praise in a warrior society. Confucius, however, changed the meaning of the term and gave it great ethical weight. He identified "manliness" (or, in non-sexist terms, the qualities associated with constructive social leadership) with the firm disposition to place the needs and feelings of others and of the community before one's own. The written graph of this term is a simple one; it combines the form for "person" on the left with the number "two" on the right; a person of Humanity, or ren, is someone who is thoroughly relational in their thoughts, feelings, and actions. (The happily illustrative graphic etymology is, unfortunately, undercut by recently unearthed manuscript texts of the late fourth century BCE, which consistently render the term with the graph for "body" placed over the graph for "heart/mind"; this may, however, have been a local scribal tradition confined to the southerly region of Chu.) Confucians often pair this term with Righteousness, and it is very often common for the two terms together to be used as a general expression for "morality". The term is closely linked in Confucian discourse with the ideal of the *junzi* (Analects 4.5: If one takes ren away from junzi, wherein is he worthy of the name?).

considers it is his to sustain—is it not heavy? Only with death does his course stop—is it not long?"

◈ [Version 2]

Ceng Zi said: "To be called a *shi* you must be open-minded as well as **resolute**, since your burden is heavy and your course is long. If you take *ren* as your burden, is it not heavy? If you continue to death, is it not long?"

resolute /ˈrezəluːt/ *adj*. determined in character, action, or ideas 坚决的，刚毅的

◈【原文】

子曰："仁远乎哉？我欲仁，斯仁至矣。"(《论语·述而》)

◈【今译】

孔子说："仁，距离我远吗？只要我想要做到仁，仁就随着心念到了。"

◈ [Version 1]

The Master said, "Is virtue a thing remote? I wish to be virtuous, and virtue is at hand."

◈ [Version 2]

The Master said: "Is *ren* far away? If I aspire for *ren* it is right here!"

◈【原文】

子曰："巧言令色，鲜矣仁！"(《论语·学而》)

◈【今译】

孔子说："花言巧语，装出和善的面孔。这种人，心里不会有多少仁德！"(这种人不会有真正的爱人之心)。

◈ [Version 1]

The Master said, "Fine words and an **insinuating** appearance are seldom associated with true virtue."

insinuate /ɪnˈsɪnjueɪt/ *v*. suggesting ideas without saying them directly 迂回，巧妙或迂回地潜入

◈ [Version 2]

The Master said: "Someone who is a clever speaker and maintains a contrived smile is seldom considered to be a really good person."

◈【原文】

子曰:"德不孤,必有邻。"(《论语·里仁》)

◈【今译】

孔子说:"世界上有道德的人是不会孤立的,一定有很多思想一致的人和他在一起。"

◈[Version 1]

The Master said, "Virtue is not left to stand alone. He who practices it will have neighbors."

◈[Version 2]

The Master said: "If you are virtuous, you will not be lonely. You will always have friends."

◈【原文】

子曰:"质胜文则野,文胜质则史。文质彬彬,然后君子。"(《论语·雍也》)

◈【今译】

孔子说:"朴实多于文采,就未免粗野;文采多于朴实,又未免虚浮。一个人的高尚的品质和外在的表现一致,然后才能成为君子。"

◈[Version 1]

The Master said, "Where the solid qualities are in excess of accomplishments, we have **rusticity**; where the accomplishments are in excess of the solid qualities, we have the manners of a clerk. When the accomplishments and solid qualities are equally blended, we then have the man of virtue."

rusticity /ˈrʌstɪsəti/ *n*. simple and often rough in appearance; typical of the countryside 乡村特点、风格或气息

◈[Version 2]

The Master said: "If raw substance dominates refinement, you will be coarse. If refinement dominates raw substance, you will be clerical. When **refinement** and raw qualities are well blended, you will be a noble man."

refinement /rɪˈfaɪnmənt/ *n*. an improvement, usually a small one, to something 精炼;改良;优雅

◈【原文】

子曰:"君子不重,则不威,学则不固。主忠信,无友不如己者,过则勿惮改。"(《论语·学而》)

惮[dàn] 动词,畏难

◈【今译】

孔子说:"君子如果不自重,就没有威严,(别人也不会尊重你),学习的知识就不会扎实。做人重要的是讲求忠诚,守信用。不要同不如自己的人交朋友。如果犯了错误,就不要害怕改正。"

◈ [Version 1]

The Master said, "If the scholar be not grave, he will not call forth any veneration, and his learning will not be solid. Hold faithfulness and sincerity as first principles. Have no friends not equal to yourself. When you have faults, do not fear to abandon them."

◈ [Version 2]

The Master said: "If the noble man lacks gravitas, then he will not inspire awe in others. If he is not learned, then he will not be on firm ground. He takes loyalty and good faith to be of primary importance, and has no friends who are not of equal (moral) **caliber**. When he makes a mistake, he doesn't hesitate to correct it."

caliber /ˈkæləbə/ *n*. the level of quality or ability that someone or something has achieved of somebody's calibre 能力,水准

◈【原文】

子曰:"志士仁人,无求生以害仁,有杀身以成仁。"(《论语·卫灵公》)

◈【今译】

孔子说:"有志之士和仁人,不会贪生怕死而损害仁德,只会勇于牺牲来成全仁德。"

◈ [Version 1]

The Master said, "The determined scholar and the man of virtue will not seek to live at the expense of injuring their virtue. They will even sacrifice their lives to preserve their virtue complete."

◈ [Version 2]

The Master said: "The earnest officer with a truly humane mind (*ren*) will not save his life if it requires him to sacrifice of his humaneness. He will even sacrifice himself to consummate his humaneness."

◈【原文】

子贡曰:“如有博施于民而能济众,何如?可谓仁乎?”子曰:“何事于仁,必也圣乎!尧舜其犹病诸!夫仁者,己欲立而立人,己欲达而达人。能近取譬,可谓仁之方也已。”(《论语·雍也》)

◈【今译】

子贡说:“假如有这么一个人,广泛地给人民以好处,又能帮助大家生活得很好,怎么样?可以说是仁道吗?”孔子说:“哪里仅是仁道!那一定是圣德了!尧舜或者都难以做到呢!仁是什么呢?自己要在社会上自立,就要使别人能在社会上自立;自己要在社会上通达,就要别人也能在社会上通达。能够就眼下的事实选择例子一步步去做,可以说是实践仁道的方法了。”

◈［Version 1］

Zi Gong said, “Suppose the case of a man extensively conferring benefits on the people, and able to assist all, what would you say of him? Might he be called perfectly virtuous?” The Master said, “Why speak only of virtue in connection with him? Must he not have the qualities of a sage? Even Yao and Shun were still **solicitous** about this. Now the man of perfect virtue, wishing to be established himself, seeks also to establish others; wishing to be enlarged himself, he seeks also to enlarge others. To be able to judge of others by what is nigh in ourselves—this may be called the art of virtue.”

solicitous /səˈlɪsɪtəs/ *adj*. very concerned about someone’s safety, health, or comfort 关心的;挂念的;热切的

◈［Version 2］

Zi Gong asked:“Suppose there were a ruler who benefited the people far and wide and was capable of bringing salvation to the multitude, what would you think of him? Might he be called humane?”The Master said, “Why only humane? He would undoubtedly be a sage. Even Yao and Shun would have had to strive to achieve this. Now the *ren* man, wishing himself to be established, sees that others are established, and, wishing himself to be successful, sees that others are successful. To be able to take one’s own feelings as a guide may be called the art of *ren*.”

◈【原文】

子曰:“饭疏食饮水,**曲肱**而枕之,乐亦在其中矣。不义而富且贵,于我如浮云。”(《论语·述而》)

曲肱［qǔ gōng］ 动词,肱,臂也。曲臂当枕小卧,多用以比喻清贫而闲适的生活

◈【今译】

孔子说:“吃粗粮,喝冷水,弯着胳膊做枕头,也有着乐趣。做不应该做的事从而做官发财,对我来

说，好比是天空浮来浮去的过眼烟云。”

◈ [Version 1]

The Master said, "With coarse rice to eat, with water to drink, and my bended arm for a pillow; I have still joy in the midst of these things. Riches and honors acquired by unrighteousness, are to me as a floating cloud."

◈ [Version 2]

The Master said: "I can live with coarse rice to eat, water for drink and my arm as a pillow and still be happy. Wealth and honors that one possesses in the midst of injustice are like floating clouds."

◈【原文】

子曰："当仁，不让于师。"(《论语·卫灵公》)

◈【今译】

孔子说："在实行仁德之事的时候，对自己的老师也不要谦让。"

◈ [Version 1]

The Master said, "Let every man consider virtue as what devolves on himself. He may not yield the performance of it even to his teacher."

◈ [Version 2]

The Master said: "It is better to value *ren* than to passively follow your teacher."

◈【原文】

子曰："君子喻于义，小人喻于利。"(《论语·里仁》)

◈【今译】

孔子说："君子懂得的是义，小人懂得的是利。"

◈ [Version 1]

The Master said, "The mind of the superior man is conversant with righteousness; the mind of the mean man is conversant with gain."

◈ [Version 2]

The Master said: "The noble man is aware of fairness, the inferior man is aware of

advantage."

◈【原文】

子曰:"过而不改,是谓过矣。"(《论语·卫灵公》)

◈【今译】

孔子说:"有了过错而不改正,这才真叫过错呢。"

◈[Version 1]

The Master said, "To have faults and not to reform them—this, indeed, should be pronounced having faults."

◈[Version 2]

The Master said: "To make a mistake and not correct it: this is a real mistake."

◈【原文】

子曰:"君子不以言举人,不以人废言。"(《论语·卫灵公》)

◈【今译】

孔子说:"君子不因为别人的话说得好就提拔他,也不因为别人的品德不好就废弃他的正确意见。"

◈[Version 1]

The Master said, "The superior man does not promote a man simply on account of his words, nor does he put aside good words because of the man."

◈[Version 2]

The Master said: "The noble man does not promote a man because of his words, and does not disregard the words because of the man."

◈【原文】

有子曰:"其为人也孝弟,而好犯上者,鲜矣;不好犯上,而好作乱者,未之有也。君子务本,本立而道生。孝弟也者,其为仁之本与!"(《论语·学而》)

◈【今译】

有子说:"他的为人,孝顺爹娘,敬爱兄长,却喜欢触犯上级,这种人是很少的;不喜欢触犯上级,却喜欢造反,这种人从来没有过。君子专心致力于基础工作,基础树立了,'道'就会产生。孝顺爹娘,敬爱兄长,这就是'仁'的基础吧!"

◈[Version 1]

The philosopher You said, "They are few who, being filial and fraternal, are fond of offending against their superiors. There have been none, who, not liking to offend against their superiors, have been fond of stirring up confusion. The superior man bends his attention to what is radical. That being established, all practical courses naturally grow up. Filial piety and fraternal submission! Are they not the root of all benevolent actions?"

◈[Version 2]

You Zi said: "There are few who have developed themselves filially and fraternally who enjoy offending their superiors. Those who do not enjoy offending superiors are never troublemakers. The noble man concerns himself with the fundamentals. Once the fundamentals are established, the proper way appears. Are not filial piety and obedience to elders fundamental to the actualization of fundamental human goodness?"

◈【原文】

子曰:"见贤思齐焉,见不贤而内自省也。"(《论语·里仁》)

◈【今译】

孔子说:"看见贤人就应想着向他看齐,看见不贤的人则应在内心自我反省有无类似缺点。"

◈[Version 1]

The Master said, "When we see men of worth, we should think of equaling them; when we see men of a contrary character, we should turn inwards and examine ourselves."

◈[Version 2]

The Master said: "When you see a good person, think of becoming like her/him. When you see someone not so good, reflect on your own weak points."

知 智 篇

◈【原文】

子曰:"人不知而不愠,不亦君子乎?"(《论语·学而》)

◈【今译】

孔子说:"别人不了解我,我并不埋怨,不也是君子吗?"

Wisdom

◈ [Version 1]

The Master said, "Is he not a man of complete virtue, who feels no **discomposure** though men may take no note of him?"

◈ [Version 2]

The Master said: "If people do not recognize me and it doesn't bother me, am I not a *noble man*?"

◈【原文】

子曰:"知者不惑,仁者不忧,勇者不惧。"(《论语·子罕》)

◈【今译】

孔子说:"聪明的人不会疑惑,实行仁德的人不会忧愁,真正勇敢的人不会畏惧。"

◈ [Version 1]

The Master said, "The wise are free from **perplexities**; the virtuous from anxiety; and the bold from fear."

---

perplexity /pə'pleksəti/ *n*. a state of confusion or a complicated and difficult situation or thing 困惑,混乱,复杂

◈ [Version 2]

The Master said: "The wise are not confused, the humane are not anxious, the brave are not afraid."

◈【原文】

子曰:"不患人之不己知,患不知人也。"(《论语·学而》)

◈【今译】

子曰:"不怕别人不了解我,怕的是自己不了解别人。"

◈ [Version 1]

The Master said, "I will not be afflicted at men's not knowing me; I will be afflicted that I do not know men."

◈ [Version 2]

The Master said:“I am not bothered by the fact that I am unknown. I am bothered when I do not know others.”

◈【原文】

子曰:“由!诲女知之乎?知之为知之,不知为不知,是知也。”(《论语·为政》)

◈【今译】

孔子说:“由!教给你对待知或不知的正确态度吧!知道就是知道,不知道就是不知道,这就是真知啊。”

◈ [Version 1]

The Master said,“You, shall I teach you what knowledge is? When you know a thing, to hold that you know it; and when you do not know a thing, to allow that you do not know it—this is knowledge.”

◈ [Version 2]

The Master said:“You, shall I teach you about knowledge? What you know, you know, what you don't know, you don't know. This is knowledge.”

◈【原文】

子曰:“君子不可小知,而可大受也;小人不可大受,而可小知也。”(《论语·卫灵公》)

◈【今译】

孔子说:“人格高尚的人不可用小事情考验他,却可以委以重任;人格低下的人不可委以重任,却可用小事情考验他。”

◈ [Version 1]

The Master said, “The superior man cannot be known in little matters; but he may be intrusted with great concerns. The small man may not be intrusted with great concerns, but he may be known in little matters.”

◈ [Version 2]

The Master said:“The noble man cannot act within the framework of lesser wisdom, but he can handle major affairs. The inferior man cannot handle major affairs, but he can act within the framework of lesser wisdom.”

◈【原文】

子曰:"知者乐水,仁者乐山。知者动,仁者静。知者乐,仁者寿。"(《论语·雍也》)

◈【今译】

孔子说:"聪明智慧的人爱水,有仁德的人爱山。聪明智慧的人爱活跃,有仁德的人爱沉静。聪明智慧的人快乐,有仁德的人长寿。"

◈[Version 1]

The Master said, "The wise find pleasure in water; the virtuous find pleasure in hills. The wise are active; the virtuous are **tranquil**. The wise are joyful; the virtuous are long-lived."

tranquil /ˈtræŋkwəl/ *adj*. pleasantly calm, quiet, and peaceful 安静的,平静的,宁静的

◈[Version 2]

The Master said: "The wise enjoy the sea, the humane enjoy the mountains. The wise are busy, the humane are tranquil. The wise are happy, the humane are eternal."

◈【原文】

子曰:"知之者不如好之者,好之者不如乐之者。"(《论语·雍也》)

◈【今译】

孔子说:"懂得它的人不如爱好它的人,爱好它的人不如以它为乐的人。"

◈[Version 1]

The Master said, "They who know the truth are not equal to those who love it, and they who love it are not equal to those who delight in it."

◈[Version 2]

The Master said: "Knowing it is not as good as loving it; loving it is not as good as delighting in it."

哲 理 篇

◈【原文】

子曰:"不在其位,不谋其政。"(《论语·泰伯》)

◈【今译】

孔子说:"不在那个职位上,就不要过问那方面的政事。"

Philosophy

◈ [Version 1]

The Master said, "He who is not in any particular office has nothing to do with plans for the administration of its duties."

◈ [Version 2]

The Master said: "If you don't have the official position, you can't plan the affairs of government."

◈【原文】

子夏为莒父宰,问政。子曰:"无欲速,无见小利。欲速,则不达;见小利,则大事不成。"(《论语·子路》)

◈【今译】

子夏做了莒父的县长,问政治。孔子说:"不求速成,不要图小利。想求速成,反而达不到目的,贪图小利就做不成大事。"

◈ [Version 1]

Zi Xia, being governor of Ju Fu, asked about government. The Master said, "Do not be desirous to have things done quickly; do not look at small advantages. Desire to have things done quickly prevents their being done thoroughly. Looking at small advantages prevents great affairs from being accomplished."

◈ [Version 2]

Zi Xia, who was serving as governor of Jufu, asked about government. Confucius said, "Don't be impatient, and don't look for small advantages. If you are impatient, you will not be thorough ("penetrating," *da* 达). If you look for small advantages, you will never accomplish anything great."

◈【原文】

子曰:"人而无信,不知其可也。大车无**輗**,小车无**軏**,其何以行之哉?"(《论语·为政》)

輗[ní] 名词,木质,外裹铁皮,竖串于辕与衡之两孔中,使辕与衡可以灵活转动

軏[yuè] 名词,古代用牛力的车叫大车,用马力的车叫小车。两者都要把牲口套在车辕上。车辕前面有一道横木,就是驾牲口的地方。那横木,大车上的叫做鬲,小车叫做衡,軏就是鬲的关键,輗就是衡的关键。

◈【今译】

孔子说:"一个人如果不守信用,不知他怎么可以做人! 譬如大车子没有安横木的輗,小车子没有按横木的軏,如何能走呢?"

◈[Version 1]

The Master said, "I do not know how a man without truthfulness is to get on. How can a large carriage be made to go without the crossbar for yoking the oxen to, or a small carriage without the arrangement for yoking the horses?"

◈[Version 2]

The Master said: "If a person lacks trustworthiness, I don't know what she/he can be good for. When a pin is missing from the yoke-bar of a large wagon, or from the collar-bar of a small wagon, how can it go?"

◈【原文】

子曰:"躬自厚而薄责于人,则远怨矣。"(《论语・卫灵公》)

◈【今译】

子曰:"凡事多责备自己而少责备别人,就可以避开怨恨了。"

◈[Version 1]

The Master said, "He who requires much from himself and little from others, will keep himself from being the object of resentment."

◈[Version 2]

The Master said, "If one sets strict standards for oneself and makes allowances for others when making demands on them, one will stay clear of ill will."

◈【原文】

子路曰:"卫君待子而为政,子将奚先?"子曰:"必也正名乎!"子路曰:"有是哉,子之迂也! 奚其正?"子曰:"野哉,由也! 君子于其所不知,盖阙如也。名不正,则言不顺;言不顺,则事不成;事不成,则礼乐不兴;礼乐不兴,则刑罚不中;刑罚不中,则民无所措手足。故君子名之必可言也,言之必可行也。君子于其言,无所苟而已矣。"(《论语・子路》)

◈【今译】

子路对孔子说:"卫君等着您去治理国政,您准备首先干什么?"孔子说:"那一定是纠正名分上的用词不当罢!"子路说:"您的迂腐竟到如此地步吗! 这又何必纠正?"孔子说:"你怎么这样鲁莽! 君子对于他所不懂的，大概采取保留态度，（你怎么能乱说呢？）用词不当，言语就不能顺理成章；言语不顺理成章，工作就不可能搞好；工作搞不好，国家的礼乐制度也就举办不起来；礼乐制度举办不起来，刑罚也就不会得当；刑罚不得当，百姓就会（惶惶不安，）连手脚都不晓得摆在哪里才好。所以君子用一个词，一定（有它一定的理由，）可以说得出来；而顺理成章的话也一定行得通。君子对于措词说话要没有一点马虎的地方才罢了。”

◈ [Version 1]

Zi Lu said, "The ruler of Wei has been waiting for you, in order with you to administer the government. What will you consider the first thing to be done?" The Master replied, "What is necessary is to rectify names." "So! indeed!" said Zi Lu. "You are wide of the mark! Why must there be such rectification?" The Master said, "How uncultivated you are, You! A superior man, in regard to what he does not know, shows a cautious reserve. If names be not correct, language is not in accordance with the truth of things. If language be not in accordance with the truth of things, affairs cannot be carried on to success. When affairs cannot be carried on to success, proprieties[①] and music will not flourish. When proprieties and music do not flourish, punishments will not be properly awarded. When punishments are not properly awarded, the people do not know how to move hand or foot. Therefore a superior man considers it necessary that the names he uses may be spoken appropriately, and also that what he speaks may be carried out appropriately. What the superior man requires is just that in his words there may be nothing incorrect."

◈ [Version 2]

Zi Lu said: "The ruler of Wei is anticipating your assistance in the administration of his state. What will be your top priority?" Confucius said, "There must be a correction of terminology." Zi Lu said, "Are you serious? Why is this so important?" Confucius said, "You are really simple, aren't you? A noble man is cautious about jumping to conclusions about that which he does not know." "If terminology is not corrected, then what is said cannot be followed. If what is said cannot be followed, then work cannot be accomplished. If work cannot be accomplished, then ritual and music cannot be developed. If ritual and music cannot be developed, then criminal punishments will not be appropriate. If criminal punishments are not appropriate, the people

---

① Li 礼 (Ritual) Commitment to ritual was the distinguishing characteristic of the Confucian School. By "ritual", or *li*, the Confucians meant not only ceremonies of grand religious or social occasions, but also the institutions of Zhou Dynasty political culture and the norms of proper everyday conduct. Although accordance with ritual was, in some senses, a matter of knowing the codes of aristocratic behavior (and knowing them better than the debased aristocrats of the later Zhou era), it was more importantly a manner of attaining full mastery of the style or pattern (wen) of civilized behavior. Confucians viewed these patterns as the essence of civilization itself. The great sages of the past has labored era after era to transform China from brutishness to refinement through the elaboration of these artistic forms of social interaction, and in the Confucian view, the epitome of human virtue was expressed only through these forms. Mastery of the outer forms was the path to inner sagehood. The ancient character for *li* shows a ceremonial vessel filled with sacrificial goods on the right, with an altar stand on the left.

cannot make a move. Therefore, the noble man needs to have his terminology applicable to real language, and his speech must accord with his actions. The speech of the noble man cannot be indefinite."

◈【原文】

子贡曰:"君子之过也,如日月之食焉:过也,人皆见之;更也,人皆仰之。"《论语·子张》

◈【今译】

子贡说:"君子的过失好比日蚀月蚀:有了过错,别人都能看到;改了,人们都会敬仰他。"

◈ [Version 1]

Zi Gong said, "The faults of the superior man① are like the eclipses of the sun and moon. He has his faults, and all men see them; he changes again, and all men look up to him."

◈ [Version 2]

Zi Gong said: "The faults of the noble man are like the eclipses of the sun and moon—everyone sees them. But when he corrects them, everyone looks up to him."

Chinese Philosophy

1.【百善孝为先】

Of all virtues, filial piety is the first In Confucian philosophy, filial piety (孝, *xiào*) is a virtue of respect for one's parents, elders and ancestors. The Confucian *Classic of Filial Piety*, thought to be written around the Qin-Han period, has historically been the authoritative source on the Confucian tenet of filial piety. The book, a purported dialogue between Confucius and his student Zengzi, is about how to set up a good society using the principle of filial piety. The term can also be applied to general obedience. Filial piety is central to Confucian role ethics.

2.【礼之用,和为贵】

In practicing the rules of propriety, a natural ease is to be prized. *Li* is a classical Chinese word which finds its most extensive use in Confucian and post-Confucian Chinese philosophy. *Li* is variously translated as "rite" or "reason", "ratio" in the pure sense of Vedic *rta* ("right", "order") when referring to the cosmic law, but when referring to its realization in the context of human social behavior it has also been translated as "customs", "measures" and "rules", among other

---

① Junzi 君子(Superior man or Noble man) This is a compound word composed of two written characters which separately mean "ruler's son". The ancient character for "ruler" (*jun*) showed a hand grasping a writing brush with a mouth placed by the side, illustrating the modes by which a ruler issued orders. In pre-philosophical writings, the word *junzi* was used to refer to someone who was heir to a ruling position by virtue of his birth. For Confucians, the hallmark of the *junzi* was his complete internalization of the virtue of *ren* and associated qualities, such as righteousness (*yi*) and full socialization through ritual skills.

terms. *Li* also means religious rites which establish relations between humanity and the gods. Confucius envisioned proper government being guided by the principles of *li*. Some Confucians proposed that all human beings may pursue perfection by learning and practising *li*. Overall, Confucians believe that governments should place more emphasis on *li* and rely much less on penal punishment when they govern.

3.【克己复礼】

To subdue one's self and return to propriety is perfect virtue. This is the Confucian virtue denoting the good feeling a virtuous human experiences when being altruistic. It is exemplified by a normal adult's protective feelings for children. It is considered the essence of the human being, endowed by Heaven, and at the same time the means by which man may act according to the principle of Heaven (天理, *Tiān lǐ*) and become one with it.

4.【德不孤,必有邻】

Virtue is not left to stand alone. He who practices it will have neighbors. *De* occurs 40 times in the Confucian *Lunyu* or *Analects*. While Confucius extolled *de* "virtue; morality"—"If you are virtuous, you will not be lonely. You will always have friends." (4: 25)—he frequently criticized his contemporaries for having lost it. He described *de* as something that one can augment, and praised sage kings who governed through its compelling powers. Confucianism is, then, a more focused virtue ethics. When confronted with moral questions, it tells us to start with a consideration of how our responses will first affect our closest loving relationships. If those are secure, then we can seek solutions that extend our responsibilities outward to others. That is how "character" is built.

Practice

I. Vocabulary

Choose a proper word or phrase to complete each of the following sentences, changing the form when necessary.

filial piety	suspicious	courses	delight	ceasing
reciprocity	perplexities	virtue	satiety	superior

1. The silent treasuring up of knowledge; learning without ________; and instructing others without being wearied: which one of these things belongs to me?
2. Mang Wu asked what ________ was. The Master said, "Parents are anxious lest their children should be sick."
3. Fair appearances are ________. The Master said, "Fine words and an insinuating appearance are seldom associated with true virtue."
4. Different stages of attainment. The Master said, "They who know the truth are not equal

to those who love it, and they who love it are not equal to those who ________in it."

5. The great principle of reciprocity is the rule of life. Tsze-kung asked, saying, "Is there one word which may serve as a rule of practice for all one's life?" The Master said, "Is not ________ such a word? What you do not want done to yourself, do not do to others."
6. The danger of specious words, and of impatience. The Master said, "Specious words confound ________. Want of forbearance in small matters confounds great plans."
7. Agreement in principle necessary to concord in plans. The Master said, "Those whose ________ are different cannot lay plans for one another."
8. The sequences of wisdom, virtue, and bravery. The Master said, "The wise are free from ________; the virtuous from anxiety; and the bold from fear."
9. How Confucius was affected by a running stream. The Master standing by a stream, said, "It passes on just like this, not ________day or night!"
10. Contrast in their feelings between the Chun-tsze and the mean man. The Master said, "The ________man is satisfied and composed; the mean man is always full of distress."

II. Translation

Translate the following sentences and the passage into English.

1. 父母在,不远游,游必有方。

____

2. 工欲善其事,必先利其器。

____

3. 君子坦荡荡,小人长戚戚。

____

4. 君子以文会友,以友辅仁。

____

5. 有德者,必有言。有言者,不必有德。仁者,必有勇。勇者,不必有仁。

____

6. 颜渊问仁。子曰:"克己复礼为仁。一日克己复礼,天下归仁焉。为仁由己,而由人乎哉?"颜渊曰:"请问其目。"子曰:"非礼勿视,非礼勿听,非礼勿言,非礼勿动。"颜渊曰:"回虽不敏,请事斯语矣。"

____

____

____

III. Critical Thinking

Discuss the following questions in groups and do your group presentation in class on the basis of your discussion.

1. The Master said, "Yu, shall I teach you what knowledge is? When you know a thing, to

hold that you know it; and when you do not know a thing, to allow that you do not know it—this is knowledge." How do you understand the difference between the real "knowledge" and the real "wisdom"?

2. Learning without thought is labor lost; thought without learning is perilous. What do you think of the relationship between the study and the reflection?

References

[1] Legge, James. The Confucian Analects [M]. 郑州：中州古籍出版社，2016.
[2] 刘殿爵. Confucius The Analects [M]. 北京：中华书局，2011.
[3] 杨伯峻. 论语译注[M]. 北京：中华书局，2009.

Unit 4

The Doctrine of the Mean①

Introduction

The Doctrine of the Mean is alleged to be written by Zi Si of the Warring States Period, listed in the Song dynasty as one of the four Confucian canonical books. Zhu Xi proposed that *The Doctrine of the Mean* should be read at last within the Four Books because of its high level theory. Confucius regarded the golden mean as the highest moral standard and the supreme wisdom in solving all problems. The Chinese word *Chung* means central, and *Yung* means common. Therefore, the two Chinese words mean the true, fair universal standard of right. Ku Hung Ming translated the title as *The Universal Order or Conduct of Life*.

The book consists of thirty-three chapters, discussing a series of problems such as *Xing*, *Dao*, *Jiao*, *Tian*, etc. From the book, Chapter One and Chapter Twenty were selected, because Chapter One is the creed of the whole book and Chapter Twenty is the most important chapter which tells us how to cultivate one's moral character, regulate one's family and administer a country.

Learning Objectives

After learning this unit, you will be able to

1. learn generally about the content and genre of *The Doctrine of the Mean* in general;
2. understand deeply the selected quotations from *The Doctrine of the Mean* in detail;
3. interpret critically the materials in English related to the theory of Mean, and the knowledge about Chinese spirit;
4. understand and develop the traditional Chinese values based on *The Doctrine of the Mean*.

① The Chinese version comes from Wang Guoxuan, the edition of Chung Hwa Book Co.; English version one is made by James Legge, who was the authority on Chinese study during 1828 – 1893; English version two is a translation of Ku Hung Ming, who was a famous Chinese scholar devoting to introduce Chinese culture to Westerners.

Selected Readings

第一章

◈【原文】

天①命之谓性;率性②之谓道;修道③之谓教④。道也者,不可须臾离也;可离,非道也。是故君子戒慎乎其所不睹,恐惧乎其所不闻。莫**见**乎隐,莫显乎微。故君子慎其独也。喜怒哀乐之未发,谓之中。发而皆**中**节,谓之和。中也者,天下之大本也。和也者,天下之达道也。致中和,天地位焉,万物育焉。

见[xiàn] 动词,同"现"

中[zhòng] 动词,符合

◈【今译】

天赋与人的禀赋叫做性,遵循天性而行叫做道,按照道的原则修养叫做教。道是不可以片刻离开的,如果可以离开,那就不是道了。所以,君子在别人看不见的地方也是谨慎的,在别人听不见的地方也是有所戒慎畏惧的。越是隐秘的事情越是容易显露,越是细微的事情越是容易显现。所以,君子在一个人独处独知的时候,更要谨慎。喜怒哀乐各种感情没有表现出来的时候,叫做中;表现出来以后符合节度,叫做和。中是天下的根本;和是天下普遍遵循的规律。达到中和的境界,天地便各在其位了,万物的生长就茂盛了。

◈ [Version 1]

Chapter One

What Heaven has conferred is called the Nature; an accordance with this nature is called The path of duty; the regulation of this path is called Instruction. The path may not be left for an instant. If it could be left, it would not be the path. On this account, the superior man does not wait till he sees things, to be cautious, nor till he hears things, to be apprehensive. There is nothing more visible than what is secret, and nothing more manifest than what is minute. Therefore the superior man is watchful over himself, when he is alone. While there are no

---

① "Tian" is a controversial issue, which contains rich connotations. In Legge's version, "Tian" is translated as "Heaven" which contains the color of religion. Ku considered "Tian" as cosmic order, thus "Tian ming" was "the ordinance of God". Sometimes, "Tian" was translated as "sky" in the natural meaning such as "Now Confucius cannot be equalled, just as no man can climb up to the sky." (*The Discourses and Sayings of Confucius* translated by Ku Hung Ming, Chapter XIX).

② "Xing" is another term difficult to be understood. Legge translated it as "Nature", while Ku limited it as "the law of our being".

③ "Dao" is also difficult to define. Legge considered it as "the path of Duty", while Ku saw it as "the moral law" which comes from the cosmic order.

④ "Jiao" in Legge's version was "instruction", while in Ku's version was "religion". Ku explained "the moral law when reduced to a system is what we call religion" which followed the logic from knowing the cosmic order to abide by the order (the moral law) to induce it as a system (religion).

stirrings of pleasure, anger, sorrow, or joy, the mind may be said to be in the state of **Equilibrium**. When those feelings have been stirred, and they act in their due degree, there ensues what may be called the state of Harmony. This Equilibrium is the great root from which grow all the human actings in the world, and this Harmony is the universal path which they all should pursue. Let the states of equilibrium and harmony exist in perfection, and a happy order will prevail throughout heaven and earth, and all things will be nourished and flourish.

equilibrium /ˌiːkwəˈlɪbriəm/ *n.* a state in which you are calm and not angry or upset 平衡,均势;平静

◈ [Version 2]

The ordinance of God is what we call the law of our being. To fulfill the law of our being is what we call the moral law. The moral law when reduced to a system is what we call religion.

The moral law is a law from whose operation we cannot for one instant in our existence escape. A law from which we may escape is not the moral law. Wherefore it is that the moral man watches diligently over what his eyes cannot see and is in fear and awe of what his ears cannot hear.

There is nothing more evident than what cannot be seen by the eyes and nothing more **palpable** than what cannot be perceived by the senses. Wherefore the moral man watches diligently over his secret thoughts.

When the passions, such as joy, anger, grief and pleasure, have not awakened, that is our true self or moral being. When these passions awaken and each and all attain due measure and degree, that is the moral order. Our true self or moral being is the great reality of existence, and moral order is the universal law in the world.

When true moral being and moral order are realized, the universe then becomes a cosmos and all things attain their full growth and development.

palpable /ˈpælpəbəl/ *adj.* *formal* a feeling that is palpable is so strong that other people notice it and can feel it around them 明白的,明显的;可感知的,摸得出的

第二十章

◈【原文】

哀公问政。子曰:"文武之政,布在方策。其人存,则其政举;其人亡,则其政息。人道敏政,地道敏树。夫政也者,蒲卢也。故为政在人,取人以身,修身以道,修道以仁。仁者人也,亲亲为大;义者宜也,尊贤为大。亲亲之杀,尊贤之等,礼所生也。在下位不获乎上,民不可得而治矣!故君子不可以不修身;思修身,不可以不事亲;思事亲,不可以不知人;思知人,不可以不知天。"

杀[shài] 名词,等级,差别

◈【今译】

鲁哀公向孔子询问政治。孔子说:"周文王、周武王的政治措施,都记载在典籍上了。这样的贤人在世,这些政事就能实施;他们去世,这些政事也就废弛了。贤人治理国家,政事就能迅速推行;沃土植树,树木就能快速生长。政事就像芦苇生长一样快速容易。所以处理好政事完全取决于用什么人,要得到适用的人在于修养自身,修养自身在于遵循道德,遵循道德要以仁为本。仁,就是人自身具有爱人之心,亲爱亲人就是最大的仁。义,就是事事做得适宜,尊重贤人是最大的义。亲爱亲人要分亲疏,尊重贤人要有等级,这就产生了礼。所以,君子不可以不修身,想要修身,不能不侍奉父母亲人;要侍奉父母亲人,不能不了解人;想要了解人,不能不知道天理。"

Chapter Twenty

◈ [Version 1]

The Duke Ai asked about government. The Master said, "The government of Wan and Wu is displayed in the records—the tablets of wood and bamboo. Let there be the men and the government will flourish; but without the men, their government decays and ceases. With the right men the growth of government is rapid, just as vegetation is rapid in the earth; and, moreover, their government might be called an easily-growing rush. Therefore the administration of government lies in getting proper men. Such men are to be got by means of the ruler's own character. That character is to be cultivated by his treading in the ways of duty. And the treading those ways of duty is to be cultivated by the cherishing of **benevolence**. Benevolence is the characteristic element of humanity, and the great exercise of it is in loving relatives. Righteousness is the accordance of actions with what is right, and the great exercise of it is in honoring the worthy. The decreasing measures of the love due to relatives, and the steps in the honor due to the worthy, are produced by the principle of **propriety**. When those in inferior situations do not possess the confidence of their superiors, they cannot retain the government of the people. Hence the sovereign may not neglect the cultivation of his own character. Wishing to cultivate his character, he may not neglect to serve his parents. In order to serve his parents, he may not neglect to acquire knowledge of men. In order to know men, he may not **dispense** with a knowledge of Heaven."

benevolence /bəˈnevələns/ *n*. kind and generous 仁慈
propriety /prəˈpraɪəti/ *n*. *formal* correctness of social or moral behaviour 礼貌;规矩;正当;合适
dispense /dɪˈspens/ *v*. *formal* to give something to people, especially in fixed amounts 分配,分给;实施,施行

◈ [Version 2]

Duke Ai (ruler of Confucius' native state) asked what constituted good government.

Confucius replied: "The principles of good government of the Emperors Wen and Wu are abundantly illustrated in the records preserved. When the men are there, good government will flourish, but when the men are gone, good government decays and becomes extinct.

"With the right men the growth of good government is as rapid as the growth of vegetation is in the right soil. Indeed, good government is like a fast growing plant.

"The conduct of government, therefore, depends upon the men. The right men are obtained by the rulers' personal character. To put in order his personal character, the ruler must use the moral law. To put in order the moral law, the ruler must use the moral sense.

"The moral sense is the characteristic attribute of man. To feel nature affection for those nearly related to us is the highest expression of the moral sense. The sense of justice is the recognition of what is right and proper. To honour those who are worthier than ourselves is the highest expression of the sense of justice. The relative degrees of natural affection we ought to feel for those who are nearly related to us and the relative grades of honour we ought to show to those worthier than ourselves: these are that which gives rise to the forms and distinctions in social life. For useless social inequalities have a true and moral basis, government of the people is an impossibility.

"Therefore it is necessary for a man of the governing class to set about regulating his personal conduct and character. In considering how to regulate his personal conduct and character, it is necessary for him to do his duties towards those nearly related to him. In considering how to do his duties towards those nearly related to him. it is necessary for him to understand the nature and organisation of human society. In considering the nature and organisation of human society, it is necessary for him to understand the laws of God."

◈【原文】

天下之达道五,所以行之者三。曰君臣也,父子也,夫妇也,昆弟也,朋友之交也:五者,天下之达道也。知、仁、勇三者,天下之达德也,所以行之者一也。或生而知之,或学而知之,或困而知之,及其知之一也。或安而行之,或利而行之,或勉强而行之;及其成功一也。子曰:"好学近乎知,力行近乎仁,知耻近乎勇。知斯三者,则知所以修身;知所以修身,则知所以治人;知所以治人,则知所以治天下国家矣。"

◈【今译】

天下共通的人伦大道有五条,用来实行这五条人伦大道的德行有三种。君臣之道、父子之道、夫妇之道、兄弟之道、朋友之道,这五项是天下共通的大道。智、仁、勇三种是天下共通的品德,用来履行这五条人道,这三种品德的实施效果都是一致。对这些道理,有的人生来就知晓,有的人通过学习才知晓,有的人经历了困苦才知晓,但只要他们最终都知道了,也就是一样的了。对于这些道理的实行,有的人心安理得地去做，有的人因为名利去做，有的人被迫勉强去做，但只要他们最终都做成了，也就是一样的了。孔子说："爱好学习就接近智了，努力行善就接近仁了，知道羞耻就接近勇了。知道这三点，就知道怎样修养自己；知道怎样修养自己，就知道怎样治理他人；知道怎样治理他人，就知道怎样治理天下和国家了。"

◈ [Version 1]

The duties of universal obligation are five and the virtues wherewith they are practiced are three. The duties are those between sovereign and minister, between father and son, between husband and wife, between elder brother and younger, and those belonging to the intercourse of friends. Those five are the duties of universal obligation. Knowledge, **magnanimity**, and energy, these three, are the virtues universally binding. And the means by which they carry the duties into practice is singleness. Some are born with the knowledge of those duties; some know them by study; and some acquire the knowledge after a painful feeling of their ignorance. But the knowledge being possessed, it comes to the same thing. Some practice them with a natural ease; some from a desire for their advantages; and some by strenuous effort. But the achievement being made, it comes to the same thing.

The Master said, "To be fond of learning is to be near to knowledge. To practice with vigor is to be near to magnanimity. To possess the feeling of shame is to be near to energy. He who knows these three things knows how to cultivate his own character. Knowing how to cultivate his own character, he knows how to govern other men. Knowing how to govern other men, he knows how to govern the kingdom with all its states and families."

magnanimity /ˌmæɡnəˈnɪməti/ *adj*. kind and generous, especially to someone that you have defeated 宽宏大量

◈ [Version 2]

The duties of universal obligation are five, and the moral qualities by which they are carried out are three. The duties are those between ruler and subject; between father and son; between husband and wife; between elder brother and younger; and those in the intercourse between friends. These are the five duties of universal obligations. Intelligence, moral character and courage: these are the three universally recognised moral qualities of man. It matters not in what way men come to the exercise of these moral qualities, the result is one and the same.

"Some men are born with the knowledge of these moral qualities; some acquire it as the result of education; some acquire it as the result of hard experience. But when the knowledge is acquired, it comes to one and the same thing. Some exercise these moral qualities naturally and easily; some because they find it advantageous to do so; some with effort and difficulty. But when the achievement is made it comes to one and the same thing,"

Confucius went on to say: "Love of knowledge is the characteristic of men of intellectual character. Strenuous attention to conduct is the characteristic of men of moral character. Sensitiveness to shame is the characteristic of men of courage or heroic character."

"When a man understands the nature and use these three moral qualities, he will then understand how to put in order his personal conduct and character. When a man understands how to put in order his personal conduct and character, he will understand how to govern men, he will then understand how to govern nations and empires."

◈【原文】

凡为天下国家有九经，曰：修身也，尊贤也，亲亲也，敬大臣也，体群臣也，子庶民也，来百工也，柔远人也，怀诸侯也。修身则道立，尊贤则不惑，亲亲则诸父昆弟不怨，敬大臣则不眩，体群臣则士之报礼重，子庶民则百姓劝，来百工则财用足，柔远人则四方归之，怀诸侯则天下畏之。

◈【今译】

凡是治理天下国家有九条原则。那就是：修养自身，尊重贤人，亲爱亲人，敬重大臣，体恤群臣，爱民如子，招纳工匠，优待远客，安抚诸侯。修养自身，就能确立正道；尊重贤人，就不会思想困惑；亲爱亲族，就不会惹得叔伯兄弟怨恨；敬重大臣，就不会遇事迷惑；体恤群臣，士人们的回报就会更加厚重；爱民如子，老百姓就会努力工作；招纳工匠，财务就会充足，优待远客，四方之人就会归顺；安抚诸侯，天下的人就会敬畏了。

◈ [Version 1]

All who have the government of the kingdom with its states and families have nine standard rules to follow, viz. the cultivation of their own characters; the honoring of men of virtue and talents; affection towards their relatives; respect towards the great ministers; kind and considerate treatment of the whole body of officers; dealing with the mass of the people as children; encouraging the resort of all classes of **artisans**; **indulgent** treatment of men from a distance; and the kindly cherishing of the princes of the states. By the ruler's cultivation of his own character, the duties of universal obligation are set forth. By honoring men of virtue and talents, he is preserved from errors of judgment. By showing affection to his relatives, there is no grumbling nor resentment among his uncles and **brethren**. By respecting the great ministers, he is kept from errors in the practice of government. By kind and considerate treatment of the whole body of officers, they are led to make the most grateful return for his courtesies. By dealing with the mass of the people as his children, they are led to **exhort** one another to what is good. By encouraging the resort of a class of artisans, his resources for expenditure are rendered ample. By indulgent treatment of men from a distance, they are brought to resort to him from all quarters. And by kindly cherishing the princes of the states, the whole kingdom is brought to revere him.

---

artisan /ˈɑːrtɪzən/ *n*. someone who does skilled work, making things with their hands 技工，工匠

indulgent /ɪn'dʌldʒənt/ *adj*. willing to allow someone, especially a child, to do or have whatever they want, even if this is not good for them 宽容的;任性的

brethren /'breðrən/ *n*. [plural] (old use) used to address or talk about the members of an organization or group, especially a religious group (旧)兄弟们,同胞

exhort /ɪg'zɔːt/ *v*. *formal* to try very hard to persuade someone to do something 劝告,劝说;倡导;勉励

◈ [Version 2]

For every one called to the government of nations and empires, there are nine cardinal directions to be attended to:

—Putting in order his personal conduct.

—Honouring worthy men.

—Cherishing affection for, and doing his duty toward his kindred.

—Showing respect to the high ministers of state.

—Identifying himself with the interests and welfare of the whole body of public officers.

—Showing himself as a father to the common people.

—Encouraging the introduction of all useful arts.

—Showing tenderness to strangers from far countries.

—Taking interest in the welfare of the princes of the Empire.

"When the ruler pays attention to putting in order his personal conduct, there will be respect for the moral law. When the ruler honours worthy men, he will not be deceived. When the ruler cherishes affection for his kindred, there will be no disaffection among the members of his family. When the ruler shows respect to the high ministers of state, he will not make mistakes. When the ruler identifies himself with the interests and welfare of the body of public officers, there will be a strong spirit of loyalty among the gentlemen of the country. When the ruler becomes a father to the common people, the mass of the people will exert themselves for the good of the state. When the ruler encourages the introduction of all useful arts, there will be sufficiency of wealth and revenue in the country. When the ruler shows tenderness to the strangers from far countries, people from all quarters of the world will flock to the country. When the ruler takes interest in the condition and welfare of the princes of the empire, he will inspire awe and respect for his authority throughout the whole world.

◈【原文】

齐明盛服,非礼不动,所以修身也。去谗远色,贱货而贵德,所以劝贤也。尊其位,重其禄,同其好恶,所以劝亲亲也。官盛任使,所以劝大臣也。忠信重禄,所以劝士也。时使薄敛,所以劝百姓也。日**省**月试,**既廪**称事,所以劝百工也。送往迎来,嘉善而矜不能,所以柔远人也。继绝世,举废国,治乱持危,朝聘以时,厚往而薄来,所以怀诸侯也。

齐[zhāi] 名词，同"斋"
省[xǐng] 动词，省察
既廪[jì lǐn] 名词，指薪水粮食

◈【今译】

像斋戒那样净心虔诚，穿着庄重整齐的服装，不符合礼仪的事坚决不做，这就是修养自身的原则。驱除小人，疏远女色，看轻钱财而重视德行，这就是尊崇贤人的原则。提高亲族的爵位，给他们以丰厚的俸禄，与他们爱恨相一致，这就是亲爱亲族的原则。官员众多足够任使，这就是劝勉大臣的原则。真心诚意地任用他们，并给他们丰厚的俸禄，这就是奖劝士人的原则。使民服役不误农时，少收赋税，这就是勉励百姓的原则。每天省察，每月考核，付给他们的薪水粮米与他们的业绩相称，这就是奖劝工匠的原则。来时欢迎，去时欢送，嘉奖有善行的人，怜恤能力差的人，这就是优待远客的原则。延续绝嗣的家族，复兴废亡的小国，治理祸乱，扶持危弱，按时接受诸侯朝见聘问，赠送丰厚，纳贡菲薄，这就是安抚诸侯的原则。

◈[Version 1]

Self-adjustment and purification, with careful regulation of his dress, and the not making a movement contrary to the rules of propriety: this is the way for a ruler to cultivate his person. Discarding slanderers, and keeping himself from the seductions of beauty; making light of riches, and giving honor to virtue: this is the way for him to encourage men of worth and talents. Giving them places of honor and large emolument and sharing with them in their likes and dislikes: this is the way for him to encourage his relatives to love him. Giving them numerous officers to discharge their orders and commissions: this is the way for him to encourage the great ministers. According to them a generous confidence, and making their emoluments large: this is the way to encourage the body of officers. Employing them only at the proper times, and making the imposts light: this is the way to encourage the people. By daily examinations and monthly trials, and by making their rations in accordance with their labors: this is the way to encourage the classes of artisans. To escort them on their departure and meet them on their coming; to commend the good among them, and show compassion to the incompetent: this is the way to treat indulgently men from a distance. To restore families whose line of succession has been broken, and to revive States that have been extinguished; to reduce to order states that are in confusion, and support those which are in peril; to have fixed times for their own reception at court, and the reception of their envoys; to send them away after liberal treatment, and welcome their coming with small contributions: this is the way to cherish the princes of the states.

seduction /sɪˈdʌkʃən/ *n*. something that strongly attracts people, but often has a bad effect on their lives 诱惑；引诱

emolument /ɪˈmɒljəmənt/ *n*. *formal* money or another form of payment for work you have done

报酬,薪水

envoy /ˈenvɔɪ/ *n*. someone who is sent to another country as an official representative 使节,外交官;全权公使;谈判代表

◈ [Version 2]

By attending to the cleanliness and purity of his person and to the propriety and dignity of his dress, and in every word and act permitting nothing which is contrary to good taste and decency, that is how the ruler puts in order his personal conduct. By banishing all flatterers and keeping away from the society of women; holding in low estimation possession of worldly goods, but valuing moral qualities in men: that is how the ruler gives encouragement to worthy men. By raising them to high places of honour and bestowing ample emoluments for their maintenance; sharing and sympathising with their tastes and opinions: that is how the ruler inspires love for his person among the members of his family. By extending the powers of their functions and allowing them discretion in the employment of their subordinates: that is how the ruler gives encouragement to the high ministers of state. By dealing loyally and punctually with them in all engagements which he makes with them and allowing a liberal scale of pay: that is how the ruler gives encouragement to men in public service. By strictly limiting the time of their service and making all imposts as light as possible: that is how the ruler gives encouragement to the mass of the people. By ordering daily inspection and monthly examination and rewarding each according to the degree of his workmanship: that is how the ruler encourages the artisan class. By welcoming them when they come and giving them protection when they go, commending what is good in them and making allowance for their ignorance: that is how the ruler shows tenderness to strangers from far countries. By restoring lines of broken succession and reviving extinguished states, putting down anarchy and disorder wherever they are found, and giving support to the weak against the strong, fixing stated times for their attendance and the attendance of their envoys at court, loading them with presents when they leave while exacting little from them in the way of contribution when they come: that is how the ruler takes interest in the welfare of the princes of the Empire.

◈【原文】

凡为天下国家有九经,所以行之者一也。凡事豫则立,不豫则废。言前定则不**跲**,事前定则不困,行前定则不疚,道前定则不穷。

跲[jiá] 动词,绊倒

◈【今译】

总而言之,治理天下和国家有九条原则,但是习惯这些原则的方法却只有一个。任何事情,事先有准备就会成功,没有准备就会失败。说话先有准备,就不会语言不畅;做事先有准备,就不会出现困

窘；行动先有准备，就不会后悔；道路预先选定，就不会走投无路。

◈ [Version 1]

All who have the government of the kingdom with its states and families have the above nine standard rules. And the means by which they are carried into practice is singleness In all things success depends on previous preparation, and without such previous preparation there is sure to be failure. If what is to be spoken be previously determined, there will be no stumbling. If affairs be previously determined, there will be no difficulty with them. If one's actions have been previously determined, there will be no sorrow in connection with them. If principles of conduct have been previously determined, the practice of them will be inexhaustible.

◈ [Version 2]

For everyone who is called to the government of nations and empire, these are the nine cardinal directions to be attended to; and there is only one way by which they can be carried out. In all matters, success depends on preparation; without preparation there will always be failure. When what is to be said is previously determined, there will be no breakdown. When what is to be done is previously determined, there will be no difficulty in carrying it out. When a line of conduct is previously determined, there will be no occasion for **vexation**. When general principles are previously determined, there will be no perplexity to know what to do.

vexation /vekˈseɪʃən/ *n*. *old-fashioned* when you feel worried or annoyed by something 烦恼；恼火

◈【原文】

在下位不获乎上，民不可得而治矣。获乎上有道：不信乎朋友，不获乎上矣。信乎朋友有道：不顺乎亲，不信乎朋友矣。顺乎亲有道：反诸身不诚，不顺乎亲矣。诚身有道：不明乎善，不诚乎身矣。

◈【今译】

在下位的人，如果得不到在上位的人的信任，就不可能治理好民众。得到在上位人的信任是有规则的：得不到朋友的信任，就得不到在上位人的信任。得到朋友的信任是有规则的：不能让父母顺心，就得不到朋友的信任。让父母顺心是有规则的：反省自己不真诚，就不能让父母顺心。使自己真诚是有规则的：不明白什么是善，就不能够使自己真诚。

◈ [Version 1]

When those in inferior situations do not obtain the confidence of the sovereign, they cannot succeed in governing the people. There is a way to obtain the confidence of the sovereign—if one is not trusted by his friends, he will not get the confidence of his sovereign. There is a way to being trusted by one's friends—if one is not obedient to his parents, he will not be true to friends.

There is a way to being obedient to one's parents—if one, on turning his thoughts in upon himself, finds a want of sincerity, he will not be obedient to his parents. There is a way to the attainment of sincerity in one's self—if a man do not understand what is good, he will not attain sincerity in himself.

◆ [Version 2]

If those in authority have not the confidence of those under them, government of the people is an impossibility. There is only one way to gain confidence for one's authority. If a man is not trusted by his friends, he will not gain the confidence for his authority. There is only one way to be trusted by one's friends. If a man does not command the obedience of the members of his family, he will not be trusted by his friends. There is only one way to command the obedience of the members of one's family. If a man, looking into his own heart, is not true to himself, he will not command the obedience of the members of his family. There is only one way for a man to be true to himself. If he does not know what is good, a man cannot be true to himself.

◆【原文】

诚者，天之道也；诚之者，人之道也。诚者，不勉而中，不思而得，从容中道，圣人也。诚之者，择善而固执之者也。博学之，审问之，慎思之，明辨之，笃行之。有弗学，学之弗能弗措也；有弗问，问之弗知弗措也；有弗思，思之弗得弗措也；有弗辨，辨之弗明弗措也；有弗行，行之弗笃弗措也。人一能之，己百之，人十能之，己千之。果能此道矣，虽愚必明，虽柔必强。

◆【今译】

真诚，是上天的原则；追求真诚，是做人的原则。天生真诚的人，不用勉强就能做到，不用思考就能拥有，从从容容就能符合中庸之道，这是圣人啊。努力做到真诚的人，就是选择好善的目标执着追求的人。广泛学习，详细询问，周密思考，明确辨别，切实实行。要么不学，学了没有学会绝不罢休；要么不问，问了没有明白绝不罢休；要么不想，想了没有所得绝不罢休；要么不分辨，分辨了没有明确绝不罢休；要么不实行，实行了没有笃实绝不罢休。别人用一分的努力就能做到的，我用一百分的努力去做；别人用十分的努力做到的，我用一千分的努力去做。如果真能够做到这样，虽然愚笨也一定可以聪明起来，虽然柔弱也一定可以刚强起来。

◆ [Version 1]

Sincerity is the way of Heaven. The attainment of sincerity is the way of men. He who possesses sincerity is he who, without an effort, hits what is right, and apprehends, without the exercise of thought—he is the sage who naturally and easily embodies the right way. He who attains to sincerity is he who chooses what is good, and firmly holds it fast. To this attainment there are requisite the extensive study of what is good, accurate inquiry about it, careful reflection on it, the clear discrimination of it, and the earnest practice of it. The superior man, while there is anything he has not studied, or while in what he has studied there is anything he cannot

understand, will not intermit his labor. While there is anything he has not inquired about, or anything in what he has inquired about which he does not know, he will not intermit his labor. While there is anything which he has not reflected on, or anything in what he has reflected on which he does not apprehend, he will not intermit his labor. While there is anything which he has not discriminated or his discrimination is not clear, he will not intermit his labor. If there be anything which he has not practiced, or his practice fails in earnestness, he will not intermit his labor. If another man succeed by one effort, he will use a hundred efforts. If another man succeed by ten efforts, he will use a thousand. Let a man proceed in this way, and, though dull, he will surely become intelligent; though weak, he will surely become strong.

requisite /ˈrekwəzət/ *adj*. *formal* needed for a particular purpose 必需品；要素，要件

◈【Version 2】

"Trust is the law of God. Acquired truth is the law of man.

"He who intuitively apprehends truth, is one who, with effort, hits what is right and without thinking, understands what he wants to know; whose life easily and naturally is in harmony with the moral law. Such a one is what we call a saint or a man of divine nature. He who acquires truth is one who finds out what is good and holds fast to it.

"In order to acquire truth, it is necessary to obtain a wide and extensive knowledge of what has been said and done in the world; to critically inquire into it; to carefully ponder over it; to clearly sift it; and earnestly carry it out.

"It matters not what you learn, but when you once learn a thing you must never give it up until you have mastered it. It matters not what you inquire into, but when you inquire into a thing you must never give it up until you have thoroughly understood it. It matters not what you try to think out, but when you once try to think out a thing you must never give it up until you have got what you want. It matters not what you try to sift out, but when you once try to sift out a thing, you must never give it up until you have sifted it out clearly and distinctly. It matters not what try to carry out, but when you once try to carry out a thing you must never give it up until you have done it thoroughly and well. If another man succeed by one effort, you will use a hundred efforts. If another man succeed by ten efforts, you will use a thousand efforts.

"Let a man really proceed in this manner, and though dull, he will surely become intelligent; though weak, he will surely become strong."

Chinese Philosophy

1.【率性之谓道】

In some people's eyes, the old order in China is passing away, we need to learn a new order from Westerners. Whereas, they don't know Chinese civilization is a moral civilization which contains a true social order aiming to attain a sense of moral obligation in men. The ideal goal of Chinese civilization is to attain "realization of true moral being—the sense of obligation—and moral order in mankind so that the Universe shall become a cosmos and all things can attain their full growth and development."

2.【致中和】

"Zhong" and "He" are the main ideas in the book. "While there are no stirrings of pleasure, anger, sorrow, or joy, the mind may be said to be in the state of Equilibrium. When those feelings have been stirred, and they act in their due degree, there ensues what may be called the state of Harmony." How to keep calm in the state of equilibrium and how to act in order to gain the state of Harmony need us to think and learn so that we can live happier and all things grow to its full development.

3.【仁者人也,亲亲为大】

"Ren" is a key word in Confucius theory. To feel natural affection for our parents is the very beginning of love towards others. The sense of morality is the recognition of what is right and proper: we have the natural love for those who are nearly related to us so that we can extend our feelings towards others and honor those who are worthier than ourselves.

4.【博学之,审问之,慎思之,明辨之,笃行之】

The law of man is to acquire truth, which can be obtained by efforts. How to acquire truth? The keys are "the extensive study of what is good, accurate inquiry about it, careful reflection on it, the clear discrimination of it, and the earnest practice of it", which are the requisites to obtain goodness and sincerity.

Practice

I. Vocabulary

Choose a proper word or phrase to complete each of the following sentences, changing the form when necessary.

utmost	distinguish	embodying	keep it	took hold of
attainment	proper	accords	contrary	cause

1. To find and get into the true central balance of our moral being, i. e., our true moral ordinary self, that indeed is the highest human ________. People are seldom capable of it for long.
2. There is no body but eats and drinks. But they are few who can ________ flavors.
3. He ________ their two extremes, determined the Mean, and employed it in his government of the people. It was by this that he was Shun!

4. We are wise; but happening to choose the course of the Mean, they are not able to ________ for a round month.
5. The superior man ________ with the course of the Mean.
6. The way of the superior man may be found, in its simple elements, in the intercourse of common men and women; but in its ________ reaches, it shines brightly through heaven and earth.
7. The superior man does what is ________ to the station in which he is; he does not desire to go beyond this.
8. In archery we have something like the way of the superior man. When the archer misses the center of the target, he turns round and seeks for the ________ of his failure in himself.
9. The mean man's acting ________ to the course of the Mean is because he is a mean man, and has no caution.
10. The superior man's ________ the course of the Mean is because he is a superior man, and so always maintains the Mean.

II. Translation

Translate the following sentences and the passage into English.

1. 君子之道,辟如行远必自迩,辟如登高必自卑。

   ____

2. 自诚明,谓之性;自明诚,谓之教。诚则明矣,明则诚矣。

   ____

3. 道不远人。人之为道而远人,不可以为道。

   ____

4. 君子中庸,小人反中庸。

   ____

5. 万物并育而不相害,道并行而不相悖。

   ____

6. 唯天下至诚,为能尽其性;能尽其性,则能尽人之性;能尽人之性,则能尽物之性;能尽物之性,则可以赞天地之化育;可以赞天地之化育,则可以与天地参矣。

   ____

   ____

   ____

III. Critical Thinking

Discuss the following questions in groups and give your group presentation in class on the basis of your discussion.

1. What is the doctrine of the Mean? How to choose the course of the Mean and keep it?

2. How do you understand "While there are no stirrings of pleasure, anger, sorrow, or joy, the mind may be said to be in the state of Equilibrium. When those feelings have been stirred, and they act in their due degree, there ensues what may be called the state of Harmony"?

References

[1] Legge, James. The Doctrine of the Mean [M]. 郑州：中州古籍出版社，2016.
[2] 辜鸿铭. 大学·中庸[M]. 王京涛. 评述. 北京：中华书局，2017.
[3] 王国轩. 大学·中庸[M]. 北京：中华书局，2016.

Unit 5

Records of the Historian[①]

Introduction

Records of the Historian is regarded as the most representative and outstanding of all history books in the Chinese tradition. In the form of a series of biographies, the book records the history of China from the Five Legendary Rulers Period (30th century—21st century BC) to around 100 BC, under the reign of Emperor Wu of the Western Han Dynasty (206 BC—25 AD). For over 2,000 years, *Records of the Historian* has been praised for its accuracy, lofty style and vivid characterization. It is still a necessary companion for Chinese intellectuals and students of Chinese history today.

As one of the most attractive narratives in *Records of the Historian*, *Xiang Yu* told the life story of a tragic hero, who rose from humble roots to the glorious throne, but was finally defeated by his opponent and committed suicide. The features of biographical literature in traditional China have been fully displayed in *Xiang Yu*, therefore it is worthwhile to be appreciated.

Learning Objectives

After learning this unit, you will be able to

1. learn about the content and genre of *Records of the Historian* in general;
2. understand the text *Xiang Yu* in detail;
3. interpret critically the materials in English related to the tragic story of how Xiang Yu has become the Conqueror but ended up killing himself;
4. explore the traditional Chinese values about the strategies of being a good leader.

---

① English version 1 is excerpted from *Selections from Records of the Historian*, translated by Yang Xianyi and Gladys Yang, and English version 2 is excerpted from *The Grand Scribe's Records*, translated by William H. Nienhauser, Jr.

Selected Readings

《项羽》节选

◈【原文】

项王军**壁**垓下，兵少食尽，汉军及诸侯兵围之数重。夜闻汉军四面皆楚歌，项王乃大惊曰："汉皆已得楚乎？是何楚人之多也！"项王则夜起，饮帐中。有美人名虞，常**幸从**；骏马名骓，常骑之。于是项王乃悲歌慷慨，自为诗曰："力拔山兮气盖世，时不利兮骓不逝。骓不逝兮可奈何，虞兮虞兮奈若何！"歌数阕，美人和之。项王泣数行下，左右皆泣，莫能仰视①。

壁[bì]　动词，修筑营垒

幸从[xìng cóng]　动词，受宠幸跟从

◈【今译】

项王军队在垓下筑起营垒，兵少粮尽，汉军及诸侯军队重重包围了他们。夜间听到汉军四面都唱着楚歌，项王就大惊道："汉军都已得到楚国的土地了吗？为什么楚人这么多呢！"项王就连夜起来，在帐中饮酒。有位美人名叫虞，经常受宠幸跟从；骏马名叫骓，项王经常骑它。于是项王慷慨悲歌，自己作诗唱道："力拔山啊气盖世，时不利啊骓不走。虽不走啊怎么办，虞姬啊虞姬啊，把你怎么办！"唱了几遍，美人伴唱。项王泪下数行，随从们都哭了，不忍抬头看他。

◈ [Version 1]

Xiang Yu's army at Gaixia, with only a handful of troops and right out of supplies, was **hemmed** in by the men of Han and the other states. At night he heard the besiegers all about him singing Chu songs.

"Has Han already conquered Chu?" he asked in dismay. "They have so many men of Chu with them!"

He rose that night to drink in his tent. With him was the lovely Lady Yu, who followed wherever he went, and Zhui, the swift steed which he always rode. Now Xiang Yu chanted a tragic air, setting words to it himself:

> My strength uprooted mountains,
> My spirit overtopped the world;

① When translating "……左右皆泣，莫能仰视", Version 1 put it as "... all his followers wept and bowed their heads in sorrow", which employed a commonly-used translation technique called shift of perspective (视角转换). "莫能仰视"is a negative sentence, but in Version 1, it is converted into an affirmative sentence to directly describe the sorrow of the soldiers. There are many examples that could be found in version 1, such as "时不利兮"is translated as "times are against me"; "江东虽小"as "there is not much land east of the Yangtze"; "今无一人还"as "now I have come back alone".

But the times are against me,
And Zhui can gallop no more.
When Zhui can gallop no more,
What can I do?
And what is to become
Of Lady Yu?

He sang this song several times and Lady Yu joined in. Tears coursed down his cheeks, while all his followers wept and bowed their heads in sorrow.

hem /hem/ *v*. to surround closely 包围

◈ [Version 2]

King Hsiang's army **fortified** their camp at Kai-hsia, but with his troops diminished and his food exhausted, (the King of) Han and the feudal lords surrounded them with several rings of troops. After dark they heard the Han army on all four sides singing Ch'u songs. King Hsiang was alarmed and said, "Has Han already secured Ch'u? Why is it that there are so many men of Ch'u out there?" He thus got up at night and drank in his tent. He has a Fine Lady, Yü 虞, whom he favored and who always kept him company, and a steed, named Piebald, which he always rode. At this, King Hsiang, in a mood both tragic and **indignant**, composed a song:

My strength uplifted a mountain,
My vigor shadowed the world.
But the times do not favor me,
And Piebald can not gallop fast enough.
Piebald can not gallop fast enough,
And what can I do about it?
Oh Yü, Oh Yü!
What can I do about you?

He sang it several times and the Fine Lady sang with him. Tears streamed down King Hsiang's cheeks and his attendants all wept; no one could life up his head.

fortify /ˈfɔːtɪfaɪ/ *vi*. to build towers, walls, etc. around an area or city in order to defend it 构筑防御工事

indignant /ɪnˈdɪgnənt/ *adj*. angry and surprised because you feel insulted or unfairly treated 愤慨的;激愤的

◈【原文】

于是项王乃上马骑，麾下壮士骑从者八百余人，直夜溃围南出，**驰走**。平明，汉军乃觉之，令骑将灌婴以五千骑追之。项王渡淮，骑能属者百余人耳。项王至阴陵①，迷失道，问一田父，田父**绐**曰："左。"左，乃陷大泽中。以故汉追及之。项王乃复引兵而东，至东城，乃有二十八骑。汉骑追者数千人②。项王自**度**不得脱，谓其骑曰："吾起兵至今八岁矣，身七十余战，所当者破，所击者服，未尝败北，遂霸有天下。然今卒困于此，此天之亡我，非战之罪也。今日固决死，愿为诸君快战，必三胜之，为诸君溃围，斩将，刈旗，令诸君知天亡我，非战之罪也。"乃分其骑以为四队，四向。汉军围之数重。项王谓其骑曰："吾为公取彼一将。"令四面骑驰下，**期**山东为三处。于是项王大呼驰下，汉军皆披靡，遂斩汉一将。是时，赤泉侯为骑将，追项王，项王瞋目而叱之，赤泉侯人马俱惊，辟易数里。与其骑会为三处，汉军不知项王所在。乃分军为三，复围之。项王乃驰，复斩汉一都尉，杀数十百人，复聚其骑，亡其两骑耳。乃谓其骑曰："何如?"骑皆伏曰："如大王言。"

驰走[chí zǒu]　动词，使劲赶马

绐[dài]　动词，欺骗

度[duó]　动词，估计，揣度，推测

期[qī]　动词，约定

◈【今译】

这时，项王骑上马，部下壮士骑马跟随的有八百多人，当夜突围往南去，骑马飞奔。天亮了，汉军才发觉，命骑将灌婴率五千骑兵追赶。项王渡过淮水，骑马能跟得上的只有一百多人。项王到了阴陵，迷失方向，问一农夫，农夫骗他说："往左。"往左走，陷入了大沼泽中。因此汉军追上了。项王又领兵向东，到了东城，只有二十八个骑兵了。汉军骑兵追赶的有数千人。项王估计自己不能脱身，对他的骑兵们说："我起兵到现在八年了，身经七十多次战役，阻挡我的被打败，我攻打的敌人都降服，不曾败过，这才霸有天下。可是现在终于被困在这里，这是天要灭我，不是作战的错误。今天一定要决一死战，想为诸君痛快一战，一定接连三次获胜，给诸君突围，斩将，拔旗，让诸君知道是上天要灭我，不是作战的过错。"于是把人马分成四队，向四方突围。汉军重重包围了他们。项王对他的骑兵们说："我为你们斩他一将。"命骑兵四面奔驰而下，约定到山的东面分三处会合。这时项王大喊着奔驰而下，汉军都溃散，就斩杀了汉军一将。这时，赤泉侯为骑将，追赶项王，项王怒目呵斥他，赤泉侯人马都受到惊吓，远避数里，项王同他的骑士们分三处会合。汉军不知项王在哪里，就兵分三路，又包围了他们。项王继续奔驰，又斩杀汉军一名都尉，杀了上百人，又聚拢他的骑兵，只损失了两名而已。项王就

---

① When translating names of places such as "阴陵、东城" and names of people such as "吕胜、杨武" into English, Version 1 followed the normal way by using their Chinese Pinyin while Version 2 not only gave their Chinese Pinyin but also placed their Chinese characters after the Pinyin, which shows the translator's respect to the original texts.

② When translating "……乃有二十八骑。汉骑追者数千人", Version 2 followed the Chinese expression and put it as "King Hsiang ... reached Tung-ch'eng with only twenty-eight horsemen. The Han horsemen in pursuit numbered several thousand." However, Version 1 converted it into "... By now only twenty-eight horsemen remained with him, **while** his pursuers numbered several thousand." By adding a logical connective "while", Xiang Yu's unfavorable condition was better presented through contrast. Sometimes we have to add some words to ensure a smooth or idiomatic translation, and this translation skill is called amplification (增译).

问骑兵们："怎么样?"骑兵们都伏在地上说："像您说的一样。"

◈ [Version 1]

Then he mounted his horse and rode into the night with little more than eight hundred staunch followers. Breaking through the enemy lines to the south, they **galloped** away.

By dawn the Han army knew that he had escaped, and the cavalry officer Guan Ying was sent with five thousand horsemen in pursuit. By the time Xiang Yu crossed the River Huai, there were little more than a hundred horsemen with him. At Yinling he lost his way and asked an old man in the fields to direct him. "Bear left!" The old man deliberately deceived him, and going left he was **bogged down** in the marshes so that the Han cavalry came up with him.

So Xiang Yu turned back east to Dongcheng. By now only twenty-eight horsemen remained with him, while his pursuers numbered several thousand. He knew that he could not escape and told his men:

"It is eight years since I rose in arms. In that time I have fought more than seventy battles. I swept all obstacles from my path, conquered every foe I attacked, and was never defeated. That is how I won the empire. But now suddenly I am hemmed in here. This is because Heaven is against me and not because my generalship is at fault. Today I shall **perish** here, but for your sake I shall fight **gallantly** and overcome the enemy three times. For you I shall break through their lines, kill their commander and cut down their flag, so that you may know it is Heaven that has destroyed me, not my generalship that is fault."

He divided his horsemen into four groups, facing in four directions. The Han forces had surrounded them on all sides.

"Watch me kill one of their commanders for you!" he cried.

He ordered his men to gallop down in four directions and reassemble in three groups east of the hill. Then with a mighty battle-cry he charged. The Han troops scattered before him and he struck down one of their commanders. A cavalry commander named Yang Xi, the **marquis** of Chiquan, pursued him. But Xiang Yu glared and bellowed at him so fiercely that Yang Xi's horse bolted and fled, terrified, for several *li*.

Xiang Yu rejoined his men, who by now had reassembled in three groups. The Han forces, not knowing which group he was in, divided into three to surround them again. Once more Xiang Yu charged through their lines and killed a military tribune as well as several dozen men. When he **rallied** his followers again, he had lost only two of them.

"How was that?" he asked.

His men bowed and replied,"You were as good as your word, Your Majesty."

---

gallop /ˈgæləp/ *v*. to run somewhere very quickly 疾驰

bog down to get stuck 陷入困境

perish /ˈperɪʃ/ *v*. die as a result of very harsh conditions 死亡
gallantly /ˈɡæləntli/ *adv*. bravely and honorably 英勇高尚地
marquis /ˈmɑːkwɪs/ *n*. nobleman ranking above a count 侯爵
rally /ˈræli/ *v*. to unit to support 召集，团结起来

◈ [Version 2]

After this, King Hsiang mounted his horse and, accompanied by some eight hundred stalwart horsemen under his banner, that same night broke out of the siege to the south and galloped away. The Han army became aware of it only when it was daylight. They had Kuan Ying, a cavalry general, pursue them with five-thousand horsemen. After King Hsiang had crossed the Huai, he had only one-hundred horsemen or so who could still keep up with him. When he reached Yin-ling 阴陵, he lost his way and asked an old farmer. The old farmer deceived him, saying: "Go left!" He went left and was bogged down in a great marsh. Thus the Han horsemen were able to catch up with them. King Hsiang led his troops to the east instead and reached Tung-ch'eng 东城 with only twenty-eight horsemen. The Han horsemen in pursuit numbered several thousand. King Hsiang, judging that he could not escape, told his horsemen:

"It has been eight years now since I rose in arms. I have personally fought more than seventy battles, in which whomever I was matched with, I **vanquished**, whomever I set upon, I **subdued**. Never once defeated, I finally became the **Hegemon** and possessed the world. Yet in the end I have now been **cornered** here. It is Heaven that destroys me. It is not any fault of mine in battle. Today, I must surely resolve to die, but let me fight a joyful battle for you first. I vow to defeat them three times, break the siege for you, cut off the heads of their general, and cut down their banners, so that you will see it is Heaven that destroys me, not any fault of mine in battle."

Thus he divided his horsemen into four squads, facing the four directions. The Han army surrounded them with several rings of troops. King Hsiang told his horsemen, "I will take one of their generals for you." He ordered his horsemen on all four sides to charge down and **converge** in three groups on the east of the hill. With this, King Hsiang charged down yelling loudly. The entire Han line bent back in disorder and he actually succeeded in cutting off the head of one Han general. At this time the Marquis of Ch'ih-ch'üan 赤泉 was a general of the **cavalry** pursuing King Hsiang. King Hsiang glared and bellowed at him. Both the Marquis of Ch'ih-ch'üan and his horse were frightened and bolted several *li*. King Hsiang joined his horsemen, who had reassembled into three groups. The Han army did not know which group he was in, thus it divided into three groups and surrounded them again. King Hsiang charged, cut off the head of a Commandant of Han again, and killed dozens of men, nearly one-hundred. When he gathered his horsemen once more, only two of them were missing. Then he said to them, "How was that?" His horsemen replied with great respect, "It was just as Your Majesty said!"

vanish /ˈvænɪʃ/ *vi*. to disappear suddenly 消失；突然不见

subdue /səbˈdu/ *vt*. to defeat or control a person or group, especially using force 征服；克制
hegemon /ˈhedʒəmɔn/ *n*. a ruler that control others 霸主；霸权主义者
corner /ˈkɔːnə/ *vt*. to force a person or animal into a place they cannot escape from 逼入困境
converge /kənˈvəːdʒ/ *vi*. come from different directions and meet at the same point to become one thing 聚集；汇集
cavalry /ˈkævlri/ *n*. the part of an army that fights on horses 骑兵（队）

◈【原文】

于是项王乃欲东渡乌江。乌江亭长舣船待，谓项王曰："江东虽小，**地方**千里，众数十万人，亦足王也。愿大王急渡。今独臣有船，汉军至，无以渡。"项王笑曰："天之亡我，我何渡为！且籍与江东子弟八千人渡江而西，今无一人还，纵江东父兄怜而王我，我何面目见之？纵彼不言，籍**独**不愧于心乎？"乃谓亭长曰："吾知公长者，吾骑此马五岁，所当无敌，尝一日行千里，不忍杀之。以赐公。"乃令骑皆下马步行，持短兵接战，独籍所杀汉军数百人。项王身亦被十余创。顾见汉骑司马吕马童，曰："若非吾故人乎？"马童**面**之，指王翳曰："此项王也。"项王乃曰："吾闻汉购我头千金，邑万户，吾为若德。"乃自刎而死。王翳取其头，余骑相蹂践争项王，相杀者数十人。最其后，郎中骑杨喜、骑司马吕马童、郎中吕胜、杨武各得其一体。五人共会其体，皆是。故分其地为五：封吕马童为中水侯，封王翳为杜衍侯，封杨喜为赤泉侯，封杨武为吴防侯，封吕胜为涅阳侯。

地方[dì fāng] 名词，古今异义，土地方圆
独[dú] 副词，难道
面[miàn] 动词，面向

◈【今译】

这时项王就想东渡乌江。乌江亭长停船靠岸，对项王说："江东虽小，地方千里，民众数十万人，也足以称王了。希望大王赶紧渡江。现在只我有船，汉军来了，无船渡江。"项王笑道："天要灭我，我还渡江干什么！况且我项籍与江东子弟八千人渡江而西，现在无一人生还，纵然江东父兄可怜我让我做王，我还有什么脸面见他们呢！纵然他们不说，项籍难道不心中有愧吗！"于是对亭长说："我知道您是长者。我骑这马五年了，所向无敌，曾经日行千里，不忍心杀它，赐给您吧。"于是命骑兵都下马步行，持短兵器交战，仅项籍就杀了汉军数百人。项王自己也受了十几处伤。回头看见汉骑司马吕马童，说："这不是我的熟人吗？"马童面对着他，指给王翳说："这是项王。"项王就说："我听说汉王悬赏千金买我的头，封邑万户，我给你们些恩德吧。"于是自刎而死。王翳取下项王的头，其余骑兵争相践踏抢夺项王躯体，相互残杀的有数十人。到最后，郎中骑杨喜、骑司马吕马童、郎中吕胜、杨武各得到项王一肢体。五人一起合上尸体，都能对上。所以把封地划分为五份：封吕马童为中水侯，封王翳为杜衍侯，封杨喜为赤泉侯，封杨武为吴防侯，封吕胜为涅阳侯。

◈[Version 1]

Xiang Yu now considered crossing the River Wujiang and going to the east of the Yangtse.

The station master there had a boat moored and waiting. "There is not much land east of the Yangtse," he said to Xiang Yu. "But a thousand square *li* and several hundred thousand men are enough for a kingdom. You must cross quickly, Your Highness! Mine is the only boat here. When the Han army comes, they will not be able to cross."

"Heaven is against me," replied Xiang Yu with a laugh. "What use is it to cross the river? Besides, I once crossed the Yangtse and went west with eight thousand young men from the east, but now I have come back alone. Even if the elders made me king out of pity, how could I face them again? Though they said nothing, how could I hold up my head?" He turned to the station master. "I can see you are a **worthy** man. For five years I have ridden this horse, sweeping all before me, often galloping a thousand *li* in one day. I cannot bear to kill him, I give him to you."

He ordered his men to dismount for hand-to-hand combat. Xiang Yu alone killed several hundred men of Han and was wounded some dozen times. Then, turning to see the cavalry officer Lü Matong, he exclaimed:

"Isn't that my old friend Lü?"

Lü Matong, facing him, pointed him out to Wang Yi.

"There is Xiang Yu!"

Xiang Yu said," I hear the king of Han has offered a reward of a thousand gold pieces and a **fief** of ten thousand families for my head. Let me do you a good turn!" With that he cut his own throat.

Wang Yi seized his head, while the other horsemen **trampled** and **jostled** each other for his body — several dozens of them fought and killed each other. Finally a cavalryman of the guard, Yang Xi, the cavalry marshal Lü Matong, and the knights Lü Sheng and Yang Wu secured one limb each. When the five of them fitted the limbs together, it was seen that they were indeed those of Xiang Yu, and the fief was divided among them. Lü Matong was made marquis of Zhongshui, Wang Yi marquis of Duyan, Yang Xi marquis of Chiquan, Yang Wu marquis of Wufang, and Lü Sheng marquis of Nieyang.

---

worthy /ˈwɜːði/ *adj*. be morally respectable or correct 值得尊敬的

fief /fiːf/ *n*. a piece of land given to someone by their lord 采邑,封地

trample /ˈtræmpl/ *v*. to step heavily and carelessly on some place 踩踏

jostle /ˈdʒɒsl/ *v*. to bump and push to get past 推搡

◈ [Version 2]

At this point, King Hsiang had intended to cross east over (the Chiang) from Wu-chiang 乌江. The head of Wu-chiang **Precinct** waited with his boat moored; he told King Hsiang, "Even though the territory east of the Chiang is small, with its area of one thousand *li* (on a side) and population of several hundred thousand people, it is good enough to rule over as king. I beg you to

cross quickly. Only I have a boat now. When the Han army arrives, there is no way for them to get across." King Hsiang laughed and replied, "Since Heaven wants me to perish, why bother to cross the river? Besides, there were eight-thousand youths from east of the Chiang who crossed it with me and marched west, but now not a single one of them has come back. Even if the elders east of the Chiang would take pity on me and make me king, how could I look them in the face? Even though they might not say a word, I would simply feel the shame in my heart."

Then he said to the precinct head, "I know you are a kind old man. I have ridden this horse for five years, and among those I have faced, none is his match. He used to run one thousand *li* a day. I cannot bear to kill him, so I shall give him to you."

He then ordered all his horsemen to dismount and go on foot, holding short weapons to engage in combat. King Hsiang alone killed several hundred men of the Han army. He himself also suffered more than ten wounds. Turning about, he saw Lü Ma-t'ung 吕马童, the Cavalry Marshal of Han, and said: "Are you not my old friend?" Lü Ma-t'ung faced him and then, pointing him out to Wang Yi 王翳, said, "This is King Hsiang."

King Hsiang said, "I have heard that Han has offered one-thousand *chin* and a fief of ten-thousand households for my head. I will do you the favor!" He then cut his own throat and died. Wang Yi laid hold of his head. The rest of the horsemen trampled over each other struggling for his body, killing a few dozen of their comrades. In the end, the Cavalry General of the Palace Attendants, Yang Hsi, the Cavalry Marshal, Lü Ma-t'ung, and the Palace Attendants, Lü Sheng 吕胜 and Yang Wu 杨武, obtained one limb each. The five men fitted together the limbs and head and verified them all [to be those of King Hsiang]. Therefore, the King of Han divided the promised fief into five, and **enfeoffed** Lü Ma-t'ung as the Marquis of Chung-shui 中水, Wang Yi as the Marquis of Tu-yen 杜衍, Yang Hsi as the Marquis of Ch'ih-ch'uan 赤泉, Yang Wu as the Marquis of Wu-fang 吴防, and Lü Sheng as the Marquis of Nieh-yang 涅阳.

precinct /ˈpriːsɪŋkt/ *n*. one of the areas that a town or city is divided into 管辖区

enfeoff /ɪnˈfef/ *vt*. put in possession of land in exchange for a pledge of service in feudal society 授予封地

Chinese Philosophy

1.【完善自我】

Xiang Yu had no intention to overcome the weaknesses in his character throughout his life, which was fatal to a hero with great ambition and high ideal. His failure was inevitable since he took no notice of the importance of improving his own character. Liu Bang, on the other hand, paid attention to improve himself in spite of his humble origin. He learned a lot from his idol Lord Xinling, a modest and prudent young leader who cherished the talented and the learned very much;

constantly refined his own character, and thus received respect from his followers.

2.【坚忍克己】

After Liu Bang took Guanzhong, he followed Fan Kuai and Zhang Liang's advice of taking not a single cent from the national treasury and promised to the people that his army was a righteous one and would do no harm to them. By doing this, Liu Bang won the support of the people in Guanzhong. Liu Bang was greedy and lustful in nature, but he managed to restrain himself in the process of achieving his goal, which was a strong contrast with Xiang Yu's savage act of looting the treasure and young ladies once he occupied a city. It teaches us a lesson that we should try to control our desire and not act by impulse in pursuit of great cause, otherwise we would be penny-wise and pound foolish.

3.【知人善任】

Judged only by their family background and personal ability, Xiang Yu seems to far more exceed Liu Bang. However, Liu Bang's leadership stood out as he was able to incorporate many talents such as Zhang Liang, Xiao He and Han Xin into his own force. Specifically speaking, he was good at discovering able people and always put them at suitable posts, cared nothing about an able person's humble origin but his talent, was willing to provide favorable work environment for these talents and to offer exceptional promotions to those outstanding staff. From Xiang Yu and Liu Bang's example, we can see that only a wise leader that attaches great importance to his personnel and treat them well can win the final battle.

Practice

I. Vocabulary

Choose a proper word or phrase to complete each of the following sentences, changing the form when necessary.

hem	gall	bog down	perish	fief
gallantly	marquis rally	worthy	trample	jostle

1. Men have to be careful what they cry at, because some subjects are more ________ of tears than others.
2. All the training in the world won't persuade a child to behave ________ if his parents become aggressive, demanding and rude at the slightest provocation.
3. Now they find themselves caught in the middle as America and Iran ________ for regional dominance.
4. A ________ is a male member of the nobility who has a rank between duke and earl.
5. He liked to be ________ around by the reporters.
6. They say loggers are destroying rain forests and ________ on the rights of natives.

7. Her cabinet colleagues have continued to _______ to her support.
8. This year, the economic recovery may _______ as government stimulus measures dry up.
9. Most of the butterflies _______ in the first frosts of autumn.
10. Once when I was a mere lad, and had never ridden a horse before, he made me mount one and _______ by his side, with no qualms about his unskilled companion.

II. Translation

Translate the following sentences and the passage into English.

1. 吾起兵至今八岁矣，身七十余战，所当者破，所击者服，未尝败北，遂霸有天下。

____

2. 今日固决死，愿为诸君快战，必三胜之，为诸君溃围，斩将，刈旗，令诸君知天亡我，非战之罪也。

____

____

3. 是时，赤泉侯为骑将，追项王，项王瞋目而叱之，赤泉侯人马俱惊，辟易数里。

____

4. 且籍与江东子弟八千人渡江而西，今无一人还，纵江东父兄怜而王我，我何面目见之！纵彼不言，籍独不愧于心乎！

____

____

5. 乃令骑皆下马步行，持短兵接战，独籍所杀汉军数百人。项王身亦被十余创。

____

6. 羽非有尺寸，乘执起陇亩之中，三年，遂将五诸侯灭秦，分裂天下，而封王侯，政由羽出，号为“霸王”。位虽不终，近古以来未尝有也。及羽背关怀楚，放逐义帝而自立，怨王侯叛己，难矣。自矜功伐，奋其私智而不师古，谓霸王之业，欲以力征经营天下，五年卒亡其国，身死东城，尚不觉寤，而不自责，过矣。乃引“天亡我，非用兵之罪也”，岂不谬哉！

____

____

____

____

III. Critical Thinking

Discuss the following questions in groups and give your group presentation in class on the basis of your discussion.

1. What characters of Xiang Yu are revealed in this passage? Find out the relevant details from the text to support your points of view.
2. Do you think Xiang Yu has made a right decision by committing suicide in his situation? Why or why not?

References

［1］Watson, Burton. Records of the Grand Historian of China［M］. New York: Columbia University Press, 1961.

［2］William, H. Nienhauser Jr & Cheng Tsai-fa. The Grand Scribe's Records: Volum Ⅰ［M］. Bloomington, Ind.: Indiana University Press, 1994.

［3］Yang, Xianyi & Dai, Naidie. Selections from Records of the Historian［M］. Beijing: Foreign Languages Press, 2007.

［4］司马迁撰,韩兆琦评注,史记：韩兆琦评注本[M].湖南：岳麓书社,2011.

Unit 6

The Art of War①

Introduction

The Art of War is a 6th Century BC Chinese treatise on military strategy and tactics, which is authored by Sun Tzu (or Sun Zi, Sun Wu), a famous military general and strategist who lived 2,500 years ago. *The Art of War* is one of the most prestigious and influential book on the subject of strategy in the world today.

The Art of War is composed of 13 chapters and each chapter explores one aspect of warfare and how that applies to military strategy and tactics. Comprising 13 chapters of numerous thoughts, *The Art of War* continues to hold good for the present times since the basic principles remain unchanged. It applies in competition and conflict in general, on every level from the interpersonal to the international and provides valuable assistance to people in the fields of business management, sports, and politics or simply in everyday life.

Learning Objectives

After learning this unit, you will be able to

1. learn generally about the content and genre of *The Art of War*;
2. understand deeply the selected quotations from *The Art of War* in detail;
3. interpret critically the selected readings related to Sun Tzu's principles about war as well as life and his wise ways to resolve conflicts in English;
4. explore the traditional Chinese values based on *The Art of War*.

---

① Both the original selected readings and English version one in this unit are excerpted from *Sunzi*: *The Art of War*; *Sun Bin*: *The Art of War* and the translator is Lin Wusun. English version two is excerpted from *The Art of War*, translated by Lionel Giles.

Selected Readings

始计第一[1]

◈【原文】

孙子曰：兵者，国之大事，死生之地，存亡之道，不可不察也。故**经**之以五事，**校**之以**计**而索其情：一曰道，二曰天，三曰地，四曰将，五曰法。道者，令民于上同意也。故可以与之死，可以与之生，而不畏危。天者，阴阳、寒暑、时制也；地者，远近、险易、广狭、死生也。将者，智、信、仁、勇、严也。法者，**曲制**、**官道**、**主用**也。凡此五者，将莫不闻，知之者胜，不知之者不胜。

经[jīng] 动词，以……为经，分析研究
校[jiào] 动词，通"较"，比较
计[jì] 名词，指下文的"主孰有道"等七计，对这七个方面情况的估计
曲制[qū zhì] 名词，军队组织编制的制度
官道[guān dào] 名词，各级将吏的职责区分、统辖管理等制度
主用[zhǔ yòng] 名词，军需物资的供应和管理

◈【今译】

孙子说：战争，是国家的大事，是军队生死的所在，国家存亡的途径，不能不认真考察。所以，要从五个方面进行分析，比较敌我双方的各种条件，以探索战争的情势：一是道，二是天，三是地，四是将，五是法。所谓"道"，就是使民众与君主的意愿一致。这样，他们就可以为君主死，为君主生，而不畏惧危险。所谓"天"，是指昼夜阴晴、寒冬酷暑、春夏秋冬的变化更替。所谓"地"，是指远途近路、险阻平地、地域宽窄、死地生地。所谓"将"，是指将帅的智谋、诚信、仁慈、勇敢、严明。所谓"法"，是指军队的组织编制、将吏的管理、军需的掌管。凡属这五个方面的情况，将帅都不能不知道。了解这些情况的就能胜利，不了解这些情况的就不能胜利。

◈ [Version 1]

Making Assessments

Sunzi said: War is a question of vital importance to the state, a matter of life and death, the road to survival or ruin. Hence, it is a subject which calls for careful study. To access the outcome of a war, we need to examine the **belligerent** parties and compare them in terms of the following five fundamental factors: The first is the way (*dao* 道); the second, heaven (*tian* 天); the third,

---

[1] "计篇" is the title of the first chapter in *the Art of War*. Giles's translation is *Laying Plans* while Lin translates as *Making Assessments*. In the original selected reading, "计" here means to make comparisons of five fundamental factors (道、天、地、将、法) of both sides involved in the war. "计" does not simply refer to *Laying Plans* as Giles renders, while *Making Assessments* can better express the process that both sides make preliminary calculations and an estimate of the situation.

earth (*di* 地); the fourth, command (*jiang* 将); and the fifth, rules and regulations (*fa* 法). By "the way", I mean moral influence, or that which causes the people to think in line with their **sovereign** so that they will follow him through every **vicissitude**, whether to live or to die, without fear of mortal peril. By "heaven", I mean the effects of night and day, of good and bad weather, of winter's cold and summer's heat; in short, the conduct of military operations in accordance with the changes of natural forces. By "earth", I mean distance, whether it is great or small; the terrain, whether it is **treacherous** or secure; the land, whether it is open or constricted; and the place, whether it **portends** life or death. By "command", I mean the wisdom, trustworthiness, benevolence, courage and firmness of the commander. By "rules and regulations", I mean the principles guiding the organization of army units, the appointment and administration of officers and management of military supplies and **expenditures**. There is no general who has not heard of these five factors. Yet it is he who masters them that wins and he who does not that loses.

belligerent /bəˈlɪdʒərənt/ *adj*. very unfriendly and wanting to argue or fight 好战的

sovereign /ˈsɒvrɪn/ *n*. a king or queen 君主

vicissitude /vəˈsɪsətjuːd/ *n*. the continuous changes and problems that affect a situation or someone's life 变化;变迁;兴衰

treacherous /ˈtretʃərəs/ *adj*. ground, roads, weather conditions, etc. that are particularly dangerous because you cannot see the dangers very easily 危险的,不可靠的

portend /pɔːˈtend/ *v*. to be a sign that something is going to happen, especially something bad 预兆,成为……的前兆

expenditure /ɪkˈspendɪtʃə/ *n*. [countable, uncountable] the total amount of money that a government, organization, or person spends during a particular period of time 开支;消耗

◈ [Version 2]

Laying Plans

Sun Tzu said: The art of war is of vital importance to the State. It is a matter of life and death, a road either to safety or to ruin. Hence it is a subject of inquiry which can on no account be neglected. The art of war, then, is governed by five constant factors, to be taken into account in one's deliberations, when seeking to determine the conditions obtaining in the field. These are: (1) The Moral Law; (2) Heaven; (3) Earth; (4) The Commander; (5) Method and discipline. *The Moral Law* causes the people to be in complete accord with their ruler, so that they will follow him regardless of their lives, **undismayed** by any danger. *Heaven* signifies night and day, cold and heat, times and seasons. *Earth* **comprises** distances, great and small, danger and security, open ground and narrow passes, the chances of life and death. *The Commander* stands for the virtues of wisdom, sincerity, benevolence, courage and strictness. By *Method and discipline* are to be understood the **marshalling** of the army in its proper **subdivisions**, the **gradations** of rank among the officers, the maintenance of roads by which supplies may reach the army, and the control of military expenditure. These five heads should be familiar to every general: he who knows them will be victorious; he who knows them not will fail.

undismayed /ˌʌndɪsˈmeɪd/ *adj*. not worried or frightened by something unpleasant or unexpected 无恐惧的;不泄气的

comprise /kəmˈpraɪz/ *v*. to form part of a larger group of people or things 构成;包含

marshal /ˈmɑːʃəl / *v*. to organize all the people or things that you need in order to be ready for a battle, election, etc. 编制,编列

subdivision /ˌsʌbdəˈvɪʒən/ *n*. [countable, uncountable] any of the parts into which something is divided, or the act of creating these 分支;细分;一部分

gradation /grəˈdeɪʃən/ *n*. a small change or difference between points on a scale 等级;渐变

始计第一

◈【原文】

兵者,**诡道**也。故**能**而示之不能,用而示之不用,近而示之远,远而示之近。**利**而诱之,乱而取之,实而备之,强而避之,怒而**挠**之,卑而骄之,**佚**而劳之,亲而离之。攻其无备,出其不意。此兵家之胜,不可先**传**也。

诡道[guǐ dào] 名词,以诡诈为道

能[néng] 名词,能力、实力

利[lì] 动词,贪利

挠[náo] 动词,扰乱

佚[yì] 形容词,通“逸”,安逸

传[chuán] 动词,传授、泄露

◈【今译】

用兵应以诡诈为原则。所以,能打而装作不能打,要打而装作不要打,向近处而装作向远处,向远处而装作向近处;敌人贪利,就引诱它;敌人混乱,就攻取它;敌人力量充实,就要防备他;敌人兵力强大,就要避开它;敌人气势汹汹,就要屈挠它;敌人辞卑慎行,就要骄纵它;敌人休整得好,就要劳累它;敌人内部团结,就要离间它。在敌人毫无防备之处发动进攻,在敌人意料不到之时采取行动。这是军事家指挥的奥妙,是不能预先呆板规定的。

◈ [Version 1]

Making Assessments

War is a game of **deception**. Therefore, **feign** incapability when in fact capable; feign

inactivity when ready to strike; appear to be far away when actually nearby, and vice versa. When the enemy is greedy for gains, hand out a bait to lure him; when he is in disorder, attack and overcome him; when he boasts substantial strength, be doubly prepared against him; and when he is **formidable**, **evade** him. If he is given to anger, provoke him. If he is timid and careful①, encourage his arrogance. If his forces are rested, wear him down. If he is united as one, divide him. Attack where he is least prepared. Take action when he is least expects you. Herein lies a strategist's **subtlety** of command which is impossible② to **codify** in hard-and-fast rules beforehand.

deception /dɪˈsepʃən/ *n.* the act of deliberately making someone believe something that is not true 欺诈;诡诈

feign /feɪn/ *v.* to pretend to have a particular feeling or to be ill, asleep, etc. 假装;装作

formidable /ˈfɔːmədəbəl/ *adj.* very powerful or impressive, and often frightening 强大的;难对付的

evade /ɪˈveɪd/ *v.* to escape from someone who is trying to catch you 逃避;躲避

subtlety /ˈsʌtlti/ *n.* the quality that something has when it has been done in a clever or skillful way, with careful attention to small details 微妙,巧妙

codify /ˈkəʊdɪfaɪ/ *v.* to arrange laws, principles, facts, etc. in a system 整理;编纂

◆ [Version 2]

Laying Plans

All warfare is based on deception. Hence, when able to attack, we must seem unable; when using our forces, we must seem inactive; when we are near, we must make the enemy believe we are far away; when far away, we must make him believe we are near. Hold out baits to **entice** the enemy. Feign disorder, and crush him. If he is secure at all points, be prepared for him. If he is in superior strength, evade him. If your opponent is of **choleric** temper, seek to **irritate** him. Pretend to be weak, that he may grow **arrogant**. If he is taking his ease, give him no rest. If his forces are united, separate them. Attack him where he is unprepared, appear where you are not

① According to the commentaries of Mei Yaochen and Wang Xi, "卑而骄之" means to "give the appearance of inferiority and weakness, to make them proud" (梅尧臣:示以卑弱,以骄其心) or to "appear to be lowly and weak, so as to make them arrogant" (王皙:示卑弱以骄之), while Lin translates "卑" as "if he (enemy) is timid and careful". However, many other translators such as Griffith and Cleary hold similar opinion with Giles. Their translations are as follows:

Pretend to be weak, that he may grow arrogant. (Lionel Giles)

Pretend inferiority and encourage his arrogance. (Samuel Griffith)

Use humility to make them haughty. (Thomas Cleary)

② "不可" in "此兵家之胜,不可先传也" is translated by Giles as *must not*, but in fact, this word stands for *being impossible* here. Thus Lin translates this sentence as follows: "Herein lies the subtlety of command which is impossible to codify in hard-and-fast rules beforehand."

expected. These military devices, leading to victory, must not be **divulged** beforehand.

---

entice /ɪnˈtaɪs/ *v*. to persuade someone to do something or go somewhere, usually by offering them something that they want 诱使;引诱

choleric /ˈkɒlərɪk/ *adj*. bad-tempered or angry 易怒的

irritate /ˈɪrɪteɪt/ *v*. to make someone feel annoyed or impatient, especially by doing something many times or for a long period of time 激怒

arrogant /ˈærəgənt/ *adj*. behaving in an unpleasant or rude way because you think you are more important than other people 傲慢自大的

divulge /daɪˈvʌldʒ/ *v*. to give someone information that should be secret 泄露

谋攻第三

Attack by stratagem

◈【原文】

故曰:知彼知己者,百战不**殆**;不知彼而知己,一胜一负;不知彼,不知己,每战必殆。

殆[dài] 形容词,危险

◈【今译】

所以说,了解敌人又了解自己,百战都不会有危险;不了解敌人而了解自己,胜败的可能各半;不了解敌人也不了解自己,那就每战都有危险了。

◈ [Version 1]

Attacking by Stratagem

Therefore I say: Know your enemy and know yourself and you can fight a hundred battles without **peril**. If you are ignorant of the enemy and know only yourself, you will stand equal chances of winning and losing. If you know neither the enemy nor yourself, you are bound to be defeated in every battle.

---

peril /ˈperəl/ *n*. [uncountable] *literary or formal* great danger, especially of being harmed or killed 危险,冒险

◈【Version 2】

Attack by Stratagem

Hence the saying: If you know the enemy and know yourself, you need not fear the result of a hundred battles. If you know yourself but not the enemy, for every victory gained you will also suffer a defeat. If you know neither the enemy nor yourself, you will **succumb** in every battle.

succumb /sə'kʌm/ *v*. to stop opposing someone or something that is stronger than you, and allow them to take control 屈从

◈【原文】

谋攻第三

孙子曰：凡用兵之法，全国为上，破国次之；全军为上，破军次之；全旅为上，破旅次之；全卒为上，破卒次之；全伍为上，破伍次之。是故百战百胜，非**善**之善者也；不战而**屈**人之兵，善之善者也。故**上兵**伐谋，其次**伐交**，其次伐兵，其下攻城。攻城之法为不得已。……故善用兵者，屈人之兵而非战也，**拔**人之城而非攻也，毁人之国而非久也，必以全争于天下，故兵不**顿**而利可全，此谋攻之法也。

善[shàn] 形容词，高明

屈[qū] 动词，使屈服

上兵[shàng bīng] 名词，用兵的上策

伐谋[fá móu] 动词，粉碎敌人的计谋而使之屈服

伐交[fá jiāo] 动词，通过外交手段瓦解、孤立敌人，使之不敢发动战争

拔[bá] 动词，攻占、夺取

顿[dùn] 形容词，通"钝"，疲惫、受挫

◈【今译】

孙子说：指导战争的法则是，使敌国完整地降服是上策，击破敌国就次一等；使敌人全"军"完整地降服是上策，击破它的"军"就次一等；使敌人全"旅"完整地降服是上策，击破它的"旅"就次一等；使敌人全"卒"完整地降服是上策，击破它的"卒"就次一等；使敌人全"伍"完整地降服是上策，击破它的"伍"就次一等。因此，百战百胜还不算高明中最高明的；不经交战而使敌人屈服，才算是高明中最高明的。所以，上策是挫败敌人的战略计谋，其次是挫败敌人的外交，再次是战胜敌人的军队，下策是攻打敌人的城池。攻城的办法是不得已的。……所以，善于用兵的人，使敌人屈服而不靠直接交战，夺取敌人的城堡而不靠硬攻，毁灭敌人的国家而不需旷日久战，一定要用全胜的战略争胜于天下，这样，军队不疲惫受挫而胜利却可完满取得。这就是以计谋攻取敌人的法则。

◈【Version 1】

Attacking by Stratagem

Sunzi said: Generally in war, the best policy is to take the enemy state whole and intact; to destroy it is not. To have the enemy's army① surrender in its entirety is better than to crush it; likewise, to take a **battalion**, a company or a five-man **squad** intact is better than to destroy it. Therefore, to fight a hundred battles and win each and every one of them is not the wisest thing to do. To break the enemy's resistance without fighting is. Thus, the best policy in war is to **thwart** the enemy's strategy. The second best is to disrupt his alliances through diplomatic means. The third best is to attack his army in the field. The worst policy of all is to attack walled cities. Attack a walled city only when there is no alternative ... Therefore, he who is skilled in war **subdues** the enemy without fighting. He captures the enemy's cities without **assaulting** them. He **overthrows** the enemy kingdom without **prolonged** operations in the field. By taking all under heaven with his "whole and intact strategy," he wins total victory without wearing out his troops. This is the method of attacking by **stratagem**.

battalion /bəˈtæljən/ *n*. a large group of soldiers consisting of several companies (company) (军队)营

company /ˈkʌmpəni/ *n*. a group of about 120 soldiers who are usually part of a larger group (军队)连

squad /skwɒd/ *n*. a small group of soldiers working together as a unit 班,小队

thwart /θwɔːt / *v*. to prevent someone from doing what they are trying to do 反对;阻碍

assault /əˈsɔːlt/ *v*. to attack someone in a violent way 袭击;突袭

overthrow /ˌəʊvəˈθrəʊ/ *v*. to remove a leader or government from power, especially by force 推翻

prolonged /prəˈlɒŋd/ *adj*. continuing for a long time 持续很久的

stratagem /ˈstrætədʒəm/ *n*. *formal* a trick or plan to deceive an enemy or gain an advantage 战略

① In *Attacking by Stratagem*, "军", "旅", "卒" and "伍" are translated differently, as shown in the following table:

	Lin	Giles	Griffith	Denma group
军	army	army	army	army
旅	battalion (现代: 营,500 人)	regiment (现代: 团,1500 人)	battalion (现代: 营,500 人)	battalion (现代: 营,500 人)
卒	company(现代: 连,120 人)	detachment(现代: 特遣队)	company(现代: 连,120 人)	company(现代: 连,120 人)
伍	five-man squad (5 人班)	company(现代: 连,120 人)	five-man squad (5 人班)	squad

According to Cao Cao's commentaries, there are 12,500 soldiers in a "军", 500 soldiers in a "旅", 100 soldiers in a "卒"and 5 soldiers in a "伍". From table 1, we can see that the translation of military units in Lin's version, as well as in some other translators' versions, is in accordance with modern military organization.

◈【Version 2】

Attack by Stratagem

Sun Tzu said: In the practical art of war, the best thing of all is to take the enemy's country whole and intact; to **shatter** and destroy it is not so good. So, too, it is better to capture an army entire than to destroy it, to capture a **regiment**, a **detachment** or a company entire than to destroy them. Hence to fight and conquer in all your battles is not supreme excellence; supreme excellence consists in breaking the enemy's resistance without fighting. Thus the highest form of generalship is to **baulk** the enemy's plans; the next best is to prevent the junction of the enemy's forces; the next in order is to attack the enemy's army in the field; and the worst policy of all is to **besiege** walled cities. The rules is, not to besiege walled cities if it can possibly be avoided ... Therefore the skillful leader subdues the enemy's troops without any fighting; he captures their cities without laying **siege** to them; he overthrows their kingdom without lengthy operations in the field. With his forces intact he will dispute the mastery of the Empire, and thus, without losing a man, his triumph will be complete. This is the method of attacking by stratagem.

shatter /ˈʃætə/ *v*. to break suddenly into very small pieces, or to make something break in this way 粉碎;毁坏

regiment /ˈredʒəmənt/ *n*. a large group of soldiers, usually consisting of several battalions (军队)团

detachment /dɪˈtætʃmənt/ *n*. a group of soldiers who are sent away from a larger group to do a special job 特遣队

baulk /bɔːlk/ *n*. the act of deliberately making someone believe something that is not true 阻止

besiege /bɪˈsiːdʒ/ *v*. to surround a city or castle with military force until the people inside let you take control 围攻;包围

siege /siːdʒ/ *n*. a situation in which an army or the police surround a place and try to gain control of it or force someone to come out of it 包围

虚实第六

◈【原文】

夫兵形象水,水之行,避高而趋下;兵之胜,避实而击虚。水因地而制流,兵因敌而制胜。故兵无常势,水无常形,能因敌变化而取胜者,谓之神。

◈【今译】

用兵的规律好像水的流动,水的流动是避开高处而流向低处;作战的规律是避开敌人雄厚的实力而攻击它的弱点。水因地势的高低而制约流向,作战则根据敌人的变化而夺取胜利。战争没有固定的态势,水流没有不变的形态。能根据敌情的变化夺取胜利的,就叫做用兵如神。

◈ [Version 1]

Weakness and Strength

Now the law governing military operations is as that governing the flow of water, which always evades high points, choosing lower ones instead. To operate the army successfully, we must avoid the enemy's strong points and seek out his weak points. As the water changes its course in accordance with the **contours** of the **terrain**, so a warrior changes his **tactics** in accordance with the enemy's changing situation. There is no fixed pattern in the use of tactics in war, just as there is no constant course in the flow of water. He who wins modifies his tactics in accordance with the changing enemy situation and this works miracles.

contour /ˈkɒntʊə/ *n*. the shape of the outer edges of something such as an area of land or someone's body 轮廓

terrain /teˈreɪn/ *n*. a particular type of land 地形

tactic /ˈtæktɪk/ *n*. a method that you use to achieve something 策略;战术

◈ [Version 2]

Weak Points and Strong

Military tactics are like **unto** water; for water in its natural course runs away from high places and hastens downwards. So in war, the way is to avoid what is strong and to strike at what is weak. Water shapes its course according to the nature of the ground over which it flows; the soldier works out his victory in relation to the **foe** whom he is facing. Therefore, just as water retains no constant shape, so in warfare there are no constant conditions. He who can modify his tactics in relation to his opponent and thereby succeed in winning, may be called a heaven-born captain.

unto /ˈʌntuː/ *prep*. *old use* to 对于

foe /fəʊ/ *n*. an enemy 仇敌

九地第十一

◈【原文】

故善用兵者,譬如率然;率然者,常山之蛇也。击其首则尾至,击其尾则首至,击其中则首尾俱至。敢问:"兵可使如率然乎?"曰:"可。"夫吴人与越人相恶也,当其同舟而济,遇风,其相救也如左右手。

◈【今译】

善于统帅部队的人,能使部队像"率然"一样。"率然"是常山的一种蛇。打它的头,尾巴就过来救

应;打它的尾,头就过来救应;打它的身子,头尾都过来救应。试问:"可以使军队如同率然一样吗?"回答是:"可以。"吴国人和越国人是互相仇恨的,他们同船渡河,遇上大风,互相救援就像一个人的左右手。

◆【Version 1】

Nine Regions

Therefore, those who are skilled in employing troops are like the snake found on Mount Chang①. If you strike at its head, its tail will come to help; if you strike at its tail, its head will come to help; and if you strike at its middle, both head and tail will come to the rescue. Asked if an army can be trained to behave like the snake of Mount Chang, I say: Yes, it can. The people of Wu and the people of Yue hate each other. Yet if they were to cross the river in the same boat and were caught in a storm, they would come to each other's assistance as the right hand helps the left.

◆【Version 2】

The Nine Situations

The skillful **tactician** may be **likened** to the shuai-ran. Now the shuai-ran is a snake that is found in the Chung mountains. Strike at its head, and you will be attacked by its tail; strike at its tail, and you will be attacked by its head; strike at its middle, and you will be attacked by head and tail both. Asked if an army can be made to imitate the shuai-ran, I should answer, Yes. For the men of Wu and the men of Yueh are enemies; yet if they are crossing a river in the same boat and are caught by a storm, they will come to each other's assistance just as the left hand helps the right.

tactician /tækˈtɪʃən/ *n*. someone who is very good at tactics 战术家

liken /ˈlaɪkən/ *v*. consider or describe as similar, equal, or analogous 比作;比拟,使……像

Chinese Philosophy

1.【知彼知己,百战不殆】

Meaning: "If you know the enemy and know yourself, you need not fear the result of a hundred

① "率然"is a legendary snake living in Mount Heng (in Quyang, Hebei province) in Chinese mythology. The name of Mount Heng was changed to "Mount Chang" during the reign of the Emperor Wen(Liu Heng) of the Han Dynasty, for it was a taboo against using the name of emperor in ancient China. In all existing works "Heng" was changed to "Chang". When translating into English, both Lin and Giles keep the Mount Chang from the original selected reading, while Sinologist John Minford and Denma translation group render it to Mount Heng and explain the reason.

battles." This strategy is from Chapter 3 *Attack by Stratagem*. As one of Sun Tzu's most famous principles, it emphasizes on knowing both your enemy and yourself in a battle. This point speaks to the importance of gathering foreknowledge about your enemy and yourself, which is one of the primary keys to victory in battle; while in business, it is critical to know fully about your competitors, your customers and yourself. It advises you to have awareness of your capabilities and surroundings and adjust your plans to suit your resources.

Take business as an example. A successful business is founded on a series of sound decisions, so the way you analyze situations and choose to react is essential. SWOT analysis (Strengths, Weaknesses, Opportunities, and Threats) is one of the good application of this principle. It focuses on the internal strengths and weaknesses of your business, your staff and your products. At the same time, it looks at the external opportunities and threats that may have an impact on your business, such as market and consumer trends, changes in technology, legislation, and financial issues, etc. The same analysis may be used on your competitors as well. Only when you develop a full awareness of all the factors may you make right decisions in business.

2.【攻其无备,出其不意】

Meaning:"Attack him where he is unprepared, appear where you are not expected." This strategy is from Chapter 1 *Laying Plans*. In war, you can be sure of succeeding in your surprise attacks if you attack places which are undefended. Examples of deception in warfare are endless, running from the attack on Pearl Harbor in the World War II up to Operation Desert Storm in the Gulf War. The attack on Pearl Harbor was a surprise military strike by Japan against the United States naval base at Pearl Harbor, Hawaii on the morning of December 7, 1941. For over an hour, in two waves, Japanese aircraft attacked the naval base, which caused 2,403 Americans, including 68 civilians, died in the attack in all. In comparison, Japan suffered relatively light causalities—it lost only 29 aircraft and a few mini-submarines. This principle of Sun Tzu extends far beyond the field of battle and his approaches can be also applied in various competitive fields from business to sports today.

3.【不战而屈人之兵】

Meaning:"... the skillful leader subdues the enemy's troops without any fighting." This strategy is from Chapter 3 *Attack by Stratagem*. Sun Tzu advises to avoid frontal attack in battles, but surpass from a different way. The Cuban Missile Crisis serves as a good example. It was a 13-day confrontation (October 16 - 28, 1962) between the United States, the Soviet Union and Cuba concerning Soviet ballistic missile deployment in Cuba. It is often regarded as the moment in which the Cold War came closest to a nuclear war. A number of missile launch facilities were constructed in Cuba by the Soviet Union and Cuba, which allowed the Soviets to target effectively most of the Continental US. Instead of taking military actions, U S and the Soviet Union reached an agreement finally in which the Soviets would remove their missiles from Cuba after tense negotiations between two sides.

In contemporary business environment, this strategy can be interpreted as avoiding competing

head on and avoiding using up resources directly against your competitors. Instead, you should aim for excellence, take the initiative and being first to market or innovate, so that no other organization would even dare compete. It is highly recommended to invent the most innovative product, process, to occupy new territory or to be the first to secure the marketplace.

4.【避实而击虚】

Meaning:"So in war, the way is to avoid what is strong and to strike at what is weak." This strategy is from Chapter 6 *Weak Points and Strong*. Sun Tzu suggests that you do not attack in force where the enemy is strongest, and throw a fierce attack at weak corners elsewhere instead.

This military strategy can be applied to our daily life, for instance, the battle for better habits. Too often, we try to build new habits and achieve big goals through sheer force. We fight our battles directly and attack the enemy—our bad habits—at the point where they are strongest. For example, we try to follow a strict diet while we are out to dinner with friends, or we try to concentrate while using a smart phone filled with social media apps, games, and other distractions. When we fail to achieve our goals, we blame ourselves for not having enough willpower. In many cases, however, failure is not a result of poor willpower, but a result of poor strategy. Good military leaders start by winning easy battles and improving their position. They wait until the opposition is weakened and morale is low before they take on their foe directly. Why start a war by fighting battles in areas that are well-defended? Why start new habits in an environment that makes progress difficult? We should make easy improvements to our habits first, build our strength, and establish a better position from which to attack the most difficult changes.

Practice

I. Vocabulary

Choose a proper word or phrase to complete each of the following sentences, changing the form when necessary.

succumb	turmoil	divine	tactician	in accordance with
subdue	siege	overthrow	shatter	intact

1. Several generals formed a conspiracy to ________ the government.
2. The town was forced to yield after a long ________ .
3. His skill in negotiating earned him a reputation as a shrewd ________.
4. Her elegance and beauty was simply ________ .
5. She ________ the cup when she dropped it on the floor.
6. His words are completely ________ his thoughts.
7. In the ________ resulting from the collision, the arrested man broke loose and ran off.
8. Don't ________ to the temptation to have just one cigarette.

9. No one has ever been able to ________ these areas.
10. The church was destroyed in the bombing but the statue survived ________.

II. Translation

Translate the following sentences and passage into English.

1. 故兵贵胜,不贵久。
____

2. 是故胜兵先胜而后求战,败兵先战而后求胜。
____

3. 投之亡地然后存,陷之死地而然后生。
____

4. 故举秋毫不为多力,见日月不为明目,闻雷霆不为聪耳。
____

5. 夫未战而庙算胜者,得算多也;未战而庙算不胜者,得算少也。多算胜,少算不胜,而况于无算乎!吾以此观之,胜负见矣。
____
____

6. 孙子曰:昔之善战者,先为不可胜,以待敌之可胜。不可胜在己,可胜在敌。故善战者,能为不可胜,不能使敌之可胜。故曰:胜可知,而不可为。不可胜者,守也;可胜者,攻也。守则不足,攻则有余。(形篇)
____
____
____

III. Critical Thinking

Discuss the following questions in groups and give your group presentation in class on the basis of your discussion.

1. *The Art of War* has been applied to many fields well outside of the military, such as business management, sports and so on. Find an example that has applied the lessons taken from the book and share it with your classmates.
2. List three of your favorite quotations from *The Art of War* and talk with your partners about their possible applications nowadays.

References

[1] Sun Tzu, Cleary, Thomas(tr.). The Art of War [M]. Boston: Shambhala Publications, 1988.
[2] Sun Tzu, Dallas Galvin (ed.), Lionel Giles (tr.). The Art of War [M]. New York: Barnes &

Noble Classics, 2003.

[3] Sun Tzu, Denma Translation Group (tr.). The Art of War [M]. Boston: Shambhala Publications, 2002.

[4] Sun Tzu, Griffith, Samuel B(tr.). The Art of War [M]. New York: Oxford University Press, 1963.

[5] 孙武撰,曹操等注,杨丙安校理.十一家注孙子[M].北京:中华书局,2017.

[6] 孙武(春秋),孙膑(战国)著,林戊荪译.孙子兵法·孙膑兵法:汉英对照[M].北京:外文出版社,2016.

Unit 7

Yellow Emperor's Canon of Medicine①

Introduction

Yellow Emperor's Canon of Medicine, a free translation of *Huangdi Neijing*, is composed of two separate books, namely *Suwen* and *Lingshu* which are often translated into *Plain Conversation* and *Spiritual Pivot* in English respectively. It is the earliest extant medical canon in China that records the achievements of medicine made by Chinese people in ancient times. In the past thousands of years, *Yellow Emperor's Canon of Medicine* guided the development of traditional Chinese medicine. All the doctors in the previous dynasties paid much attention to the study, collation and explanation of *Yellow Emperor's Canon of Medicine*, making it possible for this great classic to be passed on from generation to generation and to have saved millions of lives.

This unit, Siqi Tiaoshen Dalunpian, is selected from *Plain Conversation*, Chapter Two. It gives us a comprehensive explanation of the principles of how to regulate the spirit according to the changes of the four seasons.

Learning Objectives

After learning this unit, you will be able to

1. learn generally about the content and genre of *Huangdi Neijing*;
2. understand deeply the text, Siqi Tiaoshen Dalunpian in detail;
3. interpret critically the materials in English related to the theory of Yin and Yang and Wuxing, and the knowledge about physiology, pathology, diagnosis and treatment of the human body as well as how to cultivate health;
4. understand and develop the traditional Chinese values based on the Chinese Traditional Medicine.

---

① English version one is excerpted from *Huang Di nei jing su wen*, *An Annotated Translation of Huang Di's Inner Classic-Basic Questions*, made by Paul U. Unschuld and Hermann Tessenow. English version two is excerpted from *Yellow Emperor's Canon of Medicine. Plain conversation*, translated by Li Zhaoguo. The Chinese version is excerpted from *Huangdi Neijing*, edited by Shi Jitian.

Selected Readings

四气调神大论篇第二

Chapter 2 Comprehensive Discourse on Regulating the Spirit in Accordance with the Qi of the Four Seasons

◈【原文】

2.1 春三月，此谓**发陈**，天地俱生，万物以荣，夜卧早起，广步于庭，被发缓形，以使志生，生而勿杀，予而勿夺，赏而勿罚，此春气之应，养生之道也。逆之则伤肝，夏为寒变，奉长者少。

发陈[fā chén] 名词，指二十四节气自立春开始的三个月，为一年之始，生命萌发

◈【今译】

2.1 春季三个月，是生命萌发的时令，天地间充满生气，万物欣欣向荣。此时人们应晚睡早起，散开头发，解开衣带，在庭院散步，使形体舒缓，精神愉快。要保持万物的生机，不要滥行杀伐，要多施与，少敛夺，要多奖励，少惩罚。这是适应春季进行养生的方法。违逆了春之气则会损伤肝脏，使提供给夏长之气的条件不足，到夏季就会发生寒性病变。

◈ [Version 1]

2.1 The three months of spring, they **denote effusion** and spreading①. Heaven and earth together generate life; the myriad beings **flourish**. Go to rest late at night and rise early. Move through the courtyard with long **strides**. **Dishevel** the hair and relax the physical appearance, thereby cause the mind to orient itself on life. Give life and do not kill. Give and do not take. Reward and do not punish. This is correspondence with the qi of spring and it is the Way to **nourish** life. Opposing it harms the liver. In summer, this causes changes to cold, and there is little to support growth②.

---

① Wang Bing: "In spring the yang rises. The qi that was hidden [in winter] spreads out. It gives birth to all kinds of beings and displays their beautiful appearance. Hence, this is called 'outbreak and display.' 发 stands for 扬, 'to spread,' 'to flourish.' 陈 stands for 布, 'to spread.'" In contrast, Zhang Zhicong: "发 stands for 启, 'to open.' 陈 stands for 故, 'old.' The meaning is: 'to break up the old and follow the new.'" Yang Shangshan: "陈 stands for 旧. That is, during the three months of spring all the old roots and old seeds of herbs and trees break out again." Tanba: "发陈 has the meaning of 发散, 'to spread,' and 'to distribute.' However, given the wordings 蕃秀 and 容平 below, the text obviously refers to qi. Hence, Wang Bing's commentary must be correct." Sun Yirang: "发陈 has the meaning of 'to break open the old and substitute it by the new.' Wang Bing's commentary missed this meaning." Zhang Yizhi et al.: "陈 is 旧, 'old.' 发陈 is: to eliminate the old and bring forth the new."

② Wang Bing: "逆" is to say: to carry out the orders of autumn in contrast to the requirements of spring. The liver corresponds to wood and flourishes in spring. Hence, to carry out the orders of autumn in spring causes harm to the qi of the liver. In summer fire flourishes and wood perishes. Hence, the disease develops in summer.
Now, as for the qi of the four seasons, the qi of spring generates life and the qi of summer contributes to growth. If one counteracts the orders of spring and harms the liver, this results in diminished qi with a reduced ability to receive the order of growth in summer."

denote /dɪˈnəʊt/ *vt*. to represent or be a sign of something; to indicate 表示，表明

effusion /ɪˈfjuːʒən/ *n*. *technical* a liquid or gas that flows out of something, or the act of flowing out 渗出；泻出；渗漏物

flourish /ˈflʌrɪʃ/ *vi*. to grow well and be very healthy 繁荣，兴旺；茂盛

stride /straɪd/ *n*. a long step you make while you are walking 大步；步幅；进展

dishevel /dɪˈʃevəl/ *vt*. to disarrange (the hair or clothes) of (someone) 使(某人头发或衣服)凌乱

nourish /ˈnʌrɪʃ/ *vt*. to give a person or other living thing the food and other substances they need in order to live, grow, and stay healthy 滋养；给……营养

◈ [Version 2]

2.1 In the three months of spring, all things on the earth begin to grow. The natural world is **resuscitating** and all things are flourishing. People may sleep late in the night and get up early in the morning, taking a walk in the courtyard with hair running free to relax the body and **enliven** the mind. Such a natural resuscitating process should be activated instead of being **inhibited**, promoted instead of being deprived and encouraged instead of being destroyed. This is what adaptation to Chunqi (Spring-Qi) means and this is the Dao (the principle) for Yangsheng (cultivation of health). Any violation of this rule may impair the liver and result in cold diseases in summer due to insufficient supply for growth in summer.

resuscitate /rɪˈsʌsɪteɪt/ *vt*. to make someone breathe again or become conscious after they have almost died 使恢复呼吸；使苏醒

enliven /ɪnˈlaɪvən/ *vt*. to make something more lively or cheerful 使活泼；使有生气

inhibit /ɪnˈhɪbɪt/ *vt*. to prevent something from growing or developing well 抑制；禁止

◈【原文】

2.2 夏三月，此谓**蕃秀**，天地气交，万物华实，夜卧早起，无厌于日，使志无怒，使华英成秀，使气得泄，若所爱在外，此夏气之应，养长之道也。逆之则伤心，秋为**痎疟**，奉收者少，冬至重病。

蕃秀[fān xiù] 形容词，(万物)繁茂秀美

痎疟[jié nuè] 名词，疟疾的通称。亦指经年不愈的老疟

◈【今译】

2.2 夏季三个月，是自然界万物繁茂秀美的时令。此时，天地气相交，植物开花结实。人们应晚睡，早起，不要厌恶长日，保持愉快心情，切勿发怒，使气机宣畅，对外界事物有浓厚的兴趣，这是适应夏季气候，保护长养之气的方法。违逆了夏长之气则会损伤心脏，提供给秋收之气的条件不足，到秋天容易发生疟疾，冬季到来会再次发生重大疾病。

◈ [Version 1]

2.2 The three months of summer, they denote **opulence** and blossoming①. The qi of heaven and earth interact and the myriad beings bloom and bear fruit. Go to rest late at night and rise early. Never get enough of the sun②. Let the mind have no anger. Stimulate beauty and have your elegance perfected. Cause the qi to flow away, as if that what you loved were located outside. This is correspondence with the qi of summer and it is the Way to nourish growth. Opposing it harms the heart. In autumn this causes *jie* and **malaria**③, and there is little to support gathering. Multiple disease develops at winter solstice.

opulence /ˈɔpjuləns/ *n*. wealth as evidenced by sumptuous living 富裕;丰富

malaria /məˈlɛəriə/ *n*. a serious disease carried by mosquitoes, which causes periods of fever (内科)疟疾;瘴气

◈ [Version 2]

2.2 The three months of summer is the period of prosperity. *Tianqi* (Heaven Qi) and Diqi (Earth-qi) have **converged** and all things are in blossom. People should sleep late in the night and get up early in the morning, avoiding any **detestation** with longer hot daytime and anxiety in life, trying to delight themselves and enabling Qi to flow smoothly. Such an attitude toward life in summer is just like the outward manifestation of a cheerful state of mind. This is what adaptation to Xiaqi (Summer-Qi) means and this is the Dao for Yangsheng (cultivation of health). Violation of this rule may impair the heart and result in Jienue (malaria) in autumn and severe disease in winter due to insufficient supply for **astringency** in autumn.

converge /kənˈvɜːdʒ/ *vt*. to come from different directions and meet at the same point to become one thing 使汇聚;聚集

detestation /ˌdiːtɛsˈteɪʃən/ *n*. intense hatred; abhorrence 憎恶;嫌恶

astringe /əˈstrɪndʒ/ *vt*. 使……收缩;使……收敛

astringency /əˈstrɪndʒənsi/ *n*. 收敛性

① Wang Bing: "The generation of yang qi begins with spring. When it comes to summer, the yang qi abounds and all beings grow. Hence, the text speaks of 蕃秀. 蕃 is 茂, 'luxuriance,' 盛, 'abundance.' 秀 is 华, 'blooming,' 美, 'beauty '"

② Zhang Qi: "厌 is 倦, 'tired.'" Cheng Shide et al.: "无厌于日 is to say: in summer the days are long and mankind does not get tired. That is, in summer the qi of growth rules, hence, the human qi should not be idle." Zhang yizhi et al.: "厌 is 饱, 'satisfied.' 无厌于日 is: not satisfied with the work of one day."

③ The term *jie* 痎 appears four times in the Su wen, always in conjunction with *nüe* 疟. *Jie* may have been a term for intermittent fevers breaking out every second day; nüe may have been used initially for all types of intermittent fevers. In later times, nüe was the only term used for what today is called malaria disease. Zhang Jiebin: "When the heart is harmed, the qi of summerheat avails itself of the heart. In autumn then, the qi of metal draws everything in and the evil of summerheat is depressed internally. Now the yin wishes to enter, but the yang wards it off. Hence, there is cold. The fire wishes to leave, but the yin ties it down. Hence, there is heat. Metal and fire struggle with each other. Hence, fits of cold and heat alternate and this is malaria."

◈【原文】

2.3 秋三月，此谓**容平**，天气以急，地气以明，早卧早起，与鸡俱兴，使志安宁，以缓秋刑，收敛神气，使秋气平，无外其志，使肺气清，此秋气之应，养收之道也。逆之则伤肺，冬为**飧泄**，奉藏者少。

容平[róng píng] 形容词，成熟而平定收敛

飧泄[sūn xiè] 名词，飧(sūn)泄，本病是肝郁脾虚，清气不升所致。临床表现有大便泄泻清稀，并有不消化的食物残渣，肠鸣腹痛等

◈【今译】

2.3 秋季三个月，是万物成熟而平定收敛的时令。此时，天高风急，地气清肃，人应早睡早起，和鸡的活动时间一样，以保持神志的安宁，减缓秋季肃杀之气对人体的影响，收敛神气，以适应秋季容平的气候，不使神思外驰，保持肺气清肃，这就是适应秋令的特点而保养人体收敛之气的方法。违逆了秋收之气则会伤及肺脏，使提供给冬藏之气的条件不足，冬天就要发生飧泄。

◈ [Version 1]

2.3 The three months of autumn, they denote taking in and balance①. The qi of heaven becomes tense. The qi of the earth becomes bright. Go to rest early and rise early, get up together with the chicken. Let the mind be peaceful and tranquil, so as to **temper** the punishment carried out in autumn. Collect the spirit qi and cause the autumn qi to be balanced. Do not direct your mind to the outside and cause the lung qi to be clear. This is correspondence with the qi of autumn and it is the Way to nourish gathering. Opposing it harms the lung. In winter this causes **outflow** of undigested food and there is little to support storage.

temper /ˈtempə/ *vt*. to make something less severe or extreme 使适中；缓和，减轻

outflow /ˈautfləu/ *n*. the flow of water or air from something （水或空气的）流出，泄漏

◈ [Version 2]

2.3 The three months of autumn is the season of Rongping (ripening). In autumn it is cool, the wind blows fast and the atmosphere is clear. People should sleep early in the night and get up in the morning just like ji (hens and roosters). They should keep their mind in peace to **alleviate** the **sough**ing effect of autumn, moderating mental activity to balance Qiuqi (Autumn-Qi) and preventing outward manifestation of sentiments to harmonize Feiqi (Lung-Qi). This is what

---

① Wang Bing: "In summer the myriad beings grow and blossoms as well as fruits have reached completion. Their 容状, 'appearance,' does no longer change and is fixed by autumn." Ma shi: "The yin qi has started to rise already and the appearance of all beings is finally determined. Hence, the image of the qi [in autumn] is called 'appearance settled.'" Fang Wenhui identifies 容 as 搈 with the meaning of "movement", and 平 as 止, "to stop", 静, "quiet."

adaptation to Qiuqi (Autumn-Qi) means and this is the Dao (principle) for Yangshou (cultivation of health and regulation of daily life). Any violation of this rule will impair the lung and leads to Sunxie (diarrhea with undigested food in it) in winter due to insufficient supply for storage in winter.

---

alleviate /ə'liːvieɪt/ *vt*. to make something less painful or difficult to deal with 减轻，缓和〔痛苦或困难〕

sough /sʌf/ *vi*./*n*. (arch or fml 古或文) (make a) murmuring or whispering sound (as of wind in trees) (发出)瑟瑟声，飒飒声

◈【原文】

2.4 冬三月，此谓**闭藏**，水冰地坼，无忧乎阳，早卧晚起，必待日光，使志若伏若匿，若有私意，若已有得，去寒就温，无泄皮肤，使气**亟夺**，此冬气之应，养藏之道也。逆之则伤肾，春为**痿厥**，奉生者少。

闭藏[bì cáng] 名词，潜伏，蛰藏

亟夺[jí duó] 动词，亟，(副词)急迫，屡次；夺，失去

痿厥[wěi jué] 名词，痿，中医学名，症状见肢体痿弱，经脉迟缓；厥，亦作："厥"，逆气

◈【今译】

2.4 冬天三个月，是生机潜伏、万物蛰藏的时令，水寒成冰，大地龟裂，所以人不要扰动阳气，应早睡晚起，待到日光照耀时再起床，使神志藏于内，好像要严守个人隐秘一样，要避寒取暖，不要使皮肤开泄而损失阳气。这是适应冬季的气候而保养人体闭藏机能的方法。违逆了冬令的闭藏之气则损伤肾脏，使供给春生之气的条件不足，春天就会发生痿厥。

◈［Version 1］

2.4 The three months of winter, they denote securing and storing. The water is frozen and the earth breaks open. Do not disturb the yang qi. Go to rest early and rise late. You must wait for the sun to shine. Let the mind enter a state as if hidden, as if shut in as if you had secret intentions; as if you already had made gains. Avoid cold and seek warmth and do not allow sweat to flow away through the skin. This would cause the qi to be carried away quickly. This is correspondence with the qi of winter and it is the Way of nourishing storage. Opposing it harms the kidneys. In spring this causes **limp**ness with **reced**ing qi, and there is little to support generation.

---

limp /lɪmp/ *adj*. not firm or strong 软的；不强壮的

recede /ri'siːd/ *vi*. pull back or move away or backward 退；后退

◈ [Version 2]

2.4 The three months of winter is the season for storage. The winter freezes and the earth **cracks**. Cares must be taken not to disturb Yang. People should sleep early in the night and get up late in the morning when the sun is shining, physically maintaining quiet just like keeping private affairs or as if having obtained what one has desired. They should guard themselves against cold and try to keep warm, avoiding sweating so as to prevent loss of Yangqi. This is what adaption to Dongqi (Winter-Qi) means and this is the Dao principle for Yangcang (cultivating health and promoting the storing function of the body). Any violation will impair Shenqi (Kidney-Qi) and reduce the energy for the following season, leading to Weijue (dysfunction, weakness and coldness of the limbs) in spring due to insufficient supply for growth in spring.

crack /kræk/ *vt*. to break or to make something break, either so that it gets lines on its surface, or so that it breaks into pieces 使……破裂;破裂

◈【原文】

2.5 天气,清静光明也,藏德不止,故不下也。天明则日月不明,邪害**空窍**,阳气者闭塞,地气者**冒明**,云雾不精,则上应白露不下,交通不表,万物命故不施,不施则名木多死。恶气不发,风雨不节,白露不下,则**菀槁**不荣。贼风数至,暴雨数起,天地四时不相保,与道相失,则未央绝灭。惟**圣人**从之,故身无奇病,万物不失,生气不竭。

空窍[kōng qiào] 名词,(1)即孔窍,指人体与外界相通达的孔窍,包括九窍在内(2)山川
冒明[mào míng] 形容词,昏蒙不明
菀槁[yùn gǎo] 名词,高大的树木
圣人[shèng rén] 名词,品德最高尚、智慧最高超的人。文中指懂得健康、养生方法的人

◈【今译】

2.5 天气是清净光明的,天德隐藏不露且运行不止,所以不会下泄。如果天德暴露,就会出现日月昏暗,阴霾邪气侵害山川,阳气闭塞不通,大地昏蒙不明,云雾弥漫,相应的雨露不能下降。天地之气不能交通,万物的生命就不能绵延,这样即使是高大的树木也会死亡。恶劣的天气发作,风雨无时,雨露不能应时而降,茂盛的禾苗也会枯槁不荣。贼风频频而至,暴雨不时而作,天地四时的变化失序,违背了正常的规律,使万物的生长未及一半便夭折了。只有圣人能适应自然规律,所以身无大病。如果万物不背离自然的发展规律,生机就不会衰绝。

◈ [Version 1]

2.5 The qi of heaven is that which is clear and pure, **lustrous** and brilliant. Heaven stores its **virtue** without end. Hence, it does not let its virtue move downwards. When heaven were to shine, then sun and moon would not shine, and evil would harm the **orifices**. As for yang qi, when

it is **obstructed**, as for the qi of the earth, when its brilliance is covered, then clouds and fog are not clear. As a result, corresponding above, white dew fails to **descend**. Interaction fails to manifest itself. The life of the myriad beings, hence, no longer receives any **bestowals**. When there are no bestowals, then many **eminent** trees die. Bad qi is not **effused**①. Wind and rain are excessive. White dew does not descend. As a result, gardens wither and there is no blossoming. Robber winds arrive often and violent rains emerge frequently. Heaven, earth, and the four seasons fail to maintain their mutual relationship and lose their relationship with the Way. As a result, before it has reached its middle, life is **curtailed** and **extinguished**. Only the **sages** follow the Way; hence, their bodies have no strange diseases. They do not neglect the myriad beings. Their generative qi does not exhaust itself.

lustrous /ˈlʌstrəs/ *adj*. shining in a soft gentle way 有光泽的,光亮的

virtue /ˈvəːtjuː/ *n*. moral goodness of character and behaviour 善,德,德行

orifice /ˈɒrɪfɪs/ *n*. 1. one of the holes in your body, such as your mouth, nose etc one of the holes in your body, such as your mouth, nose etc. (身体上的)孔,洞(如嘴、鼻等) 2. a hole or entrance 洞,入口

obstruct /əbˈstrʌkt/ *vt*. to prevent someone from doing something or something from happening, by making it difficult 妨碍;阻塞

descend /diˈsend/ *vi*. move downward from a higher to a lower level 下降;下去;下来

bestow /biˈstəu/ *vt*. to give someone something of great value or importance, bestow something on/upon somebody 赠予;给予 bestowal /biˈstəuəl/ *n*.

eminent /ˈeminənt/ *adj*. tall, lofty 高的;巍峨的

effuse /iˈfjuːz/ *v*. to pour or flow out 流出

curtail /kəːˈteil/ *vt*. to reduce or limit something 缩减;剪短;剥夺……特权等

extinguish /ɪkˈstɪŋgwɪʃ/ *vt*. to make a fire or light stop burning or shining; to destroy a feeling or idea 熄灭;灭绝

◈ [Version 2]

2.5 Tianqi (Heaven-qi) is clear and pure. It contains De (power) and never stops moving. That is why it never descends. If the sky is bright, the sun and the moon will become dim. As a result, Xie (Evil) harms Kongqiao (external orifices) if Yangqi in the heavens is blocked, Diqi (Earth-Qi) Maoming, clouds and fog continue to permeate through, then dew, that corresponds

① Wang Bing: "恶 stands for 害气, 'harmful qi.' 发 is to say 散发, 'to disperse.'... That is to say, harmful qi is concealed and stored and is not effused. Hence, wind and rain exceed their standards and many fractures and injuries occur. Withered trees form heaps and there is blossoming in spring." In contrast, Zhang Zhicong: "恶气 is 忿怒之气, 'the qi of anger.'" The "qi of anger", that is, violent storm and also capital punishment, is associated with autumn and if it fails to develop the season does not show its appropriate nature.

to the Diqi (Earth-Qi) in the sky, will not fall. If this happens, the communication between the upper and the lower (the earth and the heavens) will not take place, making it impossible for all the things in the natural world to continue their development. Even the largest trees will die. If Eqi (**Virulent**-Qi) emerges, if wind, rain and dew fail to appear at the right time, grasses and trees will become withered. In addition, frequent attack of Zeifeng (Thief-Wind) and rainstorm, the disorder of Yin and Yang of the heavens and the earth in the four seasons and the violation of the Dao (the law of nature) will lead to immature death of everything. Only the sages can follow such natural changes. That is why they do not **contract** any disease when such disastrous events take place. If all the things in nature do not violate the principles of health cultivation, their vitality will never be exhausted.

contract /ˈkɒntrækt/ *vt*. to catch or develop illness 感染(疾病),患(病)

virulent /ˈvɪrələnt/ *adj*. a poison, disease, etc. that is virulent is very dangerous and affects people very quickly 剧毒的;恶性的

◈【原文】

2.6 逆春气,则少阳不生,肝气内变。逆夏气,则太阳不长,心气内洞。逆秋气,则太阴不收,肺气焦满。逆冬气,则少阴不藏,肾气独沉。

◈【今译】

2.6 悖逆了春生之气,身体内的少阳之气就不能焕发生机,以致肝气内郁发生病变。悖逆了夏长之气,身体内的太阳之气就不能旺盛,以致心气内虚。悖逆了秋收之气,身体内的太阴之气就不能发挥收敛作用,以致肺热叶焦而胀满。悖逆了冬藏之气,身体内的少阴之气就不能潜藏,就会使肾气衰弱。

◈ [Version 1]

2.6 If one acts contrary to the qi of spring, then the minor yang does not promote generation. The liver qi changes internally. If one acts contrary to the qi of summer, then the major yang does not stimulate growth. The heart qi is empty internally. If one acts contrary to the qi of autumn, then the major yin does not collect. The lung qi burns and there is fullness. If one acts contrary to the qi of winter, then the minor yin does not store. The kidney qi is **turbid** and in the depth.

turbid /ˈtɜːbɪd/ *adj*. *formal* (of liquid) full of mud, dirt, etc. so that you can not see through it 浑浊的;污浊不清的

◈ [Version 2]

2.6 Violation of Chunqi (Spring-Qi) will prevents Shaoyang from growing, leading to diseases due to **stagnation** of Ganqi (Liver-Qi). Violation of Xiaqi (Summer-Qi) will prevent Taiyang from

developing, resulting in deficiency of Xinqi (Heart-Qi). Violation of Qiuqi (Autumn-Qi) will prevents Taiyin from astringing, leading to dryness and **distension** of Feiqi (Lung-Qi). Violation of Dongqi (Winter-Qi) will prevent Shaoyin from hiding, leading to sinking of Shenqi (Kidney-Qi).

stagnate /stæg'neɪt/ *vt*. to stop developing or making progress 停滞;淤塞
stagnation /stæg'neɪʃən/ *n*. 停滞;淤塞
distension /dɪs'tenʃən/ *n*. *technical* abnormal swelling in a person's or animal's body (人或动物身体内不正常的)肿胀

◈【原文】

2.7 夫四时阴阳者,万物之根本也。所以圣人春夏养阳,秋冬养阴,以从其根,故与万物沉浮于生长之门。逆其根,则伐其本,坏其真矣。故阴阳四时者,万物之终始也,死生之本也。逆之则灾害生,从之则苛疾不起,是谓得道。道者,圣人行之,愚者佩之。

◈【今译】

2.7 四时阴阳的变化,是万物生命的根本。所以圣人在春夏季节保养阳气,在秋冬季节保养阴气,以顺从生命发展的根本规律,因此能与万物一样随着生命的规律而运动。违逆了这个规律就会损害身体,破坏真元之气。因此,阴阳四时是万物的终始,是死生存亡的根本。违逆了这个根本,就会造成灾害;顺从了这个根本,就不会引发重病。这就是养生之道。对于养生之道,圣人身体力行,愚人背离违逆。

◈ [Version 1]

2.7 Now, the yin and yang qi of the four seasons, they constitute root and basis of the myriad beings. Hence, the sages in spring and summer nourish the yang and in autumn and winter nourish the yin, and this way they follow their roots. Hence, they are in the depth or at the surface with the myriad beings at the gate to life and growth. To oppose one's root, is to attack one's basis and to spoil one's true qi. Hence, yin qi, yang qi, and the four seasons, they constitute end and begin of the myriad beings, they are the basis of death and life. Opposing them results in **catastrophe** and harms life. If one follows them, severe diseases will not emerge. This is called "to achieve the Way." As for the Way, the sages practice it; the stupid wear it for decoration only.

catastrophe /kə'tæstrəfɪ/ *n*. an unexpected event that causes great suffering or damage. 大灾难;大祸

◈ [Version 2]

2.7 The changes of Yin and Yang in the four seasons are the roots of all the things in nature. So the sages cultivate Yang in spring and summer while nourish Yin in autumn and winter in order to follow such roots (the changes of Yin and Yang in different seasons). Violation of these roots means destruction of the Ben (**primordial** base) and impairment of the body. Thus the changes of Yin and Yang in the four seasons are responsible for the growth, decline and death of all things. Violation of it brings about disasters while **abidance** by it prevents the occurrence of diseases. This is what to follow the Dao (law of nature) means. The Dao (law of nature) is followed by the sages, but violated by the foolish.

primordial /praɪˈmɔːdiəl/ *adj*. formal 1. existing at the beginning of time or the beginning of the Earth 原始的;根本的;原生的 2. primordial feelings are very strong and seem to come from the part of people's character that is ancient and animal-like (情感)原始的,本能的

abidance /əˈbaidəns/ *vi*. 持续;遵守;逗留;居住(in) abidance by 遵守,遵循

◆【原文】

2.8 从阴阳则生,逆之则死,从之则治,逆之则乱。反顺为逆,是谓**内格**。是故圣人不治已病治未病,不治已乱治未乱,此之谓也。夫病已成而后药之,乱已成而后治之,譬犹渴而穿井,斗而铸锥,不亦晚乎!

◆【今译】

2.8 顺应阴阳的消长变化,就能生存,违逆了就会死亡。顺从了四季阴阳的变化,就会正常;违逆了,就会引起紊乱。如变顺应为违逆,就会造成机体与自然环境相格拒。所以圣人不是等到疾病已经发生再去治疗,而是在疾病发生之前就进行预防;不是等到乱子已经发生再去治理,而是在它发生之前就采取防止措施,其道理就在这里。疾病发生后再去治疗,乱子发生后再去治理,那就如同口渴了才去掘井,战乱发生了才去制造兵器,不是太晚了吗?

内格[nèi gé] 病症名,阴阳上下表里闭塞不通的症状

◆ [Version 1]

2.8 If one follows yin and yang, then life results; if one opposes them, then death results. If one follows them, then order results; if one opposes them, then disorder results. To act contrary to what is appropriate, this is opposition. This is called inner obstruction①. Hence, when it is said "the sages did not treat those already ill, but treated those not yet ill, they did not put in order what was already in disorder, but put in order what was not yet in disorder," then this means just the same. Now, when drugs are employed for therapy only after a disease has become fully

① Neige(内格)means that the physiological functions of the body fail to adapt to the changes of Yin and Yang in the four seasons. Wang Bing(王冰)explained that "Ge(格)means rejection. Neige(内格)means that the interior functions cannot follow the law of nature".

developed, when attempts at restoring order are initiated only after disorder has fully developed, this is as if a well were dug when one is thirsty, and as if weapons were **cast** when the fight is on. Would this not be too late, too?

cast /kɑːst/ *vt*. to make an object by pouring liquid metal, plastic etc into a mould 浇铸

◈ [Version 2]

2.8 Following the rules of Yin and Yang ensures life while violating them leads to death. Abidance by them brings about peace while violation of them results in disorders. If the violation is taken as abidance, disease known as Neige (inner conflict) will be caused. Therefore, the sages usually pay less attention to the treatment of a disease, but more to the prevention of it. To resort to treatment when a disease has already occurred and to resort to regulation when a disorder has already been caused is just like to dig a well when one feels thirsty and to make weapons when a war has already broken out. It is certainly too late!

Chinese Philosophy

1. 【起居无节，半百而衰】

"Qiju" means "living". It refers to the daily routine. Keeping a regular schedule is very important. The sages in ancient times knew the rules of cultivating health, followed the principles for Yin and Yang and adjusted the ways to cultivate health. They were moderate in eating and drinking, regular in working and resting, avoiding any overstrain. That is why they could maintain a desirable harmony between the mind and the body, enjoy good health and a long life. However, nowadays, quite a lot of people bahave oppositely. They don't know how to keep an exuberance of Jingqi and do not know how to regulate Shen (mind and spirit), often giving themselves to sensual pleasure. Being extremely irregular in daily life, they begin to become old even at the age of fifty.

2. 【顺四时，治未病】

Plain Conversation • Siqi Tiaoshen Dalunpian says: "The changes of Yin and Yang in the four seasons are the roots of all the things in nature ..." Violation of these roots means destruction of the Ben (primordial base) and impairment of the body. And *Plain Conversation • Shanggu Tianzhen Lunpian* says: "The sages in ancient times who knew the Dao followed the rules of Yin and Yang ..., they could enjoy good health and a long life." All this stresses the importance of being regular in daily life, keeping an exuberance of Jingqi, following the laws of nature, and the prevention of the disease. The prevention of the disease is the highest principle of TCM health maintenance and it runs through the diagnosis and treatment of diseases. Health maintenance is just like fire prevention, and the treatment of disease is just like firefighting. Which is more important, prevention or treatment, is self-evident.

3.【恬淡虚无,志闲少欲】

When the sages in ancient times taught the people, they emphasized the importance of living in peace and contentment, and keeping the mind free from avarice. They did not desire for high position and lived simply and naturally. Such a behavior quite accorded with Dao. They followed the tenets of preserving health and enjoyed a long life free from disease. However, it is very important for people to properly grasp the degree of "idleness and lack of desire". Negative "nothingness" will kill people's spirit of positive innovation, which will influence the progress and development of individuals and even society. Positive "idleness and lack of desire" should be like this: with proper aspiration, reasonable pursuit and free from distress for fame and fortune.

Practice

I. Vocabulary

Choose a proper word or phrase to complete each of the following sentences, changing the form when necessary.

enliven	resuscitate	abidance by	extinguish	alleviate
inhibit	denote	myriad	permeate	curtail

1. ________ honesty, faith, just competition, equivalent exchange, opposing monopolization and other morals criterion are also inside request of market economy.
2. Overt factors used to demonstrate or ________ group membership are called ethnic boundary makers.
3. Encouraged by falling inflation, central banks are cutting interest rates, and policy makers are implementing big stimulus plans to ________ economic growth.
4. The economy is in bad shape because of too much government intervention producing ________ unintended consequences and perverse incentives.
5. Immigrants and their descendants help drive America's population growth and economic dynamism even as they enrich and ________ its cultural structure.
6. Under such circumstances, you should immediately distance yourself from the oil or water and ________ the flames after the quake stops.
7. American literature, movies, and music ________ foreign societies—especially appealing to young people in those societies.
8. If you ________ these symptoms with medications, symptoms will return when the drug is withdrawn if the body has not successfully solved the problem.
9. In this article, you have learned how to ________ some of the restrictions and problems that developers unknowingly create for their consumers during development time.
10. If you are expecting both people to grow in the same direction and in the same way, that is

unfair to both people. It will ________ curtail and suffocate both of their lives.

II. Translation

Translate the following sentences and the passage into English.

1. 生而勿杀，予而勿夺，赏而勿罚。

   ____

2. 使志安宁，以缓秋刑，收敛神气，使秋气平，无外其志，使肺气清。

   ____

3. 惟圣人从之，故身无奇病。

   ____

4. 逆之则灾害生，从之则苛疾不起，是谓得道。

   ____

5. 是故圣人不治已病治未病，不治已乱治未乱，此之谓也。

   ____

6. 上古之人，其知道者，法于阴阳，和于术数，食饮有节，起居有常，不妄作劳，故能形与神俱，而尽终其天年，度百岁乃去。今时之人不然也，以酒为浆，以妄为常，醉以入房，以欲竭其精，以耗散其真，不知持满，不时御神，务快其心，逆于生乐，起居无节，故半百而衰也。

   ____

   ____

   ____

III. Critical Thinking

Discuss the following questions in groups and do your group presentation in class on the basis of your discussion.

1. As college students, how can you achieve the better balance between the pressure of study and the regular daily life?
2. How do you understand "the adaptation to the change of Yin and Yang through the four seasons"?

References

[1] Li Zhaoguo. *Yellow Emperor's Cannon of Medicine. Plain Conversation I* [M]. Beijing: World Publishing Corporation, 2008.

[2] Paul U. Unschuld and Hermann Tessenow. *Huang Di nei jing su wen, An Annotated Translation of Huang Di's Inner Classic-Basic Questions*, Volume I Chapter 2 [M]. Berkeley: University of California Press, 2010.

[3] 曹金洪.黄帝内经[M].北京：燕山出版社，2010.

[4] 时纪田.黄帝内经彩图版[M].北京：华龄出版社，2011.

Unit 8

Strange Tales from the Liaozhai Studio[①]

Introduction

Strange Tales from the Liaozhai Studio **or** ***Strange Stories from a Chinese Studio*** is a collection of classical short stories written by Pu Songling (1640 – 1715). It comprises 491 "marvel tales" of the supernatural, including such typical denizens of the Chinese folk imagination as ghosts, fox spirits, immortals and demons. The stories are fascinating and colorful, with vivid character portrayal. The author uses the supernatural and the unexplainable to illustrate his ideas of society and government, which reflect the social contradictions and people's thoughts and wishes in that period.

There are four main themes presented in the *Strange Tales from the Liaozhai Studio*. The first is a complaint about the skewed feudal system. Secondly, it reveals the corrupt imperial examination system at that time. The third theme is a clear admiration of pure, faithful love between powerless women and poor scholars. Lastly, it criticizes some people's absurd behaviors and seeks to educate them through *Strange Stories*.

Learning Objectives

After learning this unit, you will be able to

1. learn generally about the content and the genre of *Strange Tales from the Liaozhai Studio*;
2. understand deeply the selective stories with different themes in detail;
3. interpret critically the stories related to the supernatural phenomenon and its function in English;
4. explore the traditional Chinese values about Confucianism, Taoism and Buddhism.

---

① The original texts and the first English versions in this unit are excerpted from Library Chinese Classics Chinese-English: *Selections from Strange Tales from the Liaozhai Studio*, published by Foreign Languages Press. Among the second English versions, *The Taoist Priest of Mount Lao*, *The Magic Sword and The Magic Bag*, and *The Painted Skin* are translated by John Minford, published by the Penguin Group, while *The Bureau of Examination Frauds* is translated by Sidney L. Sondergard, and published by Jain Publishing Company.

Selected Readings

劳山道士

◈【原文】

又一月，苦不可忍，而道士并不传教一术。心不能待，辞曰："弟子数百里受业仙师，纵不能得长生术，或小有传习，亦可慰求教之心。今**阅**两三月，不过早樵而暮归。弟子在家，未**谙**此苦。"道士笑曰："吾固谓不能作苦，今果然。明早当遣汝行。"王曰："弟子操作多日，师略授小技，此来为不负也。"道士问："何术之求？"王曰："每见师行处，墙壁所不能隔，但得此法足矣。"道士笑而允之。乃传以诀，令自咒毕，呼曰："入之！"王面墙不敢入。又曰："试入之。"王果从容入，及墙而阻。道士曰："**俛**首骤入，勿**逡巡**！"王果去墙数步，奔而入；及墙，虚若无物；回视，果在墙外矣。大喜，入谢。道士曰："归宜洁持，否则不验。"遂助**资斧**遣之归。

阅[yuè] 动词，经，历

谙[ān] 动词，熟悉

俛[miǎn] 动词，同"俯"，屈身；低头

逡巡[qūn xún] 动词，迟疑，犹豫

资斧[zī fǔ] 名词，旅费

◈【今译】

又过了一个月，王生实在受不了劳苦了，而道士还是连一个法术也不传授。王生心里也不想再等待了，就向道士告辞说："徒弟从几百里之外来向仙师您学习道术，即使不能学到长生不老的法术，哪怕能学到点儿小法术，也可安慰我的一片求教之心了。现在过了两三个月，天天都不过是早上去砍柴，晚上回来。徒弟在家里可从来没受过这种辛苦。"道士笑着说："我本来就认为你不能吃苦，现在果然如此。明天早晨就送你回去。"王七说："徒弟在这里劳作了多日，请师父稍微教我一点儿小本事，这次就不算白来了。"道士问："你想要学什么法术呢？"王生说："我常见师父行走的时候，墙壁也不能阻隔，能学到这个法术，我就知足了。"道士笑着答应了他。于是，道士就教他念口诀，让他自己念了咒以后，就招呼道："进去！"王生面对着墙，不敢进去。道士又说："你试着往里走一下。"王生果然慢慢地往前走，到墙根前却被阻挡住了。道士说："你低头快进，不要犹豫不前！"王生果然在离墙几步远的地方，冲着墙跑了进去。到了墙里时，好像空空的什么东西也没有，回头再一看，身子果然已经在墙外边了。王生大为惊喜，又回去拜谢师父。道士说："回去后要清白做人，否则法术就不会灵验。"于是，送了他路费让他回家。

◈ [Version 1]

The Taoist Priest of Laoshan[①]

Another month went by. The hard life had become just too much for him. Besides, the priest

① In general, the titles of the stories named after the characters in *Strange Tales from the Liaozhai Studio* are translated by transliteration. However, some foreign Sinologists adopt the free translation method. They rewrite the title according to the plot of the story in order to meet the reading habits of English readers, as well to better attract their attention. For example, "聂小倩" was translated directly as "Nie Xiaoqian" in Version 1, but John Minford translated it as "The Magic Sword and The Magic Bag" in Version 2. There are many similar examples, such as "叶生", "董生", and "婴宁" were translated to "Ye Sheng", "Dong Sheng" and "Ying Ning" in the first version, while to "Friendship beyond the Grave", "Fox Enchantment" and "The laughing Girl" in John Minford's version.

wasn't teaching him any Taoist arts. He felt he couldn't wait any longer, so he went to say goodbye to the priest, "I travelled several hundred *li* to learn Taoism from you. Even if you didn't teach me the way to **immortality**, I would be satisfied to learn a few magic tricks. I've been here for two or three months, now and all I've been doing every day is cutting firewood from morning till night. At home, I never had to do such hard chores." The priest smiled and said, "I said at the beginning that you wouldn't be able to stand the hardship. Now you've proven me right. Tomorrow, you can go." But Wang said, "I've worked for so long, I beg you, Master, to teach me some little trick so that my stay here won't all have been for nothing," "Well, what do you want to learn?" the priest asked. Wang said, "I've often seen you walk right through the wall. If I could do that, I'd be more than satisfied." The priest, smiling, consented. He taught Wang the rhyme and told him to keep repeating it. Then the priest shouted, "Go!" Wang, looked at the wall but dared not. "Go on, try!" the priest shouted again. Wang took hold of himself and slowly walked toward the wall, but he bumped into it and stopped. Then the priest said, "Lower your head, charge into it, don't hesitate!" Wang took a few steps backward and then ran at the wall. When he got here, it was like running into empty space; there seemed to be nothing in his way. When he looked back, he found himself outside the wall. Elated, Wang returned and thanked the Master. The priest said to him, "After you get back home, you must be **prudent** and avoid evil. Otherwise, the magic won't work." He then gave Wang some money and sent him off.

---

immortality /ˌɪmɔːˈtæləti/ *n*. the state of living forever or being remembered forever 永生,长存,永恒

prudent /ˈpruːdənt/ *adj*. sensible and careful, especially by trying to avoid unnecessary risks 明智谨慎的,慎重的,审慎的

◈ [Version 2]

The Taoist Priest of Mount Lao

Another month went by, and again the hardship seemed more than he could bear. And still the Master had taught him no magical secrete. He could wait no longer, and went to take his leave.

"I came here from a great distance to sit at your feet, Master. Even if I could not learn the Art of Immortality, I thought at least to acquire some minor accomplishment with which to nourish my spiritual aspirations. But alas, for these three months, I have done nothing but chop wood all day and return exhausted in the evening to sleep. Hardship such as this I have never known at home."

The priest smiled. "Did I not say it would be hard? See, you have proved me right. Tomorrow morning I will send you on your way."

"Please, Master," pleaded Wang, "for all the days I have labored, give me some trifling skills to take away with me, so that I will not go home empty-handed."

"What skill do you desire?" asked the priest.

"I have noticed that wherever you go, walls are no obstruction to you. Teach me to walk through walls, Master. That will be enough."

The priest smiled. "Very well."

He taught Wang a **mantra**, bade him recite it, then cried, "Now go!"

Wang looked at the wall in front of him, but could not bring himself to walk into it.

"Try! Go!"

Wang started slowly, but when he reached the wall, there it was, as solid as ever in front of him.

"What are you waiting for? Head down and charge!" cried the priest. "Don't **procrastinate**!"

This time, Wang took a few steps back from the wall, rushed at it full **pelt** and passed through it as if there were nothing there. Looking round him, he saw that he was indeed now on the other side of the wall. It had worked! He was delighted and returned at once to give thanks.

"When you are back home," said the monk, "be sure to lead a pure life. If not, it will not work."

The monk gave him something towards his travelling expenses and sent him on his way.

mantra /ˈmæntrə/ *n*. a word or sound that is repeated as a prayer or to help people meditate 曼怛罗(祷告或冥想时反复念唱的咒语)

pelt /pelt/ *n*. the skin of a dead animal, especially with the fur or hair still on it 生皮,带毛兽皮;(at) full pelt(British English): moving as fast as possible 全速地,开足马力地

画　　皮

◈【原文】

偶适市,遇一道士,顾生而愕。问:"何所遇?"答言:"无之。"道士曰:"君身邪气萦绕,何言无?"生又力白。道士乃去,曰:"惑哉!"世固有死将临而不悟者!"生以其言异,颇疑女。转思明明丽人,何至为妖,意道士借**魇禳**以猎食者。无何,至斋门,门内**杜**,不得入。心疑所作,乃逾**垝垣**。则室门亦闭。蹑迹而窗窥之,见一狞鬼,面翠色,齿**巉巉**如锯。铺人皮于榻上,执彩笔而绘之;已而掷笔,举皮,如振衣状,披于身,遂化为女子。睹此状,大惧,兽伏而出。急追道士,不知所往。

魇禳[yán ráng]　名词,镇压邪祟叫"魇",驱除灾变叫"禳",均属道教法术

杜[dù]　动词,关,堵

垝垣[guǐyuán]　名词,残缺的院墙。垝,坍塌。垣,墙外

巉巉[chán chán]　形容词,本意为山势高俊的样子,这里用以形容女鬼牙齿而尖利

◈【今译】

有一天，王生偶尔到街市上去，遇见了一个道士，那道士一见王生，就十分惊愕地问："你最近遇见什么人了？"王生回答说："没有呀。"道士说："你全身都被邪气缠绕着，怎么还说没有？"王生极力辩白说是没有。道士便叹息着走了，说："真让人不明白啊！世上居然有死将临头还执迷不悟的人。"王生觉得他的话非同寻常，就有些怀疑那个女子了。他又转念一想，她明明是个漂亮女子，怎么会是个妖怪呢？心想道士没准是借口镇妖除怪来谋取钱财的。不一会，他走到了书房门口，看见大门从里面插着，没法进去。他心里对这种做法有些怀疑，于是翻过一道破墙进了院子，只见内室门也关着。他就蹑手蹑脚地走到窗前偷看，只见一个面目狰狞的恶鬼，脸色发青，牙齿又尖又长像锯齿一样，正把一张人皮铺在床上，手里拿着彩色画笔在描绘。画完之后，恶鬼扔下画笔，举起人皮，像抖动衣服一样地把人皮披在身上，于是就变成了美丽的女子。王生亲眼看见这个情形后，万分恐惧，像野兽一样四肢着地爬了出去。他急忙去追寻道士，但那道士已经不知去向了。

◈ [Version 1]

Painted Skin

One day Wang went to the market place and, by chance, met a Taoist priest who looked terrified when he saw Wang. He asked, "What have you done?" "Nothing," came the reply. "How can you say nothing when you are surrounded by an evil spirit?" Wang tried his best to defend himself, but the priest walked away, saying, "What a fool! There certainly are people in this world who refuse to mend their ways even when death hangs over them!" Wang thought the words sounded strange and, for a while, suspected they might have something to do with the girl. But then he thought, she is such a beauty, how can she be a demon? He decided the priest must have been after money, pretending he could drive away evil spirits and eliminate the chance of disaster.

Not long after, Wang came to the study only to find the door locked from inside. Suspecting something was happening inside, he climbed over a broken part of the wall and went in. The door of the inner chamber was also locked. He walked **stealthily** to the window and peeped in, and what did he see but a demon with a **ferocious** face and teeth like those of a saw. The demon spread a human skin on the bed and started to paint on it. When he had finished, he put down the brush, lifted the skin, shook it a few times and wrapped it around his body. Immediately, he turned into the girl. Wang was so frightened by what he had witnessed with his own eyes, he crawled out of the courtyard like an animal and hurried off to seek the Taoist priest, but the latter was nowhere to be found.

---

stealthily /ˈstelθili/ *adv*. moving or doing something quietly and secretly 悄悄地，鬼鬼祟祟地，偷偷地
ferocious /fəˈrəʊʃəs/ *adj*. violent, dangerous and frightening 凶猛的，凶残的；可怕的

◈ [Version 2]

The Painted Skin

A few days later, in the supermarket, Wang ran into a Taoist priest, who studied his face with grave concern. "What strange thing have you encountered?"

"Why, nothing!" replied Wang.

"Nothing? Your whole being is wrapped in an evil **aura**," insisted the Taoist. "I tell you, you are **bewitched**!"

Wang protested **vehemently** that he was speaking the truth.

"Bewitched!" muttered the Taoist, as he went on his way. "Poor fool! Some men blind themselves to the truth even when death is starting them in the face!"

Something in the Taoist's strange words set Wang wondering, and he began to have serious misgivings about the young woman he had taken in. but he could not bring himself to believe that such a pretty young thing could have cast an evil spell on him. Instead he persuaded himself that the Taosit was making it all up, trying to put the wind up him in the hope of being retained for a costly rite of **exorcism**. And so he put the matter out of his mind and returned home.

He reached his study to find the outer door barred. He was unable to enter his own home. His suspicions now genuinely aroused, he climbed into the courtyard through a hole in the wall, only to find that the inner door was also closed. Creeping stealthily up to a window, he peeped through and saw the most **hideous** sight, a green-faced monster, a ghoul with great jagged teeth like a saw, leaning over a human pelt, the skin of an entire human body, spread on the bed-on his bed. The monster had a paintbrush in its hand and was in the process of touching up the skin in lifelike color. When the painting was done, it threw down the brush, lifted up the skin, shook it out like a cloak and wrapped itself in it-whereupon it was instantly transformed into his pretty young '**fugitive**' friend.

Wang was absolutely terrified by what he had seen, and crept away on all fours. He went at once in search of the Taoist, but did not know where to find him.

---

aura /ˈɔːrə/ *n*. a quality or feeling that seems to surround or come from a person or a place 气氛，气息，韵味

bewitch /bɪˈwɪtʃ/ *v*. to get control over someone by putting a magic spell on them 施魔力于；使着魔

vehemently /ˈviːəməntli/ *adv*. showing very strong feelings or opinions 感情强烈地；观点激烈地

exorcism /ˈeksɔːsɪzəm/ *n*. a process during which someone tries to make an evil spirit leave a place by saying special words, or a ceremony when this is done 驱邪，驱魔；驱邪仪式

hideous /ˈhɪdiəs/ *adj*. extremely unpleasant or ugly 极丑的，极难看的

fugitive /ˈfjuːdʒətɪv/ *adj*. literary lasting for a very short time 短暂的

聂小倩

◆【原文】

“……小倩，姓聂氏，十八**夭殂**，葬寺侧，辄被妖物威胁，历役贱务；腆颜向人，实非所乐。今寺中无可杀者，恐当以夜叉来。”宁骇求计。女曰：“与燕生同室可免。”问：“何不惑燕生？”曰：“彼奇人也，不敢近。”问：“迷人若何？”曰：“狎昵我者，隐以锥刺其足，彼即茫若迷，因摄血以供妖饮；又或以金，非金也，乃**罗刹**鬼骨，留之能截取人心肝：二者，凡以投时好耳。”宁感谢。问戒备之期，答以明宵。临别泣曰：“妾堕玄海，求岸不得。郎君义气**干云**，必能拔生救苦。倘肯囊妾朽骨，归葬安宅，**不啻再造**。”宁毅然诺之。因问葬处，曰：“但记取白杨之上，有乌巢者是也。”言已出门，纷然而灭。

夭殂[yāo cú] 动词，未成年而死。

罗刹[luó chà] 名词，梵语音译，佛教故事中食人血肉的恶鬼

干云[gān yún] 动词，冲入云霄，冲天

不啻[bù chì] 副词，不只，何止

◆【今译】

“……我小倩，姓聂，十八岁时夭折，埋葬在寺庙旁边，后被妖精威胁，做这些下贱的事情，不顾羞耻面向众人，实在不是心甘情愿的。现在寺庙中没有能杀的人了，恐怕夜叉又要来。”宁采臣害怕，请姑娘想个办法。小倩说：“与燕生同室就可以免除灾难。”宁采臣问：“你为什么不迷惑燕生呢？”小倩说：“他是个奇人，不敢接近。”又问：“怎么迷惑人呢？”小倩说：“亲昵我的人，我就暗中用锥子扎他的脚心，那时他就会昏迷不知，借此抽他的血给妖精喝。或者用金钱引诱他，其实那不是真金，而是罗刹鬼的骨头，留下就会被摘走心肝。这两种方法都是用来投其所好的。”宁采臣感谢小倩说出真相。问戒备的时间，小倩讲就在明天晚上。临别时，小倩哭着说：“我坠入了地狱之海，找不到岸边。郎君义气冲天，必定能够拔生救苦。如果肯把我的朽骨包起来，送回家安葬，不亚于再生父母。”宁采臣毅然答应下来。于是又问原来埋在哪里，小倩说：“只要请记住，有乌鸦筑巢的那颗白杨树下就是了。”说罢出门，倏然间不见了。

◆ [Version 1]

Nie Xiaoqian

“... My name is Xiao Qian, and my family name is Nie. I died at the young age of eighteen and was buried by the temple. I have constantly been threatened by demons who force me to do all sorts of low things. When I put on a smiling face and **seduce** men, it is really against my own will. Now that there's no one else left in the temple to harm, I'm afraid they will send a yaksha to harm you.” (Trans. Note: A yaksha is a malevolent spirit that deliberately harms people.) Ning felt a little **panicky**, so he asked her what he should do. Xiaoqian said, “If you stay with the scholar Yan, you'll be safe.” “Why haven't you tried to seduce him?” asked Ning, to which Xiaoqian

replied, " He is a strange man. I don't dare approach him." Ning then asked, "How do you go about seducing and harming people?" Xiaoqian said, "Whoever plays with me. I prick the sole of his feet with an awl without his knowing, and when he falls into a **coma**, I suck out his blood for the demons to drink. Sometimes I lure people with gold. Actually, it is not gold but the bone of a demon. Whoever accepts it will have his heart gouged out. Women and gold are the two things used to satisfy the lust of ordinary people." Ning thanked her and asked what time he should guard against the evil spirit. Xiaoqing said, tomorrow night. Bidding goodbye, she cried and said, "I have fallen into the dark, bitter sea① and cannot see the shore. You are upright and lofty in spirit, you can surely rescue me from the bitter sea. If you would collect my bones and bury them in a safer place, it would be as good as bringing me back to life." Ning Caichen promised her that without hesitation. He asked where her original burial place was, and she said, "Just remember there's poplar tree on which the crows have made a nest." Having said that, she floated out of sight.

---

seduce /sɪˈdjuːs/ *v*. to persuade someone to have sex with you, especially in a way that is attractive and not too direct 诱奸,勾引

panicky /ˈpænɪki/ *adj*. *informal* very nervous and anxious 惊惶的,紧张不安的

coma /ˈkəʊmə/ *n*. someone who is in a coma has been unconscious for a long time, usually because of a serious illness or injury (因重病或重伤而引起的)昏迷

◈ [Version 2]

The Magic Sword and the Magic Bag

"... My family name is Nie, and I have always been known as Little Beauty. I died when I was eighteen years old, and they buried my body just outside this temple. Then an evil spirit took control of me, and ever since he has been forcing me against my will to cast spells on men, to seduce them and do all sorts of shameful things with them. Now there is no one left in the temple to kill apart from you, and I am afraid that spirit will come looking for you. He will take the form of a yaksha-demon."

Brave though he was, Ning found this prospect somewhat **daunting**. He asked her what precautions he should take.

---

① Xuanhai(玄海) from Buddhism refers to all living beings in the six realms of Samsara, suffering all kinds of pain and torture. It's also used to refer to all the troubles and misery in the world. Therefore, the Buddhist culture emphasizes that the self-awareness can let people repent so as to help them get out of the misery life. In English version 1, it is translated into "the dark, bitter sea", which can tell the figurative meaning of "Xuan" by adding the word "bitter". In this way, the translation could be more closer to the connotation of this religious culture-loaded word in the original text. When translating such culture-bound words, a translator should be aware of the cultural difference, take the target readers' understanding into special consideration and choose the best means of translation.

"You must sleep in Mr. Yan's room," she replied. "You will be safe there."

"Why is he so special?"

"He is a strange one. Spirits don't dare go near him."

"Tell me something," he said. "Tell me how you set about bewitching men."

"I do it one of two ways," she replied." Either a man agrees to make love to me, in which case I secretly prick him in the foot with an awl so that he falls unconscious and his blood can be drawn off for the evil spirit to drink. Or else I tempt him with a piece of gold, which is really not gold at all but the spirit-bone of a raksha-demon. Once he has taken the gold, I can use it to cut out his heart and liver. I use whichever method seems most likely to work at the time."

Ning thanked her for confiding in him like this, and asked her at which times he should be specially on his guard, to which she replied that the following night would be a dangerous one for him. As she left him she wept. "I am sinking into a dark sea and cannot reach the further shore! But you are so strong! You are so bright and good, I know you can put an end to my pain. Take my bones back home with you. I beg you, and give them a decent burial. Set them at peace and bring me back to life!"

Ning gallantly agreed to her request and asked where he was to find her gave.

"At the foot of the white poplar tree, in which a crow has made its nest." With these words she went out through the door and vanished into the night.

daunting /ˈdɔːntɪŋ/ *adj*. frightening in a way that makes you feel less confident 使人气馁的

考 弊 司

◈【原文】

言次，已入城郭。至一府署，廨宇不甚弘敞，惟一堂高广；堂下两**碣**东西立，绿书大于**栲栳**，一云"孝弟忠信"，一云"礼义廉耻"。躇阶而进，见堂上一扁，大书"考弊司"。楹间，板雕翠字一联云："曰校、曰序、曰**庠**，两字德行阴教化；上士、中士、下士，一堂礼乐鬼门生。"游览未已，官已出，鬈发**鲐背**，若数百年人；而鼻孔撩天，唇外倾不承其齿。从一主簿吏，虎首人身。又十余人列侍，半狞恶若山精。秀才曰："此鬼王也。"生骇极，欲却退。鬼王已睹，降阶揖生上，便问兴居。生但诺。又问："何事见临？"生以秀才意具白之。鬼王色变曰："此有成例，即父命所不敢承！"气象森凛，似不可入一词。生不敢言，骤起告别。鬼王侧行送之，至门外始返。

碣[jié] 名词，石碑

栲栳[kǎo lǎo] 名词，用柳条编织的汲水器具，形似笆斗

庠[xiáng] 名词，古代地方所设的乡学，夏代称"校"，殷代称"序"，周代称"庠"

鲐背[tái bèi] 动词，驼背，形容老态。鲐，鱼名，体呈纺锤形，背隆起

◈【今译】

说话之间，两人已经进了城。来到一所官府，房舍不太宽敞，只有一间大堂高大宽广。堂下一东一西立着两块石碑，绿色的字比笆斗还大。一边是“孝悌忠信”，一边是“礼义廉耻”。大步跨越台阶来到堂上，只见堂上悬挂着一块匾，上面大书“考弊司”三字。堂前的柱子上，有一副在木板上雕刻的绿色大字对联，上写：“曰校、曰序、曰痒，两字德行阴教化；上士、中士、下士，一堂礼乐鬼门生。”闻人生还未游览完，当官的已经出来了。只见他卷发驼背，好像好几百岁了，而鼻孔朝天，嘴唇向外翻着，挨不上牙齿。他身后跟着一个主管文书簿籍的小吏，虎头人身。又有十余人列队侍立，长相大半面目狰狞凶恶，好像山中怪兽。秀才说：“这就是鬼王。”闻人生害怕极了，想后退。鬼王已经瞧见，他走下台阶作揖请闻生上堂，就问候起居，闻人生只有唯唯诺诺。鬼王又问：“您有什么事光临这里?”闻人生就把秀才的意思和盘托出。鬼王脸色一变说道：“这事有成例，就是父亲下命令我也不敢应承!”态度十分严厉，好像听不进一句话。闻生不敢开口，马上起身告别。鬼王侧身送客，一直送到门外才返回。

◈［Version 1］

Inspectorate of Misdeeds

What with all their talking, they were inside the walls of a city before they knew it. They came to a *yamen* housed in a none-too-spacious building, only the central hall of which was highroofed and roomy. At the foot of the raised hall, to the east and the west stood two stone tablets bearing green characters, each a square foot in size. One tablet read: "Filiality, fraternity, loyalty, faithfulness" and the other "Propriety, justice, honesty, honor." Walking up the entrance steps, they saw a **plaque** with the words "**Inspectorate** of Misdeeds" at the head of the hall. A couplet in **malachite-tinted** characters was carved on two opposing pillars: "Be they institutes, academies or schools, the essence of **subterranean** teaching is 'virtuous behavior': Be they superior, **mediocre** or inferior, the hall of music and etiquette educates ghostly disciples." Before they had finished looking the place over, an official whose frizzy hair and hunched back made him look hundreds of years old came toward them. His nostrils were turned up to the sky and his lips **protruded**, unable to contain his teeth. Behind him trailed a clerk in charge of files, who had a tiger's head and human body. Last of all came ten or so men who lined up in attendance, half of whom had the fierce ugliness of trolls.

"That is the Ghoul-King," said the bachelor of letters①. The scholar recoiled in terror, but before he could get away the Ghoul-King caught sight of him, descended the steps, invited him

① "Xiucai" refers to a person who has passed the county level imperial exam in Chinese history. The translator in the first version translates "Xiucai" into "the bachelor of letters". Actually "a bachelor" or "a bachelor degree" means an undergraduate academic degree awarded by colleges and universities upon completion of a course of study lasting three to seven years. The translator chooses "bachelor" which is from the Western education system, for it is easy for the target reader to understand the ancient imperial examination system in China. Therefore, the ancient scholar earns the fame such as "Xiucai"(秀才),"Juren"(举人)and "Jinshi"(进士) which also would be translated into "Bachelor", "Master" and "Doctorate" separately by the Western sinologists in this book.

into the hall with hands clasped **obsequiously** and inquired after his health. The scholar merely grunted in acknowledgement, whereupon the king asked, "To what do I owe the honor of this visit?"

The scholar answered by telling him exactly what the bachelor of letters had asked him to say. A displeased look came over the Ghoul-King's face as he said, "In a case like this, when there is a fixed rule to go by, I could not change things even if my father ordered me to." He delivered these words with an icy finality that made pursuing the matter seem futile. Not daring to say another word, the scholar rose abruptly and asked to be excused. The Ghoul-King saw him all the way to the door, walking sideways.

---

plaque /plɑːk/ *n*. a piece of flat metal, wood, or stone with writing on it, used as a prize in a competition or attached to a building to remind people of an event or person 匾

inspectorate /ɪnˈspektərət/ *n*. the group of inspectors who officially inspect schools, factories, etc. (学校、工厂等的)检查团,督察队

malachite /ˈmæləkait/ *n*. a green mineral that is a basic carbonate of copper used especially for making ornamental objects 孔雀石

tinted /ˈtɪntɪd/ *adj*. tinted glass is colored, rather than completely transparent 着色的,带色彩的

subterranean /ˌsʌbtəˈreɪniən/ *adj*. beneath the surface of the Earth 地下的;秘密的;隐蔽的

mediocre /ˌmiːdiˈəʊkə/ *adj*. not very good 普通的;平凡的;中等的

protrude /prəˈtruːd/ *v*. to stick out from somewhere 突出,伸出

obsequiously /əbˈsiːkwiəsli/ *adv*. eagerly to please or agree with people who are powerful-used to show disapproval 谄媚地,奉承地

◈ [Version 2]

The Bureau of Examination Frauds

In the course of their conversation, they passed through the city walls. They came to a government office, but the building wasn't very spacious, and had only a large hall; there were two stone tablets standing at the threshold of the hall, **flanking** a green book bigger than a wicker basket, with one tablet reading "Filial Piety and Fraternal Duty, Loyalty and Trustworthiness," the other reading "Propriety and Righteousness, Sense of Honor."

Wen wavered at steps leading up to the hall, then proceeded till he saw a banner hanging above the hall, displaying "Bureau of Examination Frauds" in large characters. Between the pillars, there was a plaque engraved with green characters that combined to read, "The underworld school attaches great importance to enlightening the people by educating them in moral **integrity**; students at every level gather here to learn the public ceremonies, as pupils of the King of the Ghost."

He hadn't yet finished looking at everything before an official stepped out, his hair curling out over his hunched back, as though he was several hundred years old; his nostrils were turned upwards, and his lips stuck out from his face, as though they could barely contain his teeth. Following him was the secretary in charge of the official's register, who had a tiger's head and a human body. Then more than ten men lined up to wait on them, half of them as fierce-looking as **predatory** owls.

The *xiucai* announced, "This is the King of the Ghost." Wen approached in horrified dread, though he really wanted to step back and run away. The King of the Ghosts had already noticed him, and walked down the steps towards Wen with his hands clasped in greeting, making polite inquires about him. Wen merely grunted affirmatively.

Then the King of the Ghosts asked him, "On what business have you come to visit me?" Wen then expressed what he had been told by the *xiucai*. The King's pleasant expression changed as he exclaimed, "There's a precedent for this, instructions from my father that I dare not disobey!"

The atmosphere turned frigid like the severe cold of a forest, as the King of the Ghosts implied that the matter must go no further. Wen didn't dare say anything, so he suddenly stood up to take his leave. The King of the Ghosts walked beside him, accompanying him, and didn't turn back until they were already outside the building's gates.

---

flank /flæŋk/ *v*. to be on both sides of someone or something 位于……侧面

integrity /ɪnˈtegrəti/ *n*. the quality of being honest and strong about what you believe to be right 正直诚实

predatory /ˈpredətəri/ *adj*. a predatory animal kills and eats other animals for food 掠食的，捕食其他动物为生的

Chinese Philosophy

1.【持之以恒】

The Taoist Priest of Laoshan is a folktale with a moral lesson. It introduces Wang Sheng's experience of receiving *Tao* to Laoshan, portraying a man who is tempted by immortality and is not willing to work for his goal. In fact, learning first requires a clear goal. Then we should lay a solid foundation for future study. What's more, the skills can be acquired only by diligent work and assiduously training. Finally, the persistence and the positive attitude will lead us to great success.

2.【扶正祛邪】

Nie Xiaoqian tells a love story between the ghost maiden Nie Xiaoqian and the young scholar Ning Caichen, from which Pu Songling aims to promote justice and mercilessly to criticize greed. There is a strong contrast between good and evil, beauty and ugliness, and eventually, Good defeats Evil and beauty defeats ugliness in the story. In addition, it also shows a kind of tolerant attitude. For those who have reformed themselves from the evil lives, they should be given objective assessments and opportunities to restart.

3.【由表及里】

The ideological value of *Painted Skin* lies in seeing through the appearance to perceive the essence, and not being confused by an illusion. Because sometimes the truth is beneath the surface, just like the beautiful woman turning out to be a demon underneath the woman's paint, the disgusting phlegm became a resurrected panacea in the story. Therefore, we have to be especially alert and able to identify the things that are good at camouflage in our daily lives, and avoid to judge people by their appearance.

4.【为善去恶】

Inspectorate of Misdeeds reflects the dark examination system and the unscrupulous examiners in reality through author's imagination of the Hades. It aims to expose the drawbacks of the imperial examination system, bureaucratic corruption and its imprisonment and corrosion to the intellectuals. But the story still gives people the light and hope in the darkness, in which some graceful qualities are praised by the author, such as the spirit of honesty, bravery, helpfulness, and anti-oppression. At any time, we should always have a good heart and do no evil. What's more important is that the officials must be kind to the people, be selfless, and be clean and honest.

Practice

I. Vocabulary

Choose a proper word or phrase to complete each of the following sentences, changing the form when necessary.

obsequious	bewitch	immortality	thoroughbred	stealthy
prudent	panicky	daunting	integrity	coma

1. Taoism is a mystic quest for the absolute and for ________.
2. I told him I thought it would be ________ for both of us to keep our conversation between ourselves.
3. She was making progress, but then she suddenly relapsed into a ________.
4. All this ________ praise for his actions is enough to make most normal people sick.
5. It was a thick-necked, elegant beast, with the strong legs of a ________.
6. Some, shaped like tiny globes, radiated a scarlet glow that was utterly ________.
7. Steve recently completed the ________ task of photographing 100 leading western philosophers.

8. Stories appeared that were untrue, newspapers quoted things she had not said and she began to feel ________.
9. The figure was always just ahead of him, crouched low but quick and ________.
10. She is a woman of ________ who has never abandoned her principles for the sake of making money.

II. Translation

Translate the following sentences and the passage into English.

1. 道士笑曰:“吾固谓不能作苦,今果然。明早当遣汝行。”

____

2. 临别泣曰:“妾堕玄海,求岸不得。郎君义气干云,必能拔生救苦。倘肯囊妾朽骨,归葬安宅,不啻再造。”

____

____

3. 无何,至斋门,门内杜,不得入,心疑所作,乃逾垝垣。则室门亦闭。

____

4. 堂下两碣东西立,绿书大于栲栳,一云“孝弟忠信”,一云“礼义廉耻”。

____

5. 蹑迹而窗窥之,见一狞鬼,面翠色,齿巉巉如锯,铺人皮于榻上,执彩笔而绘之。

____

6. 宫中有玉树一株,围可合抱,本莹澈如白琉璃,中有心淡黄色,稍细于臂,叶类碧玉,厚一钱许,细碎有浓阴。常与女啸咏其下。花开满树,状类薝蔔。每一瓣落,锵然作响。拾视之,如赤瑙雕镂,光明可爱。时有异鸟来鸣,毛金碧色,尾长于身,声等哀玉,恻人肺腑。生闻之,辄念乡土。

____

____

____

____

III. Critical Thinking

Discuss the following questions in groups and do your group presentation in class on the basis of your discussion.

1. Which character impresses you most in these four stories (or in other stories of this book)? Please give a character analysis of him or her.
2. Think and discuss about the differences among Confucianism, Buddhism and Taoism in China.

References

［1］ Pu Songling. Sidney L. Sondergard (trans.). *Strange Tales from Liaozhai* vol. 3 [M]. Fremont: Jain Publishing Company, 2009.

［2］ Pu Songling. Zhang Youhe(ed.). Huang Youyi, Zhang Qingnian, Zhang Ciyun, Yang Yi, Denis C. Mair, Victor H. Mair (trans.). *Selections From Strange Tales from the Liaozhai Stuido* (*I—III*) [M]. Beijing: Foreign Languages Press, 2007.

［3］ Pu Songling. John Minford (trans.). *Strange Tales from a Chinese Studio* [M]. London: Penguin Classics, 2006.

［4］ 蒲松龄,于天池注;孙通海,于天池等译.聊斋志异[M].北京:中华书局,2015.

Appendix I
Key to Practice

Unit 1

I. Vocabulary

1. simulated **2.** divination **3.** manifested **4.** begets **5.** penetrated
6. signified **7.** Symbolize **8.** moisten **9.** mingled **10.** invigorated

II. Translation

1. Therefore, they set alternation of yin and yang as the way of heaven, alternation of yieldingness and firmness as the way of earth and benevolence and righteousness as the way of man.
2. Heaven and earth determine their own positions; mountain and lake interchange with each other through air and vapor; thunder rumbles and wind blows, they echo and mix with each other; fire and water are not opponents but assistants to each other; and the eight trigrams mingle in a unity of opposites.
3. The sages faced the south and received audience under heaven. They faced light and ruled the land, and perhaps drew inspiration from this trigram.
4. Miracle means miraculous creation and development of all things of creation.
5. There are heaven and earth first, and then all things of creation come into existence. There are all things of creation first and then there are men and women. There are men and women first and then there are husbands and wives. There are husbands and wives first and then there are fathers and sons. There are fathers and sons first and then there are kings and subjects. There are kings and subjects first and then there are distinctions between superiors and subordinates. There are distinctions between superiors and subordinates first and then proprieties and righteousness can be described and an effectively implemented.
6. *The Zhou Book of Change* as a book is profound and all-inclusive: there are the way of heaven, the way of man and the way of earth. The eight trigrams, at the same time, symbols of the three cardinal ways, are doubled into different combinations of the sixty

four hexagrams. The six lines of the hexagrams symbolize nothing else but the three cardinal ways. The ways in constant change in simulation of all things of creation are, therefore, called lines. The six lines have different status, so they are compared to images of all things of creation. Mixtures of different objects and states in images, therefore, are called patterns. When the patterns are inappropriately combined, therefore, they result in good fortune and disaster.

III. Critical Thinking

1. Open.

2. Open.

Unit 2

I. Vocabulary

1. gnarled **2.** moped **3.** woolly **4.** spurned **5.** fretted

6. ape **7.** unwieldy **8.** smashed **9.** fluttered **10.** crouched

II. Translation

1. I heard from Chieh Yu (接舆) some utterances that were great but could not be justified. Once stated, there is no end of his tale.

2. I was greatly startled at what he said. It seemed to be as boundless as the Milky Way. It was very improbable and far removed from human experience.

3. I thought all these sayings were nonsense and refused to believe in them.

4. The blind have nothing to do with beauty, nor the deaf with music.

5. There are not only physical blindness and deafness, there are also the intellectual.

6. Yao wanted to cede the empire to Hsu Yu. "When the sun and moon have already come out," he said, "it's a waste of light to go on burning the torches, isn't it? When the seasonal rains are falling, it's a waste of water to go on irrigating the fields. If you took the throne, the world would be well ordered. I go on occupying it, but all I can see are my failings. I beg to turn over the world to you." Hsu Yu said, "You govern the world and the world is already well governed. Now if I take your place, will I be doing it for a name? But name is only the guest of reality will I be doing it so I can play the part of a guest? When the tailorbird builds her nest in the deep wood, she uses no more than one branch. When the mole drinks at the river, he takes no more than a bellyful. Go home and forget the matter, my lord. I have no use for the rulership of the world! Though the cook may not run his kitchen properly, the priest and the impersonator of the dead at the sacrifice do not leap over the wine casks and sacrificial stands and go take his place."

III. Critical Thinking

1. Open.
2. Open.

Unit 3

I. Vocabulary

1. satiety 2. filial piety 3. suspicious 4. delight 5. reciprocity
6. virtue 7. courses 8. perplexities 9. ceasing 10. superior

II. Translation

1. While his parents are alive, the son may not go abroad to a distance. If he does go abroad, he must have a fixed place to which he goes.
2. The mechanic, who wishes to do his work well, must first sharpen his tools.
3. The superior man is satisfied and composed; the mean man is always full of distress
4. The superior man on grounds of culture meets with his friends, and by friendship helps his virtue.
5. The virtuous will be sure to speak correctly, but those whose speech is good may not always be virtuous. Men of principle are sure to be bold, but those who are bold may not always be men of principle.
6. Yan Yuan asked about perfect virtue. The Master said, "To subdue one's self and return to propriety, is perfect virtue. If a man can for one day subdue himself and return to propriety, all under heaven will ascribe perfect virtue to him. Is the practice of perfect virtue from a man himself, or is it from others?" Yan Yuan said, "I beg to ask the steps of that process." The Master replied, "Look not at what is contrary to propriety; listen not to what is contrary to propriety; speak not what is contrary to propriety; make no movement which is contrary to propriety." Yan Yuan then said, "Though I am deficient in intelligence and vigor, I will make it my business to practice this lesson."

III. Critical Thinking

1. Open.
2. Open.

Unit 4

I. Vocabulary

1. attainment 2. distinguish 3. took hold of 4. keep it 5. accords

6. utmost **7.** proper **8.** cause **9.** contrary **10.** embodying

II. Translation

1. The way of the superior man may be compared to what takes place in traveling, when to go to a distance we must first traverse the space that is near, and in ascending a height, when we must begin from the lower ground.
2. When we have intelligence resulting from sincerity, this condition is to be ascribed to nature; when we have sincerity resulting from intelligence, this condition is to be ascribed to institution. But given the sincerity, and there shall be the intelligence; given the intelligence, and there shall be the sincerity.
3. The path is not far from man. When man tries to pursue a course, which is far from the common indications of consciousness, this course cannot be considered the path.
4. The superior man embodies the course of the Mean; the mean man acts contrary to the course of the Mean.
5. All things are nourished together without their injuring one another. The courses of the seasons, and of the sun and the moon, are pursued without any collision among them.
6. It is only he who is possessed of the most complete sincerity that can exist under heaven, who can give its full development to his nature. Able to give its full development to his nature, he can do the same to the nature of other men. Able to give its full development to the nature of other men, he can give their full development to the natures of animals and things. Able to give their full development to the natures of creatures and things, he can assist the transforming and nourishing powers of Heaven and Earth. Able to assist the transforming and nourishing powers of Heaven and Earth, he may with Heaven and Earth form a ternion.

III. Critical Thinking

1. Open.
2. Open.

Unit 5

I. Vocabulary

1. worthy **2.** gallantly **3.** jostle **4.** marquis **5.** hemmed

6. trampling **7.** rally **8.** bog down **9.** perish **10.** gallop

II. Translation

1. It is eight years since I rose in arms. In that time I have fought more than seventy battles.

I swept all obstacles from my path, conquered every foe I attacked, and was never defeated. That is how I won the empire.

2. Today I shall perish here, but for your sake I shall fight gallantly and overcome the enemy three times. For you I shall break through their lines, kill their commander and cut down their flag, so that you may know it is Heaven that has destroyed me, not my generalship that is fault.
3. A cavalry commander named Yang Xi, the marquis of Chiquan, pursued him. But Xiang Yu glared and bellowed at him so fiercely that Yang Xi's horse bolted and fled, terrified, for several li.
4. Besides, I once crossed the Yangtse and went west with eight thousand young men from the east, but now I have come back alone. Even if the elders made me king out of pity, how could I face them again? Though they said nothing, how could I hold up my head?
5. He ordered his men to dismount for hand-to-hand combat. Xiang Yu alone killed several hundred men of Han and was wounded some dozen times.
6. Xiang Yu had no inch of territory at the start, yet, taking this chance to rise in the countryside, within three years he commanded five states and overthrew the House of Qin. He carved up the empire and enfeoffed kings and barons. He was supreme, styling himself the Overlord, and though his rule did not endure his achievement was surely unique in recent times. But when he gave up the land within the Pass to return to Chu, banished the Righteous Emperor and set himself up in his stead, he could hardly complain when the kings and barons turned against him. He boasted of his conquests, trusted only his personal judgement and did not follow ancient precedents. Considering himself the overlord, he tried to win the empire by military conquest, so that within five years he lost his kingdom and met his death at Dongcheng. Yet he never realized his mistake or blamed himself for his folly. What a fool he was to say that Heaven was against him and that it was not his generalship that was at fault!

III. Critical Thinking

1. Open.
2. Open.

Unit 6

I. Vocabulary

1. overthrow **2.** siege **3.** tactician **4.** divine **5.** shattered
6. in accord with **7.** turmoil **8.** succumb **9.** subdue **10.** intact

II. Translation

1. So what is important in war is quick victory, not prolonged operations.
2. So it is that a victorious army will not engage the enemy unless it is assured of the necessary conditions for victory, whereas an army destined to defeat rushes into battle in the hope that it will win by luck.
3. Only when you throw them into life-and-death situations will they fight for survive. Only when you plunge them into places where there is no way out will they fight to stay alive.
4. It is like lifting a strand of animal hair in autumn (Animal hair is very fine and light in autumn.), which is no sign of strength; like being able to see the sun and the moon, which is no test of vision; like hearing a thunderclap, which is no indication of hearing ability.
5. He who makes full assessment of the situation at the prewar council meeting in the temple is more likely to win. He who makes insufficient assessment of the situation at the meeting is less likely to win. This being the case, what chance has he of winning if he makes no assessment at all? With my assessment method, I can forecast who is likely to emerge as victor.
6. Sunzi said: The skilled commanders of the past first made themselves invulnerable, then waited for the enemy's moment of vulnerability. Invulnerability depends on one's own efforts, whereas victory over the enemy depends on the latter's negligence. It follows that those skilled in warfare can make themselves invincible but they cannot be sure of victory over the enemy. Therefore it is said that victory can be anticipated but it cannot be forced. Invulnerability lies with defense, and opportunity of victory with attack. One defends when his strength is inadequate; he attacks when his strength is abundant.

III. Critical Thinking

1. Open.
2. Open.

Unit 7

I. Vocabulary

1. Abidance by **2.** denote **3.** resuscitate **4.** myriad **5.** enliven
6. extinguish **7.** permeate **8.** inhibit **9.** alleviate **10.** curtail

II. Translation

1. Give life and do not kill. Give and do not take. Reward and do not punish.
2. Let the mind be peaceful and tranquil, so as to temper the punishment carried out in autumn. Collect the spirit qi and cause the autumn qi to be balanced. Do not direct your

mind to the outside and cause the lung qi to be clear.

3. Only the sages follow the Way; hence, their bodies have no strange diseases.
4. Opposing them (yin qi, yang qi, and the four seasons) results in catastrophe and harms life. If one follows them, severe diseases will not emerge. This is called "to achieve the Way."
5. Hence, it is said that the sages did not treat those already ill, but treated those not yet ill, they did not put in order what was already in disorder, but put in order what was not yet in disorder.
6. The sages in ancient times who knew the Dao (the tenets for cultivating health) followed the rules of Yin and Yang and adjusted Shushu (the ways to cultivate health). They were moderate in eating and drinking, regular in working and resting, avoiding any overstrain. That is why they could maintain a desirable harmony between the Shen (mind or spirit) and the body, enjoying good health and a long life. People nowadays, on the contrary, just behave oppositely. They drink wine as thin rice gruel, regard wrong as right, and seek sexual pleasure after drinking. As a result, their Jingqi (Essence-Qi) is exhausted and Zhenqi (Genuine-Qi) is wasted. They seldom take measures to keep an exuberance of Jingqi and do not know how to regulate the Shen (mind and spirit), often giving themselves to sensual pleasure. Being irregular in daily life, they begin to become old even at the age of fifty.

III. Critical Thinking

1. Open.
2. Open.

Unit 8

I. Vocabulary

1. immortality 2. prudent 3. coma 4. obsequious 5. thoroughbred
6. bewitching 7. daunting 8. panicky 9. stealthy 10. integrity

II. Translation

1. The priest smiled and said, "I said at the beginning that you wouldn't be able to stand the hardship. Now you've proven me right. Tomorrow, you can go."
2. Bidding goodbye, she cried and said, "I have fallen into the dark, bitter sea and cannot see the shore. You are upright and lofty in spirit, you can surely rescue me from the bitter sea. If you would collect my bones and bury them in a safer place, it would be as good as bringing me back to life."
3. Not long after, Wang came to the study only to find the door locked from inside.

Suspecting something was happening inside, he climbed over a broken part of the wall and went in. The door of the inner chamber was also locked.

4. At the foot of the raised hall, to the east and the west stood two stone tablets bearing green characters, each a square foot in size. One tablet read: "Filiality, fraternity, loyalty, faithfulness" and the other "Propriety, justice, honesty, honor."
5. He walked stealthily to the window and peeped in, and what did he see but a demon with a ferocious face and teeth like those of a saw. The demon spread a human skin on the bed and started to paint on it.
6. A jade tree as big in girth as a man's embrace grew in the palace. The trunk was shimmeringly transparent, like clear glass, with a pale yellow center slightly thinner than an arm. The leaves resembled green jade and were a bit thicker than copper coins. This profuse foliage cast dense shade, in which the scholar and his bride often sang and chanted poetry. The whole tree was blooming with flowers that looked like gardenias. Each time a petal fell a distance tinkle could be heard. Upon closer inspection each gleaming, delicate petal seemed to be sculpted of red agate. Rare birds with feathers of iridescent blue and tails longer than their bodies often alighted on the tree and sang strains every bit as heart-rending as notes from a plaintive jade flute. Everything the scholar heard them, he thought of his homeland.

III. Critical Thinking

1. Open.
2. Open.

Appendix II

Glossary

abidance /ə'baidəns/ *vi*. 持续；遵守；逗留;居住（in）abidance by 遵守,遵循 U7

accommodation /əˌkɔmə'deiʃən/ *n*. making or becoming suitable; adjusting to circumstances 适应;适应性调节 U1

accord /ə'kɔːd/ *n*. *formal* a situation in which two people, ideas, or statements agree with each other 符合;一致;协议;自愿 U1

ailanthus /eɪ'lænθəs/ *n*. any of several deciduous Asian trees of the genus Ailanthus 臭椿树 U2

alkaline /'ælkəlaɪn/ *adj*. containing an alkali 碱的;碱性的 U1

alleviate /ə'liːvieɪt/ *vt*. to make something less painful or difficult to deal with 减轻,缓和(痛苦或困难) U7

allotment /ə'lɒtmənt/ *n*. the act of distributing by allotting or apportioning 分配 U1

alternation /ˌɔːltə'neɪʃən/ *n*. successive change from one condition or action to another and back again repeatedly 交替;轮流;间隔 U1

anew /ə'njuː / *adv*. *written* if you do something anew, you start doing it again 重新;再 U1

antiquity /æn'tɪkwəti/ *n*. the state of being very old or ancient 古老,古 U2

ape /eɪp/ *v*. to do sth in the same way as sb else, especially when it is not done very well 模仿,仿效 U2

approbation /ˌæprə'beɪʃən/ *n*. official praise or approval 认可,批准 U3

armor /'ɑːmə / *n*. metal or leather clothing that protects your body, worn by soldiers in battles in past times （军)装甲;盔甲 U1

arrogant /'ærəgənt/ *adj*. behaving in an unpleasant or rude way because you think you are more important than other people 傲慢自大的 U6

artisan /'ɑːrtɪzən/ *n*. someone who does skilled work, making things with their hands 技工,工匠 U4

assault /ə'sɔːlt / *v*.to attack someone in a violent way 袭击;突袭 U6

astringe /ə'strɪndʒ/ *vt*. 使……收缩;使……收敛 U7

astringency /ə'strɪndʒənsi/ *n*. 收敛性 U7

aura /'ɔːrə/ *n*. a quality or feeling that seems to surround or come from a person or a place 气氛,气息,韵味 U8

avail /ə'veɪl/ *vt*. & *vi*. use, purpose, advantage, or profit 有益于;使对某人有利 U3

barren /ˈbærən/ *adj*. land or soil that is barren has no plants growing on it 荒芜的 U1

battalion /bəˈtæljən/ *n*. a large group of soldiers consisting of several companies (company) (军队)营 U6

baulk /bɔːlk/ *n*. the act of deliberately making someone believe something that is not true 阻止 U6

beget /bɪˈget/ *vt*. (begot; begotten; begetting) 1. *old use* to become the father of a child 成为……的父亲 2. to cause something or make it happen 导致 U1

belligerent /bəˈlɪdʒərənt/ *adj*. very unfriendly and wanting to argue or fight 好战的 U6

bellyful /ˈbelɪfʊl/ *n*. an undesirable overabundance 满肚子;过分,过量 U2

benevolence /bəˈnevələns/ *n*. kind and generous 仁慈 U4

besiege /bɪˈsiːdʒ/ *v*. to surround a city or castle with military force until the people inside let you take control 围攻;包围 U6

bestow /biˈstəu/ *vt*. to give someone something of great value or importance, bestow something on/upon somebody 赠与;给与 bestowal /biˈstəuəl/ *n*. U7

bewitch /bɪˈwɪtʃ/ *v*. to get control over someone by putting a magic spell on them 施魔力于;使着魔 U8

bleach /bliːtʃ/ *v*. to make sth white or pale by a chemical process or by the effect of light from the sun; to become white or pale in this way (使)变白,漂白,晒白,退色 U2

bog down to get stuck 陷入困境 U5

bramble /ˈbræmbl/ *n*. (especially British English) a wild bush with thorns on which blackberries grow 荆棘 U2

brethren /ˈbreðrən/ *n*. (old use) used to address or talk about the members of an organization or group, especially a religious group (旧)兄弟们,同胞 U4

bumpy /ˈbʌmpi/ *adj*. (of a surface) not even; with a lot of bumps 不平的;多凸块的 U2

calabash /ˈkæləbæʃ/ *n*. a container made from the hard covering of a fruit or vegetable 葫芦 U2

calf /kɑːf / *n*. (plural calves /kɑːvz/) the baby of a cow, or of some other large animals, such as an elephant 牛犊;(大象等大型动物的)幼兽 U1

caliber /ˈkæləbə / *n*. the level of quality or ability that someone or something has achieved of somebody's calibre 能力,水准 U3

cardinal /ˈkɑːdənəl/ *adj*. (only before noun) very important or basic 首要的 U1

cast /kɑːst/ *vt*. to make an object by pouring liquid metal, plastic etc. into a mould 浇铸 U7

catastrophe /kəˈtæstrəfɪ/ *n*. an unexpected event that causes great suffering or damage 大灾难;大祸 U7

caterpillar /ˈkætəpɪlə/ *n*. a small creature like a worm with legs, that develops into a butterfly or moth 毛虫 U2

cauldron /ˈkɔːldrən/ *n*. a large round metal pot for boiling liquids over a fire (金属)大锅 U1

cavalry /ˈkævlri/ *n*. the part of an army that fights on horses 骑兵(队) U5

cede /siːd/ *v*. to give sb control of sth or give them power, a right, etc., especially unwillingly

让给;退让 U2

celestial /sə'lestiəl/ *adj*. of the sky or of heaven 天空的;天上的 U2

cessation /se'seɪʃən/ *n*. *formal* a pause or stop 停止;中止;中断 U1

chapped /tʃæpt/ *adj*.(of the skin or lips 皮肤或唇) rough, dry and sore, especially because of wind or cold weather (尤指因风吹或天冷而)皲裂的,开裂的 U2

chariot /'tʃæriət/ *n*. an open vehicle with two wheels, pulled by horses, used in ancient times in battle and for racin (古代用于战斗或比赛的)双轮敞篷马车;*v*. ride a carriage 驾驭马车 U2

choleric /'kɒlərɪk / *adj*. bad-tempered or angry 易怒的 U6

chrysalis /'krɪsəlɪs/ *n*. (also chrysalid) the form of an insect, especially a butterfly or moth , while it is changing into an adult inside a hard case, also called a chrysalis 蛹,蛹壳 U2

cicada /sɪ'kɑːdə/ *n*. a large insect with transparent wings, common in hot countries 蝉,知了 U2

circulate /'sɜːkjəleɪt/ *v*. to move around within a system, or to make something do this 循环 U1

clam /klæm/ *n*. a shellfish you can eat. It has a shell in two parts that open up 蛤蜊 U1

codify /'kəudɪfaɪ / *v*. to arrange laws, principles, facts etc in a system 整理;编纂 U6

coma /'kəumə/ *n*. someone who is in a coma has been unconscious for a long time, usually because of a serious illness or injury (因重病或重伤而引起的)昏迷 U8

company /'kʌmpəni/ *n*. a group of about 120 soldiers who are usually part of a larger group (军队)连 U6

compliance /kəm'plaɪəns/ *n*. *formal* when someone obeys a rule, agreement, or demand 顺从;服从 U1

comprise /kəm'praɪz/ *v*. to form part of a larger group of people or things 构成;包含 U6

conch /kɒntʃ / *n*. the large twisted shell of a tropical sea animal that looks like a snail 贝壳;海螺壳 U1

concubine /'kɒŋkjəbaɪn/ *n*. a woman in the past who lived with and had sex with a man who already had a wife or wives, but who was socially less important than the wives 妾;情妇;姘妇 U1

conform /kən'fɔːm / *vi*. 1. to behave in the way that most other people in your group or society behave 守规矩 2. to obey a law, rule etc (与法律、愿望等)相符合 U1

contour /'kɒntuə / *n*. the shape of the outer edges of something such as an area of land or someone's body 轮廓 U6

contract /'kɒntrækt / *vt*. to catch or develop illness 感染(疾病),患(病) U7

converge /kən'vɜːdʒ/ *vi*. come from different directions and meet at the same point to become one thing 聚集;汇集 U5

converge /kən'vɜːdʒ / *vt*. to come from different directions and meet at the same point to become one thing 使汇聚;聚集 U7

copulate /'kɒpjəleɪt/ *v*. *technical* to have sex 交配;交媾 U1

cord /kɔːd/ *n*. a line made of twisted fibers or threads 绳索 U1 corner /ˈkɔːnə/ *vt*. to force a person or animal into a place they cannot escape from 逼入困境 U5

crack /kræk/ *vt*. to break or to make something break, either so that it gets lines on its surface, or so that it breaks into pieces 使……破裂;破裂 U7

crouch /krautʃ/ *v*. to put your body close to the ground by bending your legs under you 蹲;蹲下;蹲伏 U2

curtail *vt*. /kəːˈteil/ to reduce or limit something 缩减;剪短;剥夺……特权等 U7

dagger-axe /ˈdægə æks/ *n*. a type of pole weapon that was in use from the Shang dynasty until the Han dynasty in China 戈 U1

dappled /ˈdæpəld/ *adj*. marked with spots of colour, light, or shade 斑纹的;有斑点的;花的 U1

daunting /ˈdɔːntɪŋ/ *adj*. frightening in a way that makes you feel less confident 使人气馁的 U8

deception /dɪˈsepʃən/ *n*. the act of deliberately making someone believe something that is not true 欺诈;诡诈 U6

denote /dɪˈnəut / *vt*. to represent or be a sign of something; to indicate 表示,表明 U7

dense /dens/ *adj*. stupid 愚笨的;迟钝的;笨拙的 U2

descend /diˈsend/ *vi*. move downward from a higher to a lower level 下降;下去;下来 U7

detachment /dɪˈtætʃmənt/ *n*. a group of soldiers who are sent away from a larger group to do a special job 特遣队 U6

detestation /ˌdiːtesˈteɪʃən/ *n*. intense hatred; abhorrence 憎恶;嫌恶 U7

dip /dɪp/ *v*. put something into a container and take something out 伸进(……里取东西) U2

dishevel /dɪˈʃevəl/ *vt*. to disarrange (the hair or clothes) of (someone) 使(某人头发或衣服)凌乱 U7

dispense /dɪˈspens/ *v*. *formal* to give something to people, especially in fixed amounts 分配,分给;实施,施行 U4

disperse /dɪˈspɜːs/ *v*. 1. if a group of people disperse or are dispersed, they go away in different directions 驱散;散开 2. if something disperses or is dispersed, it spreads in different directions over a wide area 使分散;扩散 U1

distension /dɪsˈtenʃən/ *n*. technical abnormal swelling in a person's or animal's body (人或动物身体内不正常的)肿胀 U7

ditch /dɪtʃ/ *n*. a long narrow hole dug at the side of a field, road etc to hold or remove unwanted water 沟渠;壕沟 U1

divination /ˌdɪvəˈneɪʃən/ *n*. the ability to say what will happen in the future, or the act of doing this 预测;占卜 U1

divulge /daɪˈvʌldʒ/ *v*. to give someone information that should be secret 泄露 U6

drain /dreɪn/ *n*. *especially British English* a pipe that carries water or waste liquids away 排水管;下水道;排水沟 U1

dumbfounded /dʌmfaʊndɪd/ *adj*. unable to speak because of surprise 惊呆的;*v*. 使发愣 U2

effuse /ɪˈfjuːz/ *v*. to pour or flow out 流出 U7

effusion /ɪˈfjuːʒən/ *n*. *technical* a liquid or gas that flows out of something, or the act of flowing out 渗出；泻出；渗漏物 U7

elm /elm/ *n*. a tall tree with broad leaves, also the hard wood of the elm tree 榆树 U2

emaciated /ɪˈmeɪʃieɪtəd/ *adj*. extremely thin from lack of food or illness 瘦弱的；憔悴的 U1

eminent /ˈeminənt/ *adj*. tall, lofty 高的；巍峨的 U7

emolument /ɪˈmɒljəmənt/ *n*. *formal* money or another form of payment for work you have done 报酬，薪水； U4

enfeoff /ɪnˈfef/ *vt*. put in possession of land in exchange for a pledge of service in feudal society 授予封地 U5

enliven /ɪnˈlaɪvən/ *vt*. to make something more lively or cheerful 使活泼；使有生气 U7

entice /ɪnˈtaɪs/ *v*. to persuade someone to do something or go somewhere, usually by offering them something that they want 诱使；引诱 U6

envoy /ˈenvɔɪ/ *n*. someone who is sent to another country as an official representative 使节，外交官；全权公使；谈判代表 U4

equilibrium /ˌiːkwəˈlɪbriəm/ *n*. a state in which you are calm and not angry or upset 平衡，均势；平静 U4

equinox /ˈiːkwənɒks/ *n*. one of the two times in a year when night and day are of equal length 昼夜平分日（指春分或秋分） U1

esoteric /ˌesəˈterɪk/ *adj*. known and understood by only a few people who have special knowledge about something 秘传的；限于圈内人的；难懂的 U1

eunuch /ˈjuːnək/ *n*. a man whose testicles have been removed, especially someone who guarded a king's wives in some Eastern countries in the past 太监；阉人 U1

evade /ɪˈveɪd/ *v*. to escape from someone who is trying to catch you 逃避；躲避 U6

excursion /ɪkˈskəːʃn/ *n*. a short journey made for pleasure, especially one that has been organized for a group of people （尤指集体）远足，短途旅行 U2

exhort /ɪgˈzɔːt / *v*. formal to try very hard to persuade someone to do something 劝告，劝说；倡导；勉励 U4

exorcism /ˈeksɔːsɪzəm / *n*. a process during which someone tries to make an evil spirit leave a place by saying special words, or a ceremony when this is done 驱邪，驱魔；驱邪仪式 U8

expenditure /ɪkˈspendɪtʃə/ *n*. （countable, uncountable） the total amount of money that a government, organization, or person spends during a particular period of time 开支；消耗 U6

extinguish /ɪkˈstɪŋgwɪʃ/ *vt*. to make a fire or light stop burning or shining; to destroy a feeling or idea 熄灭；灭绝 U7

exuberant /ɪgˈzjuːbərənt/ *adj*. happy and full of energy and excitement 繁茂的；生气勃勃的，充溢的 U1

feign /feɪn/ *v*. to pretend to have a particular feeling or to be ill, asleep, etc. 假装；装作 U6

ferocious /fəˈrəʊʃəs/ *adj*. violent, dangerous and frightening 凶猛的，凶残的；可怕的 U8

fief /fiːf/ *n*. a piece of land given to someone by their lord 采邑，封地 U2 flank /flæŋk/ *v*. to be on both sides of someone or something 位于……侧面 U8

flourish /ˈflʌrɪʃ / *vi*. to grow well and be very healthy 繁荣，兴旺；茂盛 U7

flutter /ˈflʌtə/ *v*. fly somewhere moving the wings quickly and lightly 飞来飞去 U2

foe /fəʊ/ *n*. an enemy 仇敌 U6

formidable /ˈfɔːmədəbəl/ *adj*. very powerful or impressive, and often frightening 强大的；难对付的 U6

fortify /ˈfɔːtɪfaɪ/ *vi*. to build towers, walls, etc. around an area or city in order to defend it 构筑防御工事 U5

fret /fret/ *v*. to be worried or unhappy and not able to relax 苦恼；烦躁；焦虑不安 U2

frugality /fruːˈgæləti/ *n*. prudence in avoiding waste 节俭，节约，俭朴 U1

fugitive /ˈfjuːdʒətɪv/ *adj*. literary lasting for a very short time 短暂的 U8

gale /geɪl/ *n*. an extremely strong wind 大风；飓风 U2

gallantly /ˈgæləntlɪ/ *adv*. bravely and honorably 英勇高尚地 U5

gallop /ˈgæləp/ *v*. to run somewhere very quickly 疾驰 U5

gnarled /nɑːl/ *adj*. (of trees) twisted and rough; covered with hard lumps (树木)扭曲的；多节瘤的；疙疙瘩瘩的 U2

gourd /gɔːd/ *n*. a type of large fruit, not normally eaten, with hard skin and soft flesh. Gourds are often dried and used as containers. 葫芦 U2

gradation /grəˈdeɪʃən/ *n*. a small change or difference between points on a scale 等级；渐变 U6

gratify /ˈgrætɪfaɪ/ *vt*. to make someone feel pleased and satisfied 使高兴；使满意 U3

halberd /ˈhælbəd/ *n*. a type of sword that was used as a weapon in the past 戟 U1

hegemon /ˈhedʒəmɒn/ *n*. a ruler that control others 霸主；霸权主义者 U5

helmet /ˈhelmɪt/ *n*. a strong hard hat that soldiers, motorcycle riders, the police etc wear to protect their heads 钢盔，头盔 U1

hem /hem/ *v*. to surround closely 包围 U5

hexagram /ˈhɛksəˌgræm/ *n*. any of the sixty-four possible combinations of six whole or broken lines used especially in Chinese divination(六爻)卦 U1

hideous /ˈhɪdiəs/ *adj*. extremely unpleasant or ugly 极丑的，极难看的 U8

hoard /hɔːd/ (also hoard up) *v*. to collect and save large amounts of food, money etc, especially when it is not necessary to do so 贮藏 U1

hoof /huːf/ *n*. (plural hoofs or hooves /huːvz/) the hard foot of an animal such as a horse, cow etc (马等动物的)蹄 U1

immortality /ˌɪmɔːˈtæləti/ *n*. the state of living forever or being remembered forever 永生，长存，永恒 U8

impartiality /ɪmˌpɑːʃiˈæləti/ *n*. a state of being not involved in a particular situation, and therefore able to give a fair opinion or piece of advice 公正，公平；不偏不倚 U1

impersonate /ɪmˈpɜːsəneit/ *v*. to pretend to be sb in order to trick people or to entertain them 扮演；模仿；拟人，人格化 U2

impersonator /ɪmˈpɜːsəneitə(r)/ *n*. a person who copies the way another person talks or behaves in order to entertain people 演员，模仿明星的艺人 U2

impetuosity /ɪmˌpetʃuˈɒsəti/ *n*. 性急，冲动；冲力，猛烈 U1

indignant /ɪnˈdɪgnənt/ *adj*. angry and surprised because you feel insulted or unfairly treated 愤慨的；激愤的 U5

indulgent /ɪnˈdʌldʒənt/ *adj*. willing to allow someone, especially a child, to do or have whatever they want, even if this is not good for them 宽容的；任性的 U4

inhibit /ɪnˈhɪbɪt/ *vt*. to prevent something from growing or developing well 抑制；禁止 U7

insinuating /ɪnˈsɪnjueɪtɪŋ/ *v*. suggesting ideas without saying them directly 迂回，巧妙或迂回地潜入 U3

inspectorate /ɪnˈspektərət/ *n*. the group of inspectors who officially inspect schools, factories, etc.（学校、工厂等的）检查团，督察队 U8

integrity /ɪnˈtegrəti/ *n*. the quality of being honest and strong about what you believe to be right 正直，诚实 U8

interchange /ˌɪntəˈtʃeɪndʒ/ *v*. to put each of two things in the other's place, or to be exchanged in this way 互换 U1

invigorate /ɪnˈvɪgəreɪt/ *vt*. if something invigorates you, it makes you feel healthier, stronger, and have more energy 鼓舞；增加活力 U1

irritate /ˈɪrɪteɪt/ *v*. to make someone feel annoyed or impatient, especially by doing something many times or for a long period of time 激怒 U6

jostle /ˈdʒɒsl/ *v*. to bump and push to get past 推搡 U5

kindred /ˈkɪndrəd/ *n*. family and relatives （统称）家人，亲属 U2

ladle /ˈleɪdl/ *n*. a large deep spoon with a long handle, used especially for serving soup 长柄勺；汤勺 U2

lean /liːn/ *adj*. thin in a healthy and attractive way 瘦的 U1

legume /ˈlegjuːm/ *n*. *technical* a plant such as a bean plant that has seeds in a pod (= a long thin case) 豆类；豆科植物；豆荚 U1

liken /ˈlaɪkən/ *v*. consider or describe as similar, equal, or analogous 比作；比拟；使像 U6

limp /lɪmp/ *adj*. not firm or strong 软的；不强壮的 U7

lustrous /ˈlʌstrəs/ *adj*. shining in a soft gentle way 有光泽的，光亮的 U7

magnanimity /ˌmægnəˈnɪməti/ *adj*. kind and generous, especially to someone that you have defeated 宽宏大量 U4

mail /meɪl/ *n*. armor made of small pieces of metal, worn by soldiers in the Middle Ages 盔甲 U1

malachite /ˈmæləkait/ *n*. a green mineral that is a basic carbonate of copper used especially for making ornamental objects 孔雀石 U8

malaria /məˈleəriə/ *n*. a serious disease carried by mosquitoes, which causes periods of fever （内科）疟疾；瘴气 U7 manifest /ˈmænəfest/ *vt*. *formal* to show a feeling, an attitude, etc. 证明,表明;显示 U1

mantra /ˈmæntrə/ *n*. a word or sound that is repeated as a prayer or to help people meditate 曼怛罗(祷告或冥想时反复念唱的咒语) U8

marquis /ˈmɑːkwɪs/ *n*. nobleman ranking above a count 侯爵 U5

marshal /ˈmɑːʃəl/ *v*. to organize all the people or things that you need in order to be ready for a battle, election etc. 编制,编列 U6

maw /mɔː/ *n*. *literary* an animal's mouth or throat (像吞噬一切的)大嘴 U1

mediocre /ˌmiːdiˈəʊkə/ *adj*. not very good 普通的;平凡的;中等的 U8

metamorphose /ˌmetəˈmɔːfəʊz/ *v*. to change or make sth/sb change into sth completely different, especially over a period of time(使)变形,变化,发生质变 U2

mighty /ˈmaitɪ/ *a*. large and impressive; (especially literary) very strong and powerful 巨大的;强有力的;浩瀚的 U2

mingle /ˈmɪŋgəl/ *v*. if two feelings, sounds, smells etc mingle, they mix together with each other 混合 U1

moisten /ˈmɔɪsən/ *vt*. to make something slightly wet 弄湿;使……湿润 U1

mold /məʊld/ *n*. the distinctive form in which a thing is made 模式;*v*. form in clay, wax, etc. 浇筑,塑造;shape or influence; give direction to 对……产生影响 U2

mole /məʊl/ *n*. a small animal with dark grey fur, that is almost blind and digs tunnels under the ground to live in 鼹鼠 U2

mope /məʊp/ *v*. to spend your time doing nothing and feeling sorry for yourself 闷闷不乐;自怨自艾 U2

mote /məʊt/ *n*. a very small piece of dust 尘埃;微粒 U2

myriad /ˈmɪriəd/ *adj*. (usually before noun) *written* very many 无数的;种种的 U1

neigh /neɪ/ *v*. if a horse neighs, it makes a long loud noise 马嘶 U1

nourish /ˈnʌrɪʃ/ *vt*. to give a person or other living thing the food and other substances they need in order to live, grow, and stay healthy 滋养;给……营养 U7

numinous /ˈnjuːmɪnəs/ *adj*. *literary* having a mysterious and holy quality, which makes you feel that God is present 神圣的;神秘的 U1

obedient /əˈbiː. diənt/ *adj*. doing, or willing to do, what you have been told to do by someone in authority 顺从的,服从的;忠顺的 U3

obsequiously /əbˈsiːkwiəsli/ *adv*. eagerly to please or agree with people who are powerful-used to show disapproval 谄媚地,奉承地 U8

obstruct /əbˈstrʌkt/ *vt*. to prevent someone from doing something or something from happening, by making it difficult 妨碍;阻塞 U7

opulence /ˈɒpjuləns/ *n*. wealth as evidenced by sumptuous living 富裕;丰富 U7

orifice /ˈɒrɪfɪs/ *n*. 1. one of the holes in your body, such as your mouth, nose etc one of the holes in your body, such as your mouth, nose etc. (身体上的)孔,洞(如嘴、鼻等) 2. a hole or entrance 洞,入口 U7

outflow /ˈautfləu/ *n*. the flow of water or air from something （水或空气的）流出，泄漏 U7

overthrow /ˌəuvəˈθrəu/ *v*. to remove a leader or government from power, especially by force 推翻 U6

palpable /ˈpælpəbəl/ *adj*. *formal* a feeling that is palpable is so strong that other people notice it and can feel it around them 明白的，明显的；可感知的，摸得出的 U4

panicky /ˈpænɪki/ *adj*. *informal* very nervous and anxious 惊惶的，紧张不安的 U8

pebble /ˈpebəl/ *n*. a small smooth stone found especially on a beach or on the bottom of a river 卵石 U1

pelt /pelt/ *n*. the skin of a dead animal, especially with the fur or hair still on it 生皮，带毛兽皮；(at) full pelt (British English): moving as fast as possible 全速地，开足马力地 U8

peril /ˈperəl/ *n*. [uncountable] *literary or formal* great danger, especially of being harmed or killed 危险，冒险 U6

perilous /ˈperələs/ *adj*. extremely dangerous 危险的，冒险的 U3

perish /ˈperɪʃ/ *v*. die as a result of very harsh conditions 死亡 U5

permeate /ˈpɜːmɪeɪt/ *vi*./*vt*. (liquid, gas, etc.) to enter something and spread through every part of it （液体、气体等）渗透，渗入；弥漫（于） U1

perplexity /pəˈplek. sə. ti/ *n*. a state of confusion or a complicated and difficult situation or thing 困惑，混乱，复杂 U3

perseverance /ˌpɜːsəˈvɪərəns/ *n*. determination to keep trying to achieve something in spite of difficulties 毅力；韧性；不屈不挠的精神 U3

pheasant /ˈfezənt/ *n*. a large bird with a long tail, often shot for food, or the meat of this bird 野鸡；雉科鸟 U1

picul /ˈpɪkʌl/ *n*. a unit of weight used in some parts of Asia; approximately equal to 133 pounds (the load a grown man can carry) 担（计量单位） U2

piebald /ˈpaɪbɔːld/ *adj*. a piebald animal has black and white areas on its body 花斑的；杂色的 U1

pitfall /ˈpɪtfɔːl/ *n*. a problem or difficulty that is likely to happen in a particular job, course of action, or activity 陷阱，圈套；缺陷；诱惑 U1

plaque /plɑːk/ *n*. a piece of flat metal, wood, or stone with writing on it, used as a prize in a competition or attached to a building to remind people of an event or person 匾 U8

pliancy /ˈplaiənsi/ *n*. 1. the property of being pliant and flexible 软；柔顺 2. adaptability of mind or character 适应性 U1

pod /pɒd/ *n*. a long narrow seed container that grows on various plants, especially peas and beans 豆荚 U1

portend /pɔːˈtend/ *v*. to be a sign that something is going to happen, especially something bad 预兆，成为……的前兆 U6

precinct /ˈpriːsɪŋkt/ *n*. one of the areas that a town or city is divided into 管辖区 U5

predatory /ˈpredətəri/ *adj*. a predatory animal kills and eats other animals for food 掠食的，捕食

其他动物为生的 U8

primordial /praɪˈmɔːdiəl/ *adj*. *formal* 1. existing at the beginning of time or the beginning of the Earth 原始的;根本的;原生的 2. primordial feelings are very strong and seem to come from the part of people's character that is ancient and animal-like (情感)原始的,本能的 U7

primordial /praɪˈmɔːdiəl/ *adj*. *formal* existing at the beginning of time or the beginning of the Earth 原始的;远古的 U1

prolonged /prəˈlɒŋd/ *adj*. continuing for a long time 持续很久的 U6

propriety /prəˈpraiəti/ *n*. formal correctness of social or moral behaviour 礼貌;规矩;正当;合适 U4

protrude /prəˈtruːd/ *v*. to stick out from somewhere 突出,伸出 U8

prudent /ˈpruːdənt/ *adj*. sensible and careful, especially by trying to avoid unnecessary risks 明智谨慎的,慎重的,审慎的 U8

quail /kweɪl/ *n*. a small brown bird, whose meat and eggs are used for food; the meat of this bird 鹌鹑;鹌鹑肉 U2

rally /ˈræli/ *v*. to unit to support 召集,团结起来 U5

ram /ræm/ *n*. an adult male sheep 公羊 U1

recede /riˈsiːd/ *vi*. pull back or move away or backward 退;后退 U7

reciprocally /riˈsiprəkli/ *adv*. in a mutual or shared manner 相互地;相反地;互惠地 U1

rectify /ˈrektɪfaɪ/ *vt*. to correct something or make something right 改正,校正 U3

reed /riːd/ *n*. a type of tall plant like grass that grows in wet places 芦苇 U1

refinement /rɪˈfaɪnmənt/ *n*. an improvement, usually a small one, to something 精炼,改良,优雅 U3

regiment /ˈredʒəmənt/ *n*. a large group of soldiers, usually consisting of several battalions (军队)团 U6

reign /reɪn/ *v*. to rule a nation or group of nations as their king, queen, or emperor 在位统治 U1

rejoice /rɪˈdʒɔɪs/ *v*. *literary* to feel or show that you are very happy 欣喜;使高兴 U1

requisite /ˈrekwəzət/ *adj*. *formal* needed for a particular purpose 必需品;要素,要件 U4

resolute /ˈrezəluːt/ *adj*. determined in character, action, or ideas 坚决的,刚毅的 U3

restraint /rɪˈstreɪnt/ *n*. rules or conditions that limit or restrict someone or something 限制 U1

resuscitate /rɪˈsʌsɪteɪt/ *vt*. to make someone breathe again or become conscious after they have almost died 使恢复呼吸;使苏醒 U7

roil /rɔɪl/ *v*. make turbid by stirring up the sediments of (水)激荡,翻滚,翻腾 U2

rusticity /ˈrʌs. tɪsəti/ *n*. simple and often rough in appearance; typical of the countryside 乡村特点,风格或气息 U3

sage /seɪdʒ/ *n*. *literary* someone, especially an old man, who is very wise 圣人;贤人;哲人(尤指老人) U1

salve /sælv/ *n*. a substance that you put on a wound or sore skin to help it heal or to protect it 药膏;软膏;油膏 U2

sapanwood /ˈsæpənwʊd/ *n*. a variant spelling of sappan wood, a small leguminous tree, Caesalpinia sappan, of S Asia producing wood that yields a red dye 苏木 U2

scorch /skɔːtʃ/ *v*. to burn and slightly damage a surface by making it too hot; to be slightly burned by heat 烤焦;使枯萎 U2

seduce /sɪˈdjuːs/ *v*. to persuade someone to have sex with you, especially in a way that is attractive and not too direct 诱奸,勾引 U8

seduction /sɪˈdʌkʃən/ *n*. something that strongly attracts people, but often has a bad effect on their lives 诱惑;引诱 U4

shamaness /ˈʃɑːmənɪs/ *n*. a woman in some tribes who is a religious leader and is believed to be able to talk to spirits and cure illnesses 女巫 U1

shamble /ˈʃæmbəl/ *v*. to walk slowly and awkwardly, not lifting your feet much, for example because you are tired, weak, or lazy 蹒跚地走;摇晃不稳;摇摇晃晃地走 U1

shatter /ˈʃætə/ *v*. to break suddenly into very small pieces, or to make something break in this way 粉碎;毁坏 U6

siege /siːdʒ/ *n*. a situation in which an army or the police surround a place and try to gain control of it or force someone to come out of it 包围 U6

sift /ˈsɪftɪŋ/ *v*. to put flour or some other fine substance through a sieve/sifter 筛,过滤 U2

signify /ˈsɪgnɪfaɪ/ *vt*. to represent, mean, or be a sign of something 表示;意味;预示 U1

simulate /ˈsɪmjəleɪt/ *vt*. to make or produce something that is not real but has the appearance or feeling of being real 模拟 U1

slake /sleik/ *v*. to drink so that you no longer feel thirsty 解(渴);消除;to satisfy a desire 满足 U2

smash /smæʃ/ *v*. to break sth, or to be broken, violently and noisily into many pieces (哗啦一声)打碎,打破,破碎 U2

solicitous /səˈlɪsɪtəs/ *adj*. very concerned about someone's safety, health, or comfort 关心的,挂念的,热切的 U3

solstice /ˈsɔlstis/ *n*. the time when the sun is furthest north or south of the equator 至,至日;至点 the summer/winter solstice (= the longest or shortest day of the year) 夏至/冬至 U1

sorcerer /ˈsɔːsərə/ *n*. a man in stories who uses magic and receives help from evil forces 魔术师;男巫士 U1

sough /sʌf/ *vi*./*n*. (*arch or fml* 古或文) (make a) murmuring or whispering sound (as of wind in trees) (发出)瑟瑟声,飒飒声 U7

sovereign /ˈsɒvrɪn/ *n*. a king or queen 君主 U6

sprout /spraʊt/ *v*. if vegetables, seeds, or plants sprout, they start to grow, producing shoots, buds, or leaves 发芽;长芽 U1

spurn /spɜːn/ *v*. to reject or refuse sb/sth, especially in a proud way (尤指傲慢地)拒绝 U2

squad /skwɒd/ *n*. a small group of soldiers working together as a unit 班,小队 U6

stagnate /stægˈneɪt/ *vt*. to stop developing or making progress 停滞;淤塞

stagnation /stæg'neɪʃən/ *n*. 停滞;淤塞 U7

stalk /stɔːk/ *n*. a long narrow part of a plant that supports leaves, fruits, or flowers(植物的)茎,秆;(支持叶子、果实和花的)梗,柄; U1

stealthily /'stelθili/ *adv*. moving or doing something quietly and secretly 悄悄地,鬼鬼祟祟地,偷偷地 U8

stratagem /'strætədʒəm/ *n*. *formal* a trick or plan to deceive an enemy or gain an advantage 战略 U6

stride /straɪd/ *n*. a long step you make while you are walking 大步;步幅;进展 U7

sturdiness /'stəːdinis/ *n*. the state of being vigorous and robust 坚固;强健,雄壮 U1

subdivision /ˌsʌbdə'vɪʒən/ *n*. (countable, uncountable) any of the parts into which something is divided, or the act of creating these 分支;细分;一部分 U6

subdue /səb'du/ *vt*. to defeat or control a person or group, especially using force 征服;克制 U5

submissiveness /səb'misivnis/ *n*. the trait of being willing to yield to the will of another person or a superior force, etc. 柔顺;服从 U1

subterranean /ˌsʌbtə'reɪniən/ *adj*. beneath the surface of the Earth 地下的;秘密的;隐蔽的 U8

subtlety /'sʌtlti/ *n*. the quality that something has when it has been done in a clever or skillful way, with careful attention to small details 微妙,巧妙 U6

succumb /sə'kʌm/ *v*. to stop opposing someone or something that is stronger than you, and allow them to take control 屈从 U6

tactic /'tæktɪk/ *n*. a method that you use to achieve something 策略;战术 U6

tactician /tæk'tɪʃən/ *n*. someone who is very good at tactics 战术家 U6

tailorbird /'teiləbəːd/ *n*. tropical Asian warbler that stitches leaves together to form and conceal its nest 缝叶莺 U2

tapir /'teipə(r)/ *n*. an animal like a pig with a long nose, that lives in Central and S America and SE Asia 貘(生活在中南美洲和东南亚的长鼻猪状动物) U2

temper /'tempə/ *n*. to make something less severe or extreme 使适中;缓和,减轻 U7

terrain /te'reɪn/ *n*. a particular type of land 地形 U6

the rose of Sharon /'ʃærən/ *phr*. flowering plant 鲜花 U2

thorn /θɔːn/ *n*. a sharp point that grows on the stem of a plant such as a rose 刺;(植)荆棘 U1

threefold /'θriːfəuld/ *adj*. three times as much or as many 三倍的;三重的,有三部分的 U1

thwart /θwɔːt/ *v*. to prevent someone from doing what they are trying to do 反对;阻碍 U6

tinted /'tɪntɪd/ *adj*. tinted glass is colored, rather than completely transparent 着色的,带色彩的 U8

tit /tɪt/ *n*. a small European bird (鸟)山雀 U2

trample /'træmpl/ *v*. to step heavily and carelessly on some place 踩踏 U5

tranquil /'træŋkwəl/ *adj*. pleasantly calm, quiet, and peaceful 安静的,平静的,宁静的 U3

tranquility /træŋ'kwiləti/ *n*. a state of being pleasantly calm, quiet, and peaceful 宁静;平静 U1

treacherous /'tretʃərəs/ *adj*. ground, roads, weather conditions etc. that are particularly

dangerous because you cannot see the dangers very easily 危险的,不可靠的 U6

trigram /ˈtraɪˌgræm/ *n*. any of the eight possible combinations of three whole or broken lines used especially in Chinese divination(三爻)卦 U1

turbid /ˈtɜːbɪd/ *adj*. *formal* (of liquid) full of mud, dirt, etc. so that you can not see through it 浑浊的;污浊不清的 U7

twig /twɪg/ *n*. a small very thin branch that grows out of a larger branch on a bush or tree 细枝,嫩枝 U2

undismayed /ˌʌndɪsˈmeɪd/ *adj*. not worried or frightened by something unpleasant or unexpected 无恐惧的;不泄气的 U6

unto /ˈʌntuː/ *prep*. *old use* to 对于 U6

unwieldy /ʌnˈwiːldi/ *adj*. difficult to move or control because of its size, shape or weight 笨重的;笨拙的;不灵巧的 U2

vanish /ˈvænɪʃ/ *vi*. to disappear suddenly 消失;突然不见 U5

vehemently /ˈviːəməntli/ *adv*. showing very strong feelings or opinions 感情强烈地;观点激烈地 U8

vexation /vekˈseɪʃən/ *n*. *old-fashioned* when you feel worried or annoyed by something 烦恼;恼火 U4

vicissitude /vəˈsɪsətjuːd/ *n*. the continuous changes and problems that affect a situation or someone's life 变化;变迁;兴衰 U6

virtue /ˈvɜːtjuː/ *n*. moral goodness of character and behaviour 善,德,德行 U7

virtuous /ˈvɜːtʃuəs/ *adj*. behaving in a very honest and moral way 有德行的,有道德的 U3

virulent /ˈvɪrələnt/ *adj*. a poison, disease, etc. that is virulent is very dangerous and affects people very quickly 剧毒的;恶性的 U7

wearisome /ˈwɪərisəm/ *adj*. *formal* making you feel bored, tired, or annoyed 使疲倦的;使厌倦的;乏味的 U1

weasel /ˈwiːzl/ *n*. a small wild animal with reddish-brown fur, a long thin body and short legs 鼬;黄鼠狼 U2

withered /ˈwɪðəd/ *adj*. being drier and smaller and even dead or dying 枯萎的;凋谢了的 U1

wooly /ˈwʊlɪ/ *adj*. confused and vague; used especially of thinking 糊涂的;不清楚的 U2

worthy /ˈwɜːði/ *adj*. be morally respectable or correct 值得尊敬的 U5

yak /jæk/ *n*. an animal of the cow family, with long horns and long hair, that lives in central Asia 牦牛 U2

yarrow /ˈjærəʊ/ *n*. a widely naturalized strong-scented Eurasian composite herb (Achillea millefolium) with finely dissected leaves and small usually white corymbose flowers 蓍草 U1

Appendix III

汉语词汇表

蓍[shī]　名词,(植)蓍草　U1
悖[bèi]　动词,相反;违反　U1
布[bù]　名词,古代的一种钱币　U1
参[sān]　数词,同"叁"[sān],即"三"　U1
苍筤[cāng láng]　形容词,竹色青嫩　U1
大赤[dà chì]　名词,大红色　U1
逮[dài]　动词,到;及　U1
的颡[dì sǎng]　名词,(马)白额　U1
帝[dì]　名词,(主宰大自然生机的)元气　U1
尃[fū]　名词,花朵　U1
熯[hàn]　形容词,燥热,炎热　U1
萑苇[huán wěi]　名词,两种芦类植物,蒹长成后为萑,葭长成后为苇　U1
圜[yuán]　名词,圆　U1
喙[huì]　名词,鸟嘴,"黔喙"指猛禽　U1
阍寺[hūn sì]　名词,人和寺人,指古代宫中掌管门禁的官　U1
金[jīn]　名词,青铜或纯铜(铸成的钟鼎等)　U1
丽[lì]　名词,附着;依附　U1
蓏[luǒ]　名词,瓜类植物的果实　U1
蠃[luǒ]　名词,蚌属水生物　U1
黔[qián]　形容词,黑　U1
桡[ráo]　动词,曲木;木头弯曲;泛指弯曲,此处指风吹拂万物或使抒发、或使摧折　U1
射[yì]　动词,厌弃　U1
神[shén]　名词,神奇,此处指大自然运化规律的神奇功能　U1
眚[shěng]　名词,灾异　U1
豕[shǐ]　名词,猪　U1
说[yuè]　动词,同"悦"　U1
索[suǒ]　动词,求,文中犹言"求合",指阴阳相求　U1
文[wén]　名词,纹理,花纹,文中指大地万物之色杂　U1
玄黄[xuán huáng]　名词,青黄相杂之色　U1

烜[xuān] 动词，晒干 U1
舆[yú] 名词，大车 U1
之[zhī] 代词，指代万物 U1
馵足[zhù zú] 名词，(马)白色的左后足 U1
作足[zuò zú] 名词，(马)双前足举起 U1
弊弊焉[bì bì yān] 形容词，忙忙碌碌、疲惫不堪的样子 U2
樗[chū] 名词，一种高大的落叶乔木，但木质粗劣不可用 U2
疵疠[lì] 名词，疾病 U2
恶[wū] 文言叹词，何，什么 U2
姑射[yè] 名词，传说中的山名 U2
罟[gǔ] 名词，网的总称。 U2
呺[xiāo]然 形容词，庞大而又中空的样子。 U2
鷦鷯[jiāo liáo] 名词，一种善于筑巢的小鸟。 U2
决[xuè] 名词，通作"翅"，迅疾的样子。 U2
斄[lí] 名词，牛，牦牛。 U2
乱[luàn] 这里作"治"讲，这是古代同词义反的语言现象。 U2
藐[miǎo] 形容词，遥远的样子。 U2
淖[chuò]约 形容词，柔弱、美好的样子。 U2
澼[pí] 动词，在水中漂洗。 U2
絖[kuàng] 名词，丝絮 U2
洴[píng] 动词，浮 U2
蕲[qí] 动词，通祈；求的意思 U2
抢[qiāng] 动词，突过 U2
丧[shàng] 动词，丧失、忘掉 U2
数数[shuò]然 形容词，急急忙忙的样子 U2
蜩[tiáo] 名词，蝉 U2
抟[tuán] 动词，击 U2
窅[yǎo]然 形容词，怅然若失的样子 U2
鬻[yù] 动词，卖，出售 U2
殆[dài] 名词，此字有两解释。一、危殆，亦疑。思而不学，则事无征验，疑不能定，危殆不安。二、疲怠。徒使精神疲怠，而无所得 U3
悱[fěi] 动词，口欲言而未能 U3
云尔[yún ěr] 名词，尔，如此。云尔，犹如此说 U3
惮[dàn] 动词，畏难 U3
曲肱[qǔ gōng] 动词，动词，肱，臂也。曲臂当枕小卧，多用以比喻清贫而闲适的生活 U3
輗[ní] 名词，木质，外裹铁皮，竖串于辕与衡之两孔中，使辕与衡可以灵活转动 U3
軏[yuè] 名词，古代用牛力的车叫大车，用马力的车叫小车。两者都要把牲口套在车辕上。车辕前面有一道横木，就是驾牲口的地方。那横木，大车上的叫做鬲，小车叫做衡，軏就是鬲的关键，輗就

是衡的关键 U3
见[xiàn] 动词,同“现” U4
中[zhòng] 动词,符合 U4
杀[shài] 名词,等级,差别 U4
齐[zhāi] 名词,同“斋” U4
省[xǐng] 动词,省察 U4
既廪[jì lǐn] 名词,指薪水粮食 U4
跲[jiá] 动词,绊倒 U4
壁[bì] 动词,修筑营垒 U5
幸从[xìng cóng] 动词,受宠幸跟从 U5
驰走[chí zǒu] 动词,使劲赶马 U5
绐[dài] 动词,欺骗 U5
度[duó] 动词,估计,揣度,推测 U5
期[qī] 动词,约定 U5
地方[dì fāng] 名词,古今异义,土地方圆 U5
独[dú] 副词,难道 U5
面[miàn] 动词,面向 U5
拔[bá] 动词,攻占、夺取 U6
传[chuán] 动词,传授、泄露 U6
殆[dài] 形容词,危险 U6
顿[dùn] 形容词,通“钝”,疲惫、受挫 U6
伐交[fá jiāo] 动词,通过外交手段瓦解、孤立敌人,使之不敢发动战争 U6
伐谋[fá móu] 动词,粉碎敌人的计谋而使之屈服 U6
官道[guān dào] 名词,各级将吏的职责区分、统辖管理等制度 U6
诡道[guǐ dào] 名词,以诡诈为道 U6
计[jì] 名词,指下文的“主孰有道”等七计,对这七个方面情况的估计 U6
经[jīng] 动词,以……为经,分析研究 U6
利[lì] 动词,贪利 U6
挠[náo] 动词,扰乱 U6
能[néng] 名词,能力、实力 U6
屈[qū] 动词,使屈服 U6
曲制[qū zhì] 名词,军队组织编制的制度 U6
善[shàn] 形容词,高明 U6
上兵[shàng bīng] 名词,用兵的上策 U6
校[jiào] 动词,通“较”,比较 U6
佚[yì] 形容词,通“逸”,安逸 U6
主用[zhǔ yòng] 名词,军需物资的供应和管理 U6
发陈[fā chén] 名词,指二十四节气自立春开始的三个月,为一年之始,生命萌发 U7

蕃秀[fān xiù] 形容词,(万物)繁茂秀美 U7

痎疟[jié nuè] 名词,疟疾的通称。亦指经年不愈的老疟 U7

容平[róng píng] 形容词,成熟而平定收敛 U7

飧泄[sūn xiè] 名词,飧(sūn)泄,本病是肝郁脾虚,清气不升所致。临床表现有大便泄泻清稀,并有不消化的食物残渣,肠鸣腹痛等 U7

闭藏[bì cáng] 名词,潜伏,蛰藏 U7

亟夺[jí duó] 动词,亟,(副词)急迫,屡次;夺,失去 U7

痿厥[wěi jué] 名词,痿,中医学名,症状见肢体痿弱,经脉迟缓;厥,亦作:"厥",逆气 U7

空窍[kōng qiào] 名词,(1)即孔窍,指人体与外界相通达的孔窍,包括九窍在内(2)山川 U7

冒明[mào míng] 形容词,昏蒙不明 U7

菀槁[yùn gǎo] 名词,高大的树木 U7

圣人[shèng rén] 名词,品德最高尚、智慧最高超的人,文中指懂得健康、养生方法的人 U7

内格[nèi gé] 名词,病症名,阴阳上下表里闭塞不通的症状。 U7

谙[ān] 动词,熟悉 U8

不啻[bù chì] 副词,不只,何止 U8

巉巉[chán chán] 形容词,本意为山势高俊的样子,这里用以形容女鬼牙齿而尖利 U8

杜[dù] 动词,关,堵 U8

干云[gān yún] 动词,冲入云霄,冲天 U8

垝垣[guǐ yuán] 名词,残缺的院墙。垝,坍塌。垣,墙外 U8

碣[jié] 名词,石碑 U8

栲栳[kǎo lǎo] 名词,用柳条编织的汲水器具,形似笆斗 U8

罗刹[luó chà] 名词,梵语音译,佛教故事中食人血肉的恶鬼 U8

俛[miǎn] 动词,同"俯",屈身;低头 U8

逡巡[qūn xún] 动词,迟疑,犹豫 U8

鲐背[tái bèi] 动词,驼背,形容老态。鲐,鱼名,体呈纺锤形,背隆起 U8

庠[xiáng] 名词,古代地方所设的乡学,夏代称"校",殷代称"序",周代称"庠" U8

魇禳[yán rang] 名词,镇压邪祟叫"魇",驱除灾变叫"禳",均属道教法术 U8

夭殂[yāo cú] 动词,未成年而死 U8

阅[yuè] 动词,经,历 U8

资斧[zī fǔ] 名词,旅费 U8